# A Forgotten Sisterhood

Educators and Reformers of the Southern Network of Black women, early 1900s. Front row l-r: Margaret Murray Washington (Mrs. Booker T. Washington), Mary McLeod Bethune, Lucy Craft Laney, Mary Jackson McCrorey. Second row-l-r: Janie Porter Barrett, M.L. Crosthwaite, Charlotte Hawkins Brown, Eugenia Burns Hope. Courtesy of Moorland-Spingarn Research Center, Howard University

# A Forgotten Sisterhood

*Pioneering Black Women Educators and
Activists in the Jim Crow South*

Audrey Thomas McCluskey

ROWMAN & LITTLEFIELD
Lanham • Boulder • New York • London

Published by Rowman & Littlefield
A wholly owned subsidiary of The Rowman & Littlefield Publishing Group, Inc.
4501 Forbes Boulevard, Suite 200, Lanham, Maryland 20706
www.rowman.com

16 Carlisle Street, London W1D 3BT, United Kingdom

British Library Cataloguing in Publication Information Available

**Library of Congress Cataloging-in-Publication Data**

Library of Congress Cataloging-in-Publication Data Available

ISBN 978-1-4422-1138-4 (cloth : alk. paper) -- ISBN 978-1-4422-1140-7 (electronic)

∞™ The paper used in this publication meets the minimum requirements of American National Standard for Information Sciences Permanence of Paper for Printed Library Materials, ANSI/NISO Z39.48-1992.

Printed in the United States of America

To the Rising Generation of Hope and Promise:
Annan, Thomasina, Langston, & August

# Contents

# Acknowledgments

This project has taken several years to come together. That is partly due to the nature of this work that attempts to unite, in a single volume, a small group of women who each deserves a full-scale examination of her individual life and work. It is also due to interruptions and fortuitous professional diversions that were fulfilling and necessary as well as time consuming. Along the way, several people have been instrumental in supporting me and my work by providing crucial advice and encouragement in many different and unique ways. The list of generous acts by good people is long in names and years and this shout-out is just a small token of thanks.

Christie Farnham Pope and Darlene Clark Hine are high on that list. They were early mentors who have provided helpful commentary on my work. I have gained so much from their friendship and scholarly insights over the years. Linda M. Perkins is another scholar whose work informs mine and who has been supportive over the long haul. Maxine LeGall, Q. T. Jackson, Karen Y. House, Vicki Roberts, Gladys DeVane, and Margaret McDay are longtime friends who were always there when needed. I also appreciate the helpful feedback from organizers and participants at the Association for the Study of African American Life and History conferences where I first presented the beginnings of this research. Both ASLAH and the National Council for Black Studies have remained true to their mission—over these many years—of being a platform for interchange among scholars of the black experience—its history and culture.

I thank former graduate assistant Crystal Keels for her assistance along with other former graduate students and assistants—some of whom are now professors themselves, including Tanisha Ford and Ebony Utley, or on their way to that goal, including Nana Amoah, Katie Dieter, and Yakari Shinagawa. I have been enriched by my work with highly motivated graduate and undergraduate students such as Jeremy Gilmore, Shana Brodnax, Linda Paul Karessy, Shana Riddick, Mzilikaze Kone, Lynette Anigbo, among many others. I appreciate the sounding board offered by reader/writer/friend Janet Cheatham Bell as well as the helpful editorial assistance of Leora Baude. I want to also acknowledge the longtime support of Indiana University colleagues Jean Robinson and Eileen Julien as well as the Indiana University Presidential Fellowship committee for bestowing the award that helped me complete this project. My residency at the Institute for Advanced Study during the fellowship period provided splendid accommodations in a work-inspiring environment. I thank former IAS director John Bodnar, and especially assistant director, my friend, Ivona Hedin.

A special thanks goes to the staff of Howard University's Moorland-Spingarn Research Center for their helpful research and speedy response to my queries about photographs, especially Jo-Ellen El Bashir and Kenvi Phillips. The Lucy Craft Laney Museum and its director, Christine Betts, were most helpful as were Frachelle Scott, the director of the Charlotte Hawkins Brown Museum, and staff member Kara Deadmon. The staff at the Mary McLeod Bethune Council House was helpful at the beginning of this project and Margaret Gardner of the U.S. Park Service was especially accommodating and supportive.

A most special thanks to former students at Palmer Memorial Institute who allowed me to interview them and shared their time and precious memories, including Alice and Tony Hurley, who were my first interviewees, and William "Bill" Brooks, who provided photographs and additional interview sources as well. For the generosity of their time and memories, I thank the Palmerites who agreed to be interviewed including Alma Grace Moreland Motley, Robert Lipscombe, Olvin McBarnette, the brother-sister dynamo Dr. Ida Daniel Dark and Dr. William Daniel, John Scarborough, Olga Black Fluker, Henry "Mickey" Michaux Jr., Naomi Mannigault Holmes, and Jeanne Lanier Rudd. A special debt and thanks is owed to longtime friend Eleanor Baker whose late sister, Nina Jones Boyd, was a Palmer graduate, for her help in connecting me with this group of outstanding Palmerites. I also extend thanks to the former leadership team of the Nannie Helen Burroughs School, including Shirley G. Hayes and Alberta T. Ford for access to important school documents.

Last but not least, I send love and adoration to my extended family for their faith in me and for their loving ways of being there. A special thanks to Malik McCluskey for busting the ghosts that reside inside my computer.

# ONE

# The World They Inherited

*We have to do more than other women.*

—Mary Church Terrell

What makes the black women in this study of school founders in the South during the period between the late 1800s and the mid-1900s worthy subjects for historical recovery and popular interest in their lives and work? Time, place, and circumstance combine to render the most complete answer. These women, daughters of slavery, and less than a generation removed from it, witnessed the lingering effects that engulfed their southern birthplaces. The post Reconstruction animus of the vanquished white South against its black citizens was meant to terrorize them and keep them in near servitude. Being among the first of their race and sex to receive formal education, the school founders were collectively committed to education as a counteroffensive to racial degradation and an instrument of uplift for themselves and their race. Using the motto of the National Association of Colored Women (NACW), they aimed to organize and "lift as they climb[ed])." The NACW, founded in 1896 as the first national organization of African Americans, enlisted women educators, activists, and social reformers in this effort. It was urged on by its first national president, Mary Church Terrell, who told her organization, "We have to do more than other women."[1] As members of the black women's club movement, school founders were in synch with this mission. They are an often forgotten subset of clubwomen whose response to the world of disadvantage and danger that African Americans inherited from enslavement was to place faith in God and themselves and bring about change by building institutions of learning. In addition to the four school founders who are the subject of this study, a considerable number of other southern black women of this period founded schools with similar inspiration and purpose. Among them were Elizabeth E. Wright, who

1

founded Voorhees Normal and Industrial School in Denmark, South Carolina, in 1897. In 1896, Mary McLeod Bethune's mentor, Emma Wilson, founded the Mayesville Educational and Industrial School in South Carolina. Georgia Washington founded People's Village School in 1893, in Mt. Meigs, Alabama. Grace Morris Allen Jones cofounded the Piney Woods School in Braxton, Mississippi, with her husband, Clarence Jones, in 1912. Other founders were Jennie Dean of the Manassas Industrial School in Virginia in 1894, and Cornelia Bowen, founder of Mt. Meigs Colored Institute in Alabama in 1888.[2] This incomplete list illustrates the great importance attached to education for race uplift as well as the fact that women assumed leadership in providing it.

This recovery of this forgotten sisterhood of like-minded women although not uncritical or complete, aims to illuminate the lives and work of four women in this group of school founders, whose relationship to each other is most well documented. In order of their birth, the women are: Lucy Craft Laney (1854–1933), founder of Haines Institute; Mary McLeod Bethune (1875–1955), founder of Bethune-Cookman College and the National Council of Negro Women; Nannie Helen Burroughs (1879–1961), founder of the National Training School for Negro Women and Girls; and Charlotte Hawkins Brown (1883–1961), founder of Palmer Memorial Institute. They shared a resolute belief in their vision of a world transformed by the work that they, and others like them, could do. Their sisterhood—spiritual, intellectual, and visionary—was part of a larger mission undertaken by the newly educated, rising class of black women during the post-Reconstruction period and into the early twentieth century. Defined by neither Greek letter sorority nor blood ties, it emerged from a shared response to the challenging circumstances of their young adulthood in the post-Reconstruction South and their maturation in the Jim Crow era of racial violence and segregation.

These women were among the striving class of blacks who had gained access to education through a combination of mentorship, diligence, and bountiful faith. Collectively, they embraced the broader, self-imposed mandate shared by their generation who united to form organizations and build schools. It took an audacious sense of agency for them, especially women of very limited means, to persevere despite tremendous obstacles. Living in an era of harsh racial repression, as well as a social order that constricted and confined women, they embraced teaching. Purported to be the "natural" role for women, teaching children provided the opportunity for useful service that they sought. Founding their own schools gave them a platform upon which to expand their individual authority and grow their collective vision for uplift.

## THE SOUTHERN LANDSCAPE

After the Civil War (1861–1865) and Reconstruction (1865–1876) ended, the post-Reconstruction years through the beginning of World War I (1877–1915) constituted one of the most tumultuous periods in American history. The strong hopes of Reconstruction embodied the aspirations of the formerly enslaved, but were dashed by equally strong and repressive measures meant to contain them. Those measures included lynching and other extralegal activities intended to maintain the pre-Emancipation racial order. Blacks had gained their freedom, but in real terms, they had come to question the meaning of that freedom. There were restrictions on every aspect of their lives, including where and how they lived, worked, and even died. Yet they clung to the promise of freedom that was delineated in the constitutional amendments following the end of the war in 1865. The Thirteenth, Fourteenth, and Fifteenth Constitutional Amendments ended slavery, offered equality under the law, and granted black males voting rights. These amendments were at the core of the optimism of the post-emancipation generations. Historian James M. McPherson reminds us of what blacks faced in trying to act upon it: "Since the beginning of the antislavery movement [there had been] arguments that Negroes belonged to a separate, inferior species of mankind; that they would work only under compulsion; that they could not take care of themselves in freedom and would revert to barbarism."[3] Overcoming such arguments became a major concern for blacks and their allies even after slavery was abolished. Some believed that black achievement in education, politics, family life, along with social and moral comportment, would lay to rest lingering suspicions of black inferiority. As descendants of the enslaved, black women educators accepted this task by embracing the spirit of President Abraham Lincoln's 1862 Gettysburg Address, in which he declared that "all men [human beings] are created equal." Having the president utter such words reinforced equality as an undeniably American concept, however elusive. Black leaders realized that their cause could be greatly served by situating their aims within the constitutional principles of democracy, equality, and justice.[4] They held onto these principles in the face of legislative, judicial, and extralegal setbacks. Such setbacks included the Jim Crow laws of racial confinement that historian C. Vann Woodward dates as beginning in 1877, the end of Reconstruction. It was a time, he states, when white men of the South "determined [that the country would] remain a white man's country."[5] A perfect storm of legal and extralegal events made that determination a reality. The *Plessy v. Ferguson* Supreme Court decision of 1896 established the separate but equal doctrine that remained in place until the 1954 *Brown v. the Board of Education* Supreme Court decree, and the epidemic of lynching terrorized blacks throughout the South. Mary McLeod Bethune recalled her own close encounter with domestic terrorism. As a

child, she witnessed a lynching while accompanying her father on a trip
to town. She saw a drunken white man shove a flaming match into a
black man's face. He instinctively flung his arm to protect his face from
being burned, inadvertently striking the white man. Other nearby whites
grabbed the black man and started yelling, "String him up!" As Mary's
father rushed her toward their wagon to escape the gathering mob, she
looked back and saw pure fear on the black man's face as he was herded
off to be lynched.[6]

Few blacks of the first or second generation after emancipation, even
the relatively privileged few who had access to education, could escape
the direct and brutal effects of the race-based intimidation and violence
that eviscerated many of the gains blacks had achieved during the fren-
zied twelve years of Reconstruction. For women, voting rights would be
contested and deferred until passage of the Nineteenth Amendment in
1919. It took two more generations for the civil rights movement to blos-
som and help black Americans gain long denied political rights. In the
intervening years, the recalcitrant attitudes of white Southerners who
underfunded and even burned down black schools, made initiatives to
educate black children even more crucial. Such opposition spurred
among the black masses a resolve and a hunger for education.[7] In the
words of Tuskegee Institute founder Booker T. Washington, it was "a
whole race trying to go to school."[8]

Having once had to subvert laws that punished them for the trans-
gression of learning to read, formerly enslaved people were zealous in
their pursuit of what they had been long denied, and what they considered a true marker of their freedom. Getting an education was a strike
against the old planter aristocracy and was viewed by blacks in general
as the best weapon against entrenched bigotry. Because blacks embraced
the American creed of "justice for all," education was also the way to
ensure a brighter future for themselves and their children.

Although only about 100,000 emancipated blacks were in school in
1867, by 1900, scholar W. E. B. Du Bois reported that over 1.5 million
black children were enrolled.[9] Among the number who received an education and dedicated themselves to improving the conditions and plight
of their people, no group was more involved in uplift and education
efforts than black women. It has been noted that overlapping memberships in black women's clubs at both the local and national level meant
that the goal of school founders and clubwomen was the same. Historian
Stephanie Shaw shows that rather than being a new initiative in organizing, nationalizing their efforts was the logical next step in a long tradition
that began with black women working together in their local communities for self-help, self-improvement, and education since the early to
mid-1800s.[10] Finding eager students, black teachers approached their
work with religious zeal. Joining their inspired ranks were black and
white teachers from the North who were committed to helping freed

people achieve the sought-after prize of literacy. Researchers have found, however, that black teachers had a stronger sense of commitment to the cause, as measured by their personal identification with the plight of their black pupils and their willingness to stay with the job much longer than their white counterparts.[11]

A tradition of black women committing themselves to teaching and equating it with freedom emerged long before emancipation or the work of the aforementioned school founders. Historian Gerda Lerner recovered the story of Milla Granson, a slave woman who ran a midnight school in the slave quarters; some of her pupils wrote their own freedom passes and headed for Canada.[12] At the dawn of emancipation, Fannie Coppin Jackson, the pioneering principal of Philadelphia's Institute for Colored Youth, made her mark as a community-minded educator who helped to establish a model of black women's activism in education. Among black women who provided schooling before Emancipation, Mary S. Peake also stands out. Her school in Fortress Monroe, Virginia, opened at the beginning of the Civil War in 1861, and was the first one supported by the American Missionary Association (AMA), which along with the Freedman Bureau, was the most prodigious supporter of black schools in the South. AMA schools and colleges produced the majority of the black teaching corps for the next several generations, with black women comprising up to 70 percent of those entering the profession.[13] This number included trailblazers as well as followers and supporters who felt self-empowered by their faith in God and in themselves, and by their belief that education would lead to a better future for the race and secure their rights as equal citizens.

## A WOMEN'S MOVEMENT

The four school founders in this study were born between 1854 and 1883, and their youth and young adulthood coincided with the worst years of the aforementioned race-based violence that characterized the post-Reconstruction era, referred to by historians as "the nadir" for black people in America.[14] As young women, they were brimming with optimism about what their race and sex could accomplish. Their collective lifespan extended to the beginning of the civil rights movement, making them participants in, as well as witnesses to, what was perhaps the most tumultuous and defining century of transgenerational change for black Americans—and for the nation.

There were close personal friendships among these women, who shared memberships in some of the same organizations. The oldest of the school founders, Lucy Laney, was born free before slavery ended to parents who had managed to purchase their freedom. She served as a role model and mentor to an upcoming generation of dedicated women, including the women under discussion here. In this grouping, there was nearly a thirty-year difference in age between the oldest and youngest, yet their connections were firm. Their common motivation was race uplift—to help their fellow African Americans overcome the debilitating circumstances brought on by centuries of enslavement, and to clear their path to full American citizenship through education. Their schools were exemplars of the imperative among black women to organize and establish institutions that directly addressed what they considered the most basic needs of their people. Although black self-help clubs were a staple of post-emancipation life, beginning in 1896, the National Association of Colored Women brought together the work that had begun long before at the grass roots level. Local women's clubs took on the work of providing child care, home management classes, and other "uplifting" activities for women in lower class circumstances. However, as historian Deborah Gray-White describes, class and skin color issues too often divided leaders from followers[15] and led to charges of elitism. Although these four school founders held leadership positions in local, regional, and national women's organizations, the fact that they were of darker complexion than most of the club movement leadership is probably coincidental. There is no evidence that it affected their decision to strike out on their own to open schools, and one of them, Mary McLeod Bethune, even founded her own women's organization, the National Council of Negro Women. However, Nannie Helen Burroughs, a transplant to Washington, D.C., early on expressed the view that Washington's "politics"[16] got in the way of her getting hired in the D.C. school system, where light-skinned women teachers such as Mary Church Terrell, Anna Julia Cooper, and Mary Jane Patterson held sway.

Despite such obstacles, the zeal for uplift among women who became teachers and leaders transcended barriers of skin color and created a strong bond. The women held compatible ideas and beliefs about education and race progress, although they took different paths to achieve that goal. They believed that the intelligence, morality, and abilities of black women had been maligned and, indeed, misrepresented. As a whole, the larger group of educated black women of this period inserted themselves into the role of defender of their sex and race and pushed back at detractors by showing what black women could do and achieve. For example, Anna Julia Cooper (1858–1964), the prominent Oberlin-educated intellectual, wrote about the need for women to develop qualities of leadership while adhering to high moral standards.[17] In her classic early feminist treatise, *A Voice from the South* (1892), Cooper advocated for higher education for women as a racial solution. According to her, black women possessed all the necessities for race leadership, and only when they should be totally free could the entire race experience freedom.[18] She noted that the feminine principles of nurture and service combined with higher education would create leaders more willing to assume the responsibility for educating and serving others. Yet the prevailing mores of female sexual purity and Christian modesty and morality tended to discourage leadership roles for women.[19] Cooper's advocacy of women's leadership was based upon what she called their human and spiritual values, which would serve as an antidote to society's ills and would expose the fallacy of black inferiority.[20]

Such arguments created an expectation of a female vanguard that was actualized through black women's organizations and institution building. NACW president, Mary Church Terrell, carried this sentiment forward in a speech at a women's meeting in 1916: "Those of us fortunate enough to have education must share it with the less fortunate of our race."[21] Lucy Laney had sounded the same theme years earlier when she urged "educated Colored women" to accept the burden of uplift of the less fortunate among them. Quoting Scripture, she said, "Bear ye one another's burdens," addressing women at the Hampton Institute Negro Conference in 1899.[22] In her speech, Laney blamed the poor conditions in black homes on eight generations of enslavement and, like Terrell, called for educated black women to rise to the challenge and assume the responsibility for guiding and lifting the race above those conditions.

Laney's message resonated broadly, especially among the women who followed her example by founding schools. The education they were inclined to offer was, as at Laney's Haines Institute, infused with Christian values and practical skills that were important to uplift the home as well as the larger community. Their aim was to build character along with marketable skills. For black women who had to defend their character from attacks, this aspect of their activism was very important.

Clubwoman Fannie Barrier Williams, noting that black male leaders had not always defended their women from character assassination, believed that an educated cadre of black women leading the race toward social uplift would vindicate black women, as well as the race.[23] Another public voice of advocacy and activism in this period, who began her career as a teacher but made her mark as an investigative journalist and anti-lynching activist, was Ida B. Wells-Barnett. The outspoken and uncompromising co-founder of the National Association for the Advancement of Colored People and anti-lynching leader, lost the presidency of the NACW to the more diplomatic Mary Bethune in the election of 1924. Although they did not elect her as their president, clubwomen had given earlier financial support to Wells for the publication of her booklet "Southern Horror," an investigation into the lynching of blacks in the South.[24]

These examples show the constancy of activism and organizing among women who began their professional lives as teachers and followed that path into a more public arena. Teachers were considered "the best organizers,"[25] because it was the profession that inspired them to "do more." Yet despite such confidence in their ability to lead, and the general optimism about advancements in "the woman's era," the world the educators and school founders inherited presented daunting challenges from the start.

The teaching profession, according to some estimates, attracted 90 percent of educated black women in the half century following Emancipation.[26] This attraction to teaching reflected not only the closed market for black professional women, but also the fact that it was a "safe and respected career that offered the opportunity to show commitment to racial progress."[27] Being "respectable" carried great weight among educated black women. Whether influenced by the vestiges of Victorian prudery or as a strategy for "resisting and defeating oppression,"[28] or both, a goal of the black women's club movement was for black women to be treated as equals among all women. Among the teachers and school founders, the curriculums and protocols in their schools show the emphasis they placed on proper decorum and conduct. Still, the need to acknowledge the history of black women's exploitation under slavery and its social consequences, while at the same time preparing them to take their place in the broader world, made black women school founders and teachers less ideological in their educational philosophy than some of their male counterparts. On the one hand, black women sought acceptance by advocating puritanical dictates of female purity and domesticity that were devised with white women in mind.[29] Yet they also recognized the need to fight the injustice that was continuing to oppress their people. Their activism was based in this dual reality.

The sisterhood that emerged from these circumstances was forged as they passionately sought to extend an education like those they had received and the human rights they desired to their people. Both individually and collectively, these school founders worked for a common cause. The women in this study are linked not only by their common mission, but also as teachers and mentors, clubwomen, friends, and confidantes who faced persistent obstacles in advancing their cause. Each of their educational and professional journeys shows similar themes, as well as divergence in their life and work.

## THE SCHOOL FOUNDERS

Mary Bethune's formerly enslaved parents were farmers in Mayesville, South Carolina, and she was among the youngest of their seventeen children. A natural leader and organizer of her siblings, Mary was spared from chores on their small farm to walk five miles to a one-room school, and later received a scholarship from a white missionary to attend Scotia Seminary in North Carolina, before completing her education at Moody Bible Institute in Chicago in 1896. After being denied a missionary post in Africa, she returned home to teach for a year, then moved on to teach at

Haines Institute under Lucy Craft Laney, where she determined that she could follow in the footsteps of her mentor, whom she called the "greatest Negro woman educator in the history of the race."[30] Bethune, showing organizational genius and leadership skills that would catapult her onto the national stage, started her own school for girls in Daytona Beach, Florida, in 1904, and grew it into Bethune-Cookman College.[31]

Bethune's North Carolina-born friend, Charlotte Hawkins Brown, moved to Cambridge, Massachusetts, at an early age and grew up in its liberal, less racially charged atmosphere. She attended school and college in integrated settings and under the influence of New England educational ideas, styles, and manners. Wellesley College President Alice Palmer, in whose memory Brown named her school, helped her to gain entrance to Salem State University in Massachusetts. After being inspired by a lecture in which she heard of the work of Lucy Laney in Georgia, she received her mother's blessing and left Salem at age eighteen to return to North Carolina to teach. In 1901, with sponsorship from the American Missionary Association, Brown opened a school in rural North Carolina for the children of black farmers. She soon ventured out on her own, evolving the curriculum into a college preparatory focus in order to attract the sons and daughters of the black middle class—who could pay the new private school's tuition.[32] In a hand-written response to a questionnaire from *Ebony* magazine for a special feature on the school that showed a financial formula dependent upon students who could pay and her own fundraising skills, Brown noted that almost two thirds of the $100,000 budget came from tuition, room, and board, while the other third was raised by herself.[33]

Nannie Helen Burroughs' widowed mother moved the family from Virginia to Washington, D.C., in search of better schooling, but found little change in the racial segregation laws. Burroughs graduated in 1896 (the same year the National Association of Colored Women was organized) from the highly respected M Street High School, where NACW President Mary Church Terrell, an Oberlin College graduate, was one of her teachers. Anna Julia Cooper was also on the faculty and was, for a time, principal. Although the M Street School boasted of the number of its graduates who attended prestigious colleges and universities, Burroughs pursued a teaching job rather than college. It took several years before she could convince the National Baptist Convention to sponsor her school for girls and women and to locate it in the nation's capital. Her activism in the church, outspoken editorials, and the practical curriculum she installed led some to describe her as a mix between W. E. B. Du Bois, Booker T. Washington, and Marcus Garvey.[34] Her gift of speaking truth to power and standing up for women was shown when at age twenty-one, she presented a speech at the National Baptist Convention in 1900 entitled "How the Sisters are Hindered from Helping."[35] Burroughs, the last survivor among this group of activist educators, had a direct link to the civil rights movement and was an admired elder and friend of Dr. Martin Luther King, Jr. After she contacted him by phone in 1958 to ask him to speak to her Baptist youth program in Chicago, King wrote her to confirm that he would be "very happy to" accept the invitation. He added that, "we are eternally grateful to you for the great work you are doing for the Baptists of America and for the whole of Christendom."[36] Burroughs' activism was most notable in advancing the interest of the school she founded under the auspices of the Southern Baptist Convention. Showing the independent mindset that would later cause tensions within the convention, she named the school the "National," rather than "Baptist," Training School for Negro Women and Girls.[37]

Lucy Craft Laney, the first among equals, the oldest of this sisterhood, and a pioneer among women school founders, mentored or inspired a generation of black women educators, including Bethune, Brown, and Burroughs. Her school, Haines Institute in Augusta, opened in 1886, just three years after the more famous Tuskegee Institute, co-founded by her contemporaries Booker T. Washington and Olivia Davidson. Laney's own education at the American Missionary Association's Lewis High School (later Ballard High) for blacks in Macon, Georgia, and subsequent graduation in the first class of the newly instituted Atlanta University, was aided, as were Bethune and Brown, by white beneficence.[38] At Atlanta University, the classical curriculum installed by Edmund Asa Ware, along with support from the AMA and the Freedman's Bureau, gave her a broad, liberal education. It was more in tune with such schools as Oberlin College than fledging black institutions in the South that depended upon northern industrial philanthropists who encouraged them to adopt the Hampton-Tuskegee model of industrial education.[39]

Laney's reputation as a transformative teacher and change agent was burnished by reports from her students and those who worked with her to confirm that she not only "knew where every nail was" in the stately campus buildings, but she also taught, during her long tenure, almost every course in the curriculum, including Latin, Greek, English literature, and mathematics.[40] Her immersion in the classics did not prevent her from also instituting industrial education courses and lecturing to women at teacher workshops at Hampton Institute, the center for the dissemination of industrial education.[41]

Each of the women in this sisterhood of purposeful women faced a different set of circumstances but dedicated herself to a common cause. They were black women born during a thirty-year period of rapid change and national upheaval that began before the end of slavery and continued through the Reconstruction and the post-Reconstruction eras. Receiving an education through rare and fortunate fate inclined them to seek it broadly for their people, impoverished after centuries of enslavement, discriminated against, and maligned—especially black women. Collectively, they had a gift for inspiring others with their own dreams and skill for organizational work, especially among other women. They were members of their local women's clubs and the National Association of Colored Women. Laney was a founder of the Augusta chapter of the National Association of Colored People. Bethune, active in a number of organizations including women's clubs, served two terms as NACW president from 1924–1928. She later founded the National Council of Negro Women in 1935. Brown, like Bethune, was active in the Southeastern Federation of Colored Women's Clubs and president of the North Carolina branch. She later became a vice president of Bethune's NCWW. Burroughs' leadership was shown when she rose to become corresponding secretary, then president of the Women's Conference of the National Baptist Convention. In addition, all four women were members of the unofficial "Southern Network" of black women activists who emerged during the first decades of the twentieth century. Their work focused on improving conditions for black workers, health services, easing racial disparities in education, police and sanitation services, and a number of other issues that affected the black community. [42] Historian Jacqueline Rouse reminds us of the long history of organizing by southern black women, citing Lugenia Burns Hope of the Neighborhood Union in Atlanta, Margaret Murray Washington and Jennie Moton of Tuskegee, and Maggie Lena Walker of Virginia, all of whom were also members of this extended network of activist black women who viewed their race and gender not solely according to the restrictive dictates of southern history, but also according to the change they believed race uplift through education would bring. [43]

While the recorded history of the quest for education by African Americans reflects this hopeful outlook, it does not adequately present the work and ideas of black women who have a long tradition of espousing education to remediate racial injustice. In their advocacy and sense of mission, black women educators embraced and echoed W. E. B. Du Bois' call for a "talented tenth" to arise and lead. They also endorsed the "bootstrap philosophy" of Booker T. Washington. The overlap evident even between Du Bois and Washington was easily discernible in curriculums of the schools founded by these women. Because they believed that rejuvenation of the race would be led by women, [44] and that their needs had been neglected by male leaders, they placed emphasis on women. They especially emphasized the need to remove the stigma of immorality, branded upon their persons by mainstream culture. This concern, coupled with the economic motive of preparing women to be self-supporting, remained a paramount consideration among the school founders. They had an implicit understanding of the "multiple jeopardy" that the mass of black women who were subjected to gender, race, and class oppression faced, and found no contradiction in advocating both for black women and the race as a whole. They joined in interracial alliances with white women, but realized that their own organizations and schools offered the best hope for the progress they sought.[45]

The four southern women in this study deserve to have their stories told, especially in a connected way that links them to each other and their common purpose. This attempt to recover this "forgotten sisterhood" presents a progression of nonlinear chapters that examines the lives of these four influential women leaders, focusing on their activist leadership in education and institution building. It connects them to a larger network that constituted a social movement for uplift among black women from the post-Reconstruction period through the first half of the twentieth century.

The second chapter, "Moving like a Whirlwind," presents the lesser-known Lucy Craft Laney as an innovative educator and local activist who was among the first of her race and sex to found and sustain a school for nearly a half century. As a generationally bridging figure who combined Victorian ethos and efficiency with advanced educational ideas, her personal example became an inspiration to the next generation of black women educators and school founders. Chapter 3, "The Best Secondary School in Georgia," continues the focus on Laney and the origins, curriculum, campus life, and social impact of the growth and development of Haines Institute during the early twentieth century. Although most of Laney's papers were burned in a fire, surviving letters, interviews, and other documents help to reconstruct how Laney's improbable accomplishment took shape and affected the larger community. Laney's mentee, Mary McLeod Bethune, who as a young woman worked beside her at Haines, is the subject of chapter 4, "Ringing Up A School." It was reworked and expanded from an earlier published essay that appeared in the *Florida Historical Quarterly* (1994). It follows Bethune's early years in Daytona Beach, the beginnings and growth of her school for black girls, and her rising status and impact on the larger community—particularly as she navigated the racial divide and began to earn her reputation as a champion of racial diplomacy. In chapter 5, "Show Some Daylight Between You," former students, now in their seventies and eighties, recall their matriculation at Palmer Memorial Institute during the 1940s and 1950s, including memories of founder Charlotte Hawkins Brown. These student perspectives provide a rich new dimension to existing records of campus life and Brown's charismatic and idiosyncratic leadership. "Telling Some Mighty Truths," chapter 6, focuses on the activism of school founder Nannie Helen Burroughs and her work in building her school and being an outspoken voice for racial accountability and justice in the years preceding the Civil Rights movement. "The Masses and the Classes," chapter 7, recounts how women's networks and friendships both black and white, provided crucial support and stability to the school founders, particularly Charlotte Hawkins Brown and Mary McLeod Bethune. Their correspondence reveals how they cultivated donors, especially women, and the complexities of their friendship. The final chapter, "Passing into History: Commemorations, Memorials, and the Legacies of Black Women School Founders," offers a summative reading of how these four women are presented as historical figures and occupy public space in popular and institutional memory. "Milestones: A Chronology" presents selected dates that highlight significant events in the interconnected lives of Laney, Bethune, Brown, and Burroughs.

## NOTES

1. Deborah Gray White, *Too Heavy a Load: Black Women in Defense of Themselves, 1894–1994* (New York: W. W. Norton), 22.

2. Dorothy Salem, *To Better Our World: Black Women in Organized Reform, 1890–1920* (Brooklyn: Carlson Publishing, 1990).

3. James M. McPherson, *The Struggle for Equality: Abolitionists and the Negro in the Civil War and Reconstruction* (Princeton, N.J.: Princeton University Press, 1964), 134.

4. Richard Hofstadter, *Social Darwinism in American Thought* (Philadelphia: University of Pennsylvania Press, 1955), 44.

5. C. Vann Woodward, *The Strange Case of Jim Crow* (New York: Oxford University Press, 1957), 7.

6. Milton Metzer, *Mary McLeod: Voice of Black Hope* (New York: Viking, 1987), 9.

7. James D. Anderson, *The Education of Blacks in the South, 1860–1935* (Chapel Hill, N.C.: University of North Carolina Press, 1988), 5.

8. Anderson, *Education of Blacks*, 5.

9. W. E. B. Du Bois, *Black Reconstruction*, reprint of Harcourt, Brace edition (Millwood, N.Y.: Kraus Thomson, 1935), 701.

10. Stephanie J. Shaw, "Black Club Women and the Creation of the National Association of Colored Women," in *"We Specialize in the Wholly Impossible": A Reader in Black Women's History*, ed. Darlene Clark Hine, Wilma King, and Linda Reed (Brooklyn, N.Y.: Carlson Publishing, 1995), 434.

11. Adam Fairclough, *A Class of their Own: Black Teachers in the Segregated South* (Cambridge, Mass.: Harvard University Press, 2007), 42.

12. Gerda Lerner, ed., *Black Women in White America: A Documentary History* (New York: Vintage Books, 1973), 32–33.

13. Linda M. Perkins, "Education," in *Black Women in America: An Historical Encyclopedia*, eds. Darlene Clark Hine et al. (New York: Carlson Publishing, 1993), 383.

14. Rayford W. Logan, *The Negro in American Life and Thought: The Nadir, 1877–1901* (New York: Dial, 1954), 3–11.

15. Gray White, *Too Heavy a Load*, 75–78.

16. Earl L. Harrison, *The Dream and the Dreamer: An Abbreviated Story of the Life of Dr. Nannie Helen Burroughs and the National Trade School* (Washington, D.C.: unknown binding, 1956), in undated, untitled school records from files of Nannie Helen Burroughs School, n.p. courtesy of school principal Aurelia R. Downey.

17. Karen A. Johnson, *Uplifting the Women and the Race: The Lives, Educational Philosophies, and Social Activism of Anna Julia Cooper and Nannie Helen Burroughs* (New York: Garland Publishing, 2000), xxix–xxx.

18. Anna Julia Cooper, *A Voice from the South: By a Black Woman of the South* (Xenia, Ohio: Aldine Printing House, 1892; New York: Oxford University Press, 1988), 29. Citations refer to 1988 reprint.

19. Anne Hogan and Andrew Bradstock, eds., *Women of Faith in Victorian Culture: Reassessing the Angel in the House* (New York: St. Martin's Press, 1998), 1.

20. Anna J. Cooper, *Voice from the South*, 144.

21. Mamie Garvin Fields with Karen Fields, *Lemon Swamp and Other Places: A Carolina Memoir* (New York: Free Press, 1983), 189.

22. Lucy Craft Laney, "The Burden of the Educated Colored Woman," *Southern Workman* 28, no. 9 (September 1899): 341–44.

23. Fannie Barrier Williams, "The Club Movement among Negro Women," in J. W. Gibson and W. H. Crogman, *Progress of A Race* [1902] (Miami: Mnemosyne Publishing Co., 1969), 204.

24. Paula Giddings, *When and Where We Enter: The Impact of Black Women on Race and Sex in America* (New York: William Morrow, 1984), 30.

25. Gray White, *Too Heavy a Load*, 52.

26. Jeanne L. Noble, *The Negro Woman's College Education* (1956; repr., New York: Garland Publishing, 1987), 18.

27. Noble, *Negro Woman*, 52.

28. Hazel V. Carby, "'On the Threshold of Woman's Era': Lynching, Empire, and Sexuality in Black Feminist Theory," *Critical Inquiry* 12 (Autumn 1985): 264.

29. Linda M. Perkins, "The Impact of the Cult of True Womanhood on the Education of Black Women," *Journal of Social Issues* 39, no. 3 (1983): 17–28.

30. Mary McLeod Bethune, "A Century of Progress of Negro Women," n.d., Mary McLeod Bethune Paper Collection, Amistad Research Center, Tulane University.

31. Audrey Thomas McCluskey, "Mary McLeod Bethune and the Education of Black Girls in the South, 1904–1923," (PhD diss., Indiana University, 1991). Bethune moved her school from the very rural Palatka, Florida, to Daytona in order to attract rich donors who spent their winters nearby. The school, continuing to evolve, is now Bethune-Cookman University.

32. Sandra N. Smith and Earle H. West, "Charlotte Hawkins Brown," *Journal of Negro History* 51, no. 3 (Summer 1983): 197.

33. "*Ebony* Questionnaire," Charlotte Hawkins Brown Papers, Schlesinger Library.

34. Sharon Harley, "Nannie Helen Burroughs: The Black Goddess of Liberty," *Journal of Negro History* 18 (Winter–Autumn, 1996): 68–70.

35. "A Brief Note on the Lives of Anna Julia Cooper and Nannie Helen Burroughs: Profiles of African Women Educators," *Global African Community History Notes.* http://aalbc.com/reviews/anna.htm (12 Mar. 2009).

36. Martin Luther King, Jr., to Nannie Burroughs, March 8, 1958, in *The Papers of Martin Luther King, Jr,. Vol. 4: Symbol of the Movement*, January 1957–December 1957, ed. Clayborne Carson (Berkeley: University of California Press, 1992), 378.

37. Nannie Helen Burroughs Papers, "A Register of Her Papers in the Library of Congress," prepared by Audrey Walker et al., Manuscript Division, 1982, 6–95.

38. Audrey Thomas McCluskey, "Manly Husbands and Womanly Wives: The Educational Leadership of Lucy Craft Laney," in *Post Bellum, Pre-Harlem Renaissance: African American Literature and Culture, 1877–1919*, eds. Carolyn Gebhard and Barbara McCaskill (New York: NYU Press, 2006), 7.

39. Anderson, *The Education of Blacks in the South, 1860–1935*,), 35–78.

40. Britt Edward Cottingham, "The Burden of the Educated Colored Woman: Lucy Craft Laney and the Haines Institute, 1886–1933," (master's thesis, Georgia State University, 1995), 72–73.

41. Cottingham, "Burden."

42. Jacqueline Anne Rouse, *Lugenia Burns Hope: Black Southern Reformer* (Athens, Ga.: University of Georgia Press, 1989), 5–6.

43. Rouse, *Lugenia Burns Hope*, 5–6.

44. "Womanhood: A Vital Element in the Regeneration and Progress of a Race," in Cooper, *Voice from the South*, 9–48; Mary McLeod Bethune, "President's Address to the Fifteenth Biennial Convention of the National Association of Colored Women," in *Mary McLeod Bethune Building a Better World*, eds. Audrey Thomas McCluskey and Elaine M. Smith (Bloomington: Indiana University Press, 2000), 154–62.

45. Cynthia Neverdon-Morton, *Afro-American Women of the South and the Advancement of the Race, 1895–1925* (Knoxville: University of Tennessee Press, 1989), 201.

# TWO

## "Moving Like a Whirlwind"

### Lucy Craft Laney, Activist Educator

*The educated Negro woman must teach the 'Black Babies'; she must come forward and inspire our men and boys to make a successful onslaught upon sin, shame, and crime.*

—Lucy C. Laney

In the city of Augusta, Georgia, a high school and a museum and conference center[1] both bear her name. Her portrait hangs in the state capitol in Atlanta, recognizing her as a woman of achievement.[2] She and Dr. Martin Luther King, Jr., are the only two native Georgians whose gravesites are alight with an eternal flame. In her day, people far beyond the state of Georgia heralded Lucy Craft Laney (1854–1933) as the visionary founder of Haines Normal and Industrial Institute in Augusta in 1883, calling her a "race leader." She was revered by friends and acquaintances and was clearly one of the most influential black women of her era. At her funeral in 1933, news sources noted the many dignitaries who spoke at her funeral or sent messages of tribute and reported that between 5,000 and 10,000 mourners passed her bier.[3] Among black leaders who spoke at her funeral or sent telegrams were several women school founders who considered her their role model. Charlotte Hawkins Brown, founder of Palmer Memorial Institute in North Carolina, described Laney as "the outstanding model of Negro womanhood in the world . . . and the woman who was the inspiration of my childhood dreams, the fulfillment of my ideals for a useful life."[4] Mary McLeod Bethune, founder of the school that became Bethune-Cookman University, called Laney "our heroine in the field of Christian education. Our youth have lost a fearless champion. She blazed the way to higher things. [Laney] was my early inspiration. Her work can never die."[5] Lucy Laney was "a spiritual symbol of vision, sacrifice and devotion,"[6] said her friend Nannie Helen Burroughs, founder of the National Training School for Women and Girls.

Several educators, including Bethune and Janie Porter Barrett, founder of the Virginia Industrial School for Colored Girls, had been apprentice teachers under Laney at Haines. What these women praised Laney for in life and death, they sought to emulate in their own schools: an uplifting mission in the black community, a special focus on the education of girls and young women, and a mixture of academic and vocational courses, melded with a strong Christian ethic. College presidents John Hope of Atlanta University (AU) and Mordecai Johnson of Howard University also eulogized Laney as a superior teacher. In 1930, the "capstone" of black higher education, Howard, bestowed an honorary master of arts degree on Laney, and President Johnson called her a "farseeing spirit" and the "mother of the children of the people."[7] This is a somewhat ironic appellation given that Laney, who never married and had no children of her own, became the "other mother" to so many. She gained near-legendary status among her peers during her lifetime, but notably without self-promotion. In his memorial tribute to Laney, A. C. Griggs, a longtime teacher at Haines who, after Laney died, was elected principal in 1935, offered this Dickensian quote as the apotheosis of Laney's spirit: "Do all the good you can and make no fuss about it."[8]

Lucy Craft Laney led a full life of activism and purpose dedicated to racial advancement, but her first love was the work of building Haines Institute and being its sustaining force for nearly a half century. Laney was still warmly remembered nearly seventy years later—in 2003—by a surviving student and namesake. Native Augustan Mrs. Lucille Laney Ellis Floyd attended Haines in the early 1930s, and her mother was a good friend and neighbor of the educator. Having interviewed her when she was in her eighties, Ellis Floyd recalled that Lucy Laney was always moving around "like a whirlwind, teaching all the subjects and making sure everyone was behaving."[9] Ellis Floyd remembered that "I want to wear out, not rust out" was one of Laney's favorite sayings.

Yet despite abundant praise from contemporaries and a secure legacy,[10] there is still more to be learned about her, especially as an activist educator who advocated for women, education, and social change. That task is made more difficult by the fact that before she died, most of her papers were destroyed in a fire at her school.[11] Reconstructing and assessing her life and work require a reliance on the few extant papers and speeches she left and the memories and documents of contemporaries whose lives intersected with hers.

## LANEY'S BIOGRAPHY

Lucy Craft Laney was born in Macon, Georgia, in 1854[12] and reached adulthood during the Reconstruction period. It was a time when women were largely confined to the domestic sphere. She was one of ten siblings whose parents also took in orphans. Her father, David Laney, was an accomplished carpenter. He bought his own freedom and later that of his wife, Louisa, who was owned by a prominent family in Macon.[13] David became an ordained Presbyterian minister in 1867 and was reported to have rung the church bell "to call Negroes together to tell them that they were free"[14] when General Robert E. Lee surrendered to General Ulysses S. Grant. Louisa, who had been taught to read by her mistress, encouraged her daughter's intellectual growth, and often excused her from chores so that she could read. Louisa's former owners, for whom she continued to work, allowed Lucy free rein in their library and supported her admission to the American Missionary Association's Lewis High School that opened in 1865. (It was renamed Ballard High in 1888.)[15] Laney continued her education at the age of fifteen at newly established Atlanta University. When she entered the AMA-sponsored university, she had already read Shakespeare, George Eliot, and other classics and could read and translate Latin.[16] At AU she completed the Higher Normal (teacher training) along with three other females and became a member of the first graduating class in 1873.[17] Laney, by all reports, was a brilliant student, but the university's restriction on women prevented her from entering the regular college program. Because of her family's relatively fortunate circumstances—having access to literacy at a time when almost 90 percent of blacks did not[18]—she did not have to be a "rebel literate," the term used by historian James D. Anderson in referring to the extraordinary lengths that some blacks had to go to get an education.[19] Descriptions of Laney often noted that she was a "little woman," or a "small woman,"[20] who "put first things first," and was "staunchly Christian."[21] Her classmate at Atlanta University, Richard R. Wright, recalled her as being "the loveliest, most energetic and attractive brown skin girl he had ever met."[22] She intrigued him by her unwillingness to give up and how she challenged him when she thought he was erring. The few extant photographs of Laney show that even as a young woman, she was unpretentious and straightforward in style and dress. Although she had a no-nonsense reputation as a disciplinarian, her students described her as joyful and loving. "She was the biggest child in the bunch, safely playing the games of love and life building,"[23] recalled one of her students.

Laney possessed a captivating voice that made her a popular guest speaker, and her celebrity helped in fundraising for Haines. She had a command of classical literature and languages and sprinkled the names of classical texts and authors into her speeches.[24] Given the opportunity, she also touted black advancement and spoke against the naysayers:

> It has been forty years since Emancipation . . . but we are hearing from some quarters that it is no good, that money and men and time have been wasted, and we would be better to do something for the other exceptional race and let the Negro go. I don't believe that Christian men and women believe anything of the kind; they know a great deal has been accomplished. The work is hard. For 250 years the Negro was held in slavery, and before that were centuries of heathenism against [just] forty years of freedom.[25]

Despite the obvious prejudice against African cultures that can be attributed to her acceptance of Christian missionary dogma about civilizing "Dark Africa," she is clearly a "race woman," who always extolled the great contributions and aspirations of black people. In the same speech, she refuted the charge of Negro shiftlessness by listing the number of black-owned farms and businesses, and by praising black institutions of higher learning, professionals, homeowners, and the "thousands of books written by Negroes."[26] Laney believed that formerly enslaved people could throw off the mental and social deficits of enslavement through education, moral rejuvenation, and Christian living. After graduating from Atlanta University at the age of eighteen, in the midst of post-Reconstruction repression and racial violence, she began her teaching career in Georgia's segregated public school system. Following teaching stints in Macon, Milledgeville, Savannah, and Augusta,[27] she settled in the latter, where the intent to open her own school became etched in her mind.

Initially, she was invited by prominent black leaders in Augusta to run the Fourth Ward Grammar School. There she earned a sterling reputation and was one of only two black teachers in the city to receive a second-level teaching certificate.[28] After ten years of experience in the public system and with a growing sense that "the public school cannot take the place of the mission school,"[29] she founded what was informally called "Miss Laney's School" in Augusta. Laney was greatly incensed by the widely held perception among whites that black women were unfit to teach children, and she wanted her school to focus on black girls and disprove the charge[30] that they were unfit for the classroom. She began with minimal resources and fewer prospects, partly because of existing perceptions that favored male leadership. Also, Laney did not strictly adhere to the industrial education philosophy that was favored by the Slater Fund and the General Education Board, prominent funding organizations for black education. These philanthropies wanted the Hampton-Tuskegee model of industrial education, installed and popularized by Booker T. Washington, to be the model for their support. With few resources, Laney opened her primary school for both girls and boys in a church basement, and developed it into a high school and junior college before its decline after her death in 1933. Her success was due, in no small measure, to constant nurturing and great personal sacrifice, including frequent travel for fundraising that affected her health.[31]

Her earliest and most important fundraising appeal was one that a local minister encouraged her to make at the Minnesota meeting of the 95th General Assembly of the Presbyterian Church in 1899. The odds were against her, because men dominated the Assembly and women seldom spoke up. She received nothing but moral support and train fare back home until the leader of the women's conference, Francina Haines of New Jersey, came to her aid. As a memorial to her benefactor, Laney named the fledgling school in her honor.[32] After receiving glowing reports about the school, the Presbyterian Church also joined in supporting Laney's effort. A $10,000 grant from the Presbyterians was the largest gift the school had received. Laney garnered support from other white northerners and Presbyterian Church members, as well as from black donors. For example, hair care magnate Madame C. J. Walker reportedly instructed her attorney to send a $1,000 check to Haines.[33] Another important source of revenue for Haines Institute was the alumni who organized Lucy Laney Circles in several cities.

## A SOCIAL MISSION

As her school grew in stature, Laney developed a reputation as an activist, becoming a cofounder of the Augusta branch of the National Association of Colored People in 1919, and a member of the "Southern Network" of black women reformers of the early twentieth century. Their work to improve poor black communities through education while fighting for racial and gender equality was infused with strong ideas about acceptable conduct.[34] The network included the other women school founders in this study who were inspired by Laney's example—Mary McLeod Bethune, Charlotte Hawkins Brown, and Nannie Helen Burroughs—as well as Atlanta-based organizer Lugenia Burns Hope,[35] educator Janie Porter Barrett, and banker Maggie Lena Walker, and several other prominent black women

Laney's clearest articulation of the social reforms that she believed were needed for a race stained by the corrupt habits of the slave plantation—especially the role that women should play—is spelled out in excerpts of her speeches and remembered sayings, especially two surviving speeches, "Address Before the Women's Meeting" in 1898 in Atlanta, and "The Burden of Educated Colored Women" in 1899 in Hampton, Virginia. In the Atlanta speech at her alma mater, she addressed the women's conference with the prediction that a "glorious future" was ahead for the black race. The future Laney envisioned would be built upon progress in education, politics, and religion. She told the gathered women that the future also rested upon the "God-given authority" of mothers, who must develop the young lives in their care into noble men and women. "Women of today, awake to your responsibilities and privileges,"[36] she exhorted. Laney continued this theme of women's special endowment and duty the next year at the Hampton Negro Conference, where, in her speech, she reminded the assembled women of the centuries of "dark despair" that befell our enslaved ancestors. The resulting immorality and neglect of the home must, and can only, be lifted by the educated colored woman who accepts the "burden" of racial leadership. She continued:

> We know the history; we think a correct diagnosis has often been made—let us attempt a cure. We would prescribe: homes—better homes, clean homes, pure homes; schools—better schools; more culture; more thrift; and work in large doses; put the patient at once on this treatment and continue through life. Can woman do this work? She can; and she must do her part, and her part is by no means small.[37]

Laney's views reflected Victorian notions of a vital motherhood in which the woman's role was to be at the center of family life and the arbiter of social acceptance and female empowerment.[38] She believed that the absence of habits of hygiene and discipline that should be taught in the home intensified, if not created, prejudice against the black race. She believed that the stability of black family life, molded and guided by loving mothers, would lead to a transformed and improved social and racial climate. Educated mothers would "instill lessons of cleanliness, truthfulness, loving kindness, love for nature, and love for Nature's God . . . and can lead the race away from "sin and crime."[39] She called upon women to become teachers because they are better with children and natural "nurturers and civilizers." To Laney, the home was the foundation of society, and she believed that the black race must be rid of "untidy and filthy" homes that bred death and moral decay. Laney invoked historical examples, including Phyllis Wheatley and Sojourner Truth, to show what the race was capable of achieving. In the Hampton speech, she also assailed the injustice that landed black men in jail for stealing two "fish hooks" and blamed the courts for their practice of handing down stiffer punishment to black offenders.[40] Her vision of a transformed society required blacks to do three things: develop the right kind of mother-centered Christian home life; fight racial discrimination; and gain access to a good education. Embedded in her message to women was her optimism about their expanding role: "Nothing in the present century is more noticeable than the tendency of women to enter every hopeful field of wage earning and philanthropy, and attempt to reach a place in every intellectual arena."[41]

More than a "politics of respectability,"[42] Laney's views about women's traditional roles encompassed both a domestic and public function.

She adhered to scholar Carol Allen's observation that black women intellectuals of the period often held traditional views about women but modified or expanded them."[43] For example, while Laney subscribed to the view that women have a special endowment for nurturing professions such as teaching and nursing, she also viewed this work as part of a strategy for race progress. Scholars such as Kevin Gaines have argued that many leaders of this period accepted patriarchy as the natural order.[44] Laney did accept Victorian-inspired gender divisions and women's primacy in the home, but she also wanted change. She argued that educated women's "burden" to inspire, teach, and lead the race toward dignity and self-sufficiency made them agents of transformation, not the patriarchal status quo. Women were not to be cloistered in the domestic sphere, as was the expectation of the Victorian era's cult of true womanhood ideology.[45] Rather, she believed that women should enter every field of human endeavor "without trepidation."[46]

To Laney and to others among the first generations of formally educated black women, education provided a social and racial equalizer. Her own education allowed her to teach others and to be an advocate for change. Mary White Ovington, a white woman who was a founder of the NAACP, admired Laney for standing up for her ideals and noted her refusal to bow to male authority even in the hierarchical Presbyterian Church, or to others who thought a woman should not run a school. Ovington concluded that Laney was "ahead of her time."[47]

## SETTING A STANDARD

Laney greatly influenced younger women such as Mary Bethune, who spent the 1895–1896 school year teaching at Haines before opening her own school in Daytona Beach, Florida, in 1904. That influence can be seen in the initiatives and ideas that Bethune borrowed from Laney. Community outreach programs, early childhood education, and the cultivation of both black and white female support were all ideas and concepts that Bethune saw executed at Haines. For these, Bethune continually sang Laney's praises, and she even enrolled her son and only child, Albertus, at Haines. One of Bethune's early biographers recounted that following her disappointment at being rejected for a missionary post in Africa, Bethune found in her apprenticeship with Laney a mentor and friend twenty years her senior and a new inspiration and mission. This is illustrated in the following passage that a biographer attributed to Bethune: "The corridors [of Haines] were teeming with happy children who had been gathered up, washed up, and guided into better lives. It made Bethune realize that she was needed, too."[48]

Laney aroused such a call to service because she dedicated her own life to the work of social reclamation by focusing on children. "We have nothing to make women and men [of] but girls and boys" is a saying widely attributed to Laney. The success of Haines—led by a black woman in a field dominated by men—earned Laney gravitas in the larger black community, particularly among women. Having started her school in 1883, only two years after Booker T. Washington began at Tuskegee, she showed black women what could be achieved.[49]

Another mentee inspired by Laney's example was school founder Janie Porter Barrett. Seeing that Laney's work was not being recognized beyond her own group, in 1929 Barrett nominated her for the William Harmon Foundation's annual award for distinguished achievement among Negroes. Barrett, who won the award the same year she nominated Laney, taught briefly at Haines after graduating from Hampton Institute.[50] In her letter of nomination, she asked the organization to "please look up Miss Lucy Laney's work. . . . [S]he has done a wonderful job in inspiring young people . . . [and] splendid work in the field of education through the years. I wish her to have this public recognition for she worked so unselfishly, but she works quietly. . . ."[51] Laney did not receive this national award, but was recognized with honorary degrees from black universities attended by many Haines graduates, including recognition by Atlanta University in 1898, Lincoln University in 1904, and South Carolina State in 1925.

The work for which she was being honored began with a curriculum of basic primary-level work, but there is no documentation of what she taught the five girls and one boy who were her first students. We do know that Laney developed a pioneering kindergarten program and steadily expanded and upgraded the courses. By the 1890s the curriculum included English, mathematics, the Bible, biology, physics, sociology, French, Latin, Greek, and political science. There were several courses in music and history—ancient history, United States history, and Negro history. Haines also had a debate team, a dramatic group, a choral ensemble, and a literary society, as well as the first organized football team in the city.[52]

Haines also offered vocational courses in cosmetology, mechanical arts, shorthand, and bookkeeping that sought to prepare students for the existing job market without sacrificing their academic potential. The mix of industrial or vocational courses with a college preparatory curriculum earned Laney accolades from both sides of the ideological divide over black education in this period. Tuskegee Institute founder Booker T. Washington and scholar-activist W. E. B. Du Bois—famously at odds over the best way to ensure black progress, including whether industrial or liberal (classical) education was the best choice—both praised Laney. Washington noted that she was doing "interesting and important work."[53] Du Bois criticized some unnamed person or persons for trying to undermine Laney's school, writing that the educator was "waging war . . . against entrenched prejudice, traitors and hypocrites of her own

race: men who know how to work white tourists for tidy sums by cring-
ing and kowtowing." Du Bois called Laney "brave and wholehearted."[54]

It was a shared assessment among many blacks in different regions of
the country that Lucy Laney was a "great leader of our group."[55] Haines
was successfully graduating well-prepared students and sending many
of them on to higher education. Laney's style as a leader was understated
but direct and did not court controversy. Although Haines never emulat-
ed Tuskegee by focusing exclusively on industrial and domestic training,
Laney, like some other school founders in the South, was astute enough
to place "industrial" in the name to defuse any accusation of blacks being
educated out of their "natural station," and thus avoid the white backlash
that a classical curriculum could cause. Her intent from the start was to
provide "a complete education for the child,"[56] applying what she had
experienced at Atlanta University, combined with a Christian emphasis.
"Christian education" was the term Laney used for her focus on character
development along with vocational courses integrated into a classical
curriculum. While this combination worked at Haines, it was not often
duplicated. In some black schools, industrial education was an empty
shell used to attract white donors.[57]

## INTELLECTUAL GROUNDING

Haines also reflected Laney's own intellectual mentors and academic
background. She studied a classical curriculum at the American Missionary Association-sponsored Lewis High School in Macon and at Atlanta
University, both of which were once led by Edmund Asa Ware. Ware, a
Yale-educated native of Massachusetts, was president of AU from its
founding in 1865 until his death in 1885. He believed that blacks should
be educated for race leadership, and that would come from equipping
teachers with a broad liberal education.[58] In his work with the Freedman's Bureau and as superintendent of the American Missionary Association schools, Ware favored educational programs that would identify
and train promising black youth to become teachers and preachers and
"disseminate civilization among the untaught masses."[59]

As one of those promising youth, Laney's intellectual trajectory was
markedly different from the educational experience of her contemporary,
Booker T. Washington. He attended Hampton Normal and Agricultural
Institute under the tutelage of a Civil War general in the Union Army,
Samuel Chapman Armstrong, who founded the school in 1868. The Ohio
native also believed in black education, but unlike Ware, Armstrong opposed education beyond what he considered their menial capacities.[60]
Although Armstrong graduated from Williams College, a private eastern
liberal arts institution, he rejected that path for blacks, believing that they
lacked the moral and intellectual stamina for such an education. Ware, on

the other hand, believed that there were few limits to what blacks could achieve, as evidenced by the Atlanta University motto, "I will find a way, or make one." Atlanta University's liberal arts curriculum was modeled upon the New England schools Ware knew best. He recruited Yale class-mates and other northerners to join him as teachers and promoted an egalitarian spirit in campus life by integrating the dining hall where the mostly white faculty and the black student body ate.[61]

At Hampton, which was supported by the AMA and also charged with developing teachers, the schooling under Armstrong was ideologi-cal, with racial segregation and manual labor viewed as necessary for the moral development of an inferior race.[62] To spread his gospel of the "dignity of work," Armstrong nominated his devoted and enterprising student Booker T. Washington for the job of building Tuskegee Institute, which was done with student labor. It opened in 1881.

While the comparison between these two white mentors of Laney and Washington can provide some context, so does a comparison between the two black educators. They were born within two years of each other in the South while slavery still reigned in the Confederate states—Laney in 1854 in Georgia, and Washington in 1856 in Virginia. Both were aided by white benevolence in their fierce determination to become educated but were directed toward different paths by family background and the type of education each received. Washington, the son of an enslaved woman and a white man, possibly her master, labored in a salt mine as a child. He viewed Armstrong, who recognized his potential, as a savior and role model.[63] He embraced the Hampton-type industrial education that fo-cused on practical pursuits such as agriculture and trades, while Laney was exposed to a classical education of higher mathematics, physics, an-cient history, literature, philosophy, composition, Latin, and Greek,[64] which broadened her view of the world while she maintained her practi-cal outlook. In addition to liberal arts, her courses in the women's divi-sion of AU also included household science, sewing, cooking, and nurs-ing. At graduation the class was reminded by commencement speaker Reverend Erasmus Cravat (a white American Missionary Association of-ficial who later became president of Fisk University), "of the great work to be done" as teachers of their race. He concluded by exhorting the class "to prove faithful in the discharge of your every duty; to your God first, your friends and pupils next, and to yourselves."[65] The message resonat-ed with Laney. She treated her own educational experience as a spiritual calling to minister to others. Similarly, Washington responded with zeal to Armstrong's exhortation about the benefits of industrial education and to what he had experienced as a student at Hampton. He then applied them at Tuskegee. Laney's views overlapped with Washington's about the value of property ownership and she agreed with him in urging blacks to also acquire cash, which Laney called, along with education, "the most substantial coupler,"[66] or equalizer.

Thus the widely reported ideological clash over education among blacks can be misleading. Differences that do exist, to a certain extent, are traceable to white benefactors and mentors and educational ideas to which black educators had early exposure. Similarly, an appreciation of Du Bois's northern liberalism, Fisk University education, and Harvard doctoral degree deepens our understanding of his preference for classical education and building a leadership class from among the most gifted black students. Still, these leading advocates for education were never diametrically opposed to each other, and one can find overlaps in their educational philosophies.[67]

## ACTIVISM IN GEORGIA AND BEYOND

Laney's admiration for Du Bois and his ideas was also evident. As convener of the Amenia Farm Retreat in Duchess County, New York, hosted by Mr. and Mrs. Joel Spingarn, Laney was one of the fifty black leaders whom Du Bois invited to join him in charting a new direction for black America following Washington's death in 1915. Her roommate in one of the twelve tents erected on the sprawling farm surrounding a two-acre pond was good friend Nannie Helen Burroughs. Du Bois, when he was recruited to teach at Atlanta University, had reached out to its graduates, including Lucy Laney, to help him document the living conditions among black Georgians. Their findings were reported at the Atlanta University Conferences beginning in 1896 and published the year before Du Bois arrived. Laney's contribution in the first series was a report titled "General Conditions of Mortality" in 1896. She called attention to the terrible living conditions among the urban poor, such as living in dilapidated houses, having absent parents, and being paid starvation wages, and concluded that those conditions "nourish disease, moral and physical." She expressed hope and prayer that the conferences would provide a solution to these problems.[68] Her "Address Before the Women's Meeting," mentioned earlier, drew from these findings to stress the importance of enlightened leadership by mothers in the home. During a time when women were expected to be "true" women, judged by high standards of morality, domesticity, and sexual purity, Laney was an advocate of the modern idea that mothers should hold their boys to the same standard of morality and conduct as girls.[69]

Laney's political views were also in line with the so-called black radicals such as Du Bois. She opposed segregation, scolding her students and staff for patronizing segregated facilities in Augusta. "Don't pay to be kicked," she told them.[70] The well-read Laney also embraced some of the views of an earlier generation of black intellectuals whom she admired, notably Frances E. W. Harper (1825–1911), the abolitionist poet and author of one of the first published black novels, *Iola Leroy, or Shadows*

*Uplifted* (1892). Harper's main character establishes a school for freed slaves. She writes, "The school was beginning to lift up the home, for Iola was not satisfied to teach her children only the rudiments of knowledge. She had tried to lay the foundation of good character."[71] Harper's view that the schoolhouse must replace the slave-pen and auction block[72] was also an idea proposed by Laney in her speech at Hampton exhorting mothers to protect "the black babies."[73]

One of the emerging factors in examining Lucy Craft Laney's life and work is the need to place her in the context of the racial climate in the state of Georgia at the time. Although she was active as a "whirlwind," travelling widely to give speeches and raise funds for her school, Laney lived her entire life within a 300-mile radius within the state. After Reconstruction, blacks made up nearly half the population in Georgia but were subjected to the most severe repression and hostility that the recalcitrant white South had to offer.[74] Du Bois considered the state not only the geographical center of black America, but also the epicenter of black problems.[75] Whether the issue was the convict lease system that used the prison system to re-enslave blacks and hire out their labor, black disenfranchisement, lynching, or denial of public education, the state usually adopted an anti-black stance. Throughout the state, draconian laws were enacted to deny not only political rights, but also human dignity. In Macon, for example, women were arrested and fined for violating an ordinance that mandated that all black women be employed, regardless of whether their husbands could support them.[76] This was a drastic and pitiful effort to force black women to stay in domestic service to whites.

Despite these challenging circumstances, James D. Anderson reports how formerly enslaved citizens started their own schools and provided land and other resources to build them, often with little help from the white southern political establishment.[77] Georgia, reluctant to support public schooling in general, was particularly wary of black public schools, especially those that went beyond the elementary level. In some counties that meant hiring the least qualified applicants to teach in them.[78] An Augusta judge in a grand jury hearing questioned the value of spending public money on educating blacks, and also lamented the existence of any schooling for blacks, stating that "it spoils good farm hands." He was quickly assured that "they" were receiving only "rudiments" of an education.[79]

The situation did not change substantially during the early years of the twentieth century and provides another example of why Lucy Laney's work in educating blacks was brave and fraught with challenges. The government reform, trust-busting, and moral uplift that historians have described as characterizing the Progressive Era constituted mainly a "for whites only"[80] enterprise. Georgia was a particularly harsh environment for progressive racial ideas during the period that coincided with black mass migration, from its stifling southern racism to racial violence.

The Laneys, showing their optimism about change in their state, were not among the many blacks who left Georgia and other southern states to head north. Some of the family members attended and/or worked at Haines, including Lucy Laney's brother, David, who oversaw new construction, and her niece, Margaret, who served as principal immediately after Laney's death.[81]

## EDUCATION IN AUGUSTA

Despite the poor conditions in Georgia, Laney saw opportunities for fomenting desired social change. When she incorporated Haines in 1886, the rapidly growing coastal city of Augusta had a 45 percent black population.[82] The city became the focus of her life's work as an activist educator, a role she filled until her death from hypertension in 1933. During her lifetime, she witnessed Augusta's vacillation between paternalism and benevolence, and gross hostility towards its black citizens.[83] Laney set out to change the chilly climate for blacks in the city through her outreach to various churches. She emphasized philosophically compatible ideas about self-discipline and temperance as she worked with white authorities to improve living conditions in the black community known as the "Terri." It was an area of the city that suffered from poverty and lack of city services. Working with the white Civic League and the Augusta interracial alliance, Laney saw that improvements were made in housing and drainage in black neighborhoods.[84] Laney also joined NAACP field secretary, James Weldon Johnson, to establish the Augusta chapter of the organization in 1917. After the passage of the Nineteenth Amendment, Laney headed a drive to register black women voters in Augusta, in spite of robust efforts to disenfranchise black voters in the state.[85] Laney was also active in the Young Women's Christian Association, and the black women's club movement as well as the aforementioned "Southern Network."[86]

Such activism was, nevertheless, a defiant stand against Augusta's white power structure that refused to respect the rights and wishes of its black citizens. In the 1890s, little more than a decade after Haines Institute was founded, a showdown between the white power structure and Augusta's black elite occurred. A group of leading black citizens brought a suit against the city's school board for its decision to close Ware High School, the high-performing black-led institution that was the pride of black Augusta. Laney had helped to recruit her friend and classmate Richard R. Wright for the job of principal of what was then the only public black high school in the state. But Wright resigned in 1891, sensing a slackening of support and meddling by the school board, which wanted to restrict the curriculum and the school's growth. Wright named the school Asa Edmund Ware High, in honor of the founder of Atlanta University, and under his leadership, it was easily on par with or exceeded the quality of Augusta's white high schools.[87] This reversal of fortune for Ware High may have convinced Laney that blacks could not depend on public education and needed to have their own mission schools with their own agenda. She expressed this sentiment in 1917:

> These boys and girls, if they would take the place of men and women, must not only be thoroughly educated as teachers, but must . . . have character, and mission teaching in order that they be thoroughly consecrated before they can do the service for themselves. This is what I plead for the Negro teachers of the city.[88]

Laney's attitude fueled rumors that she supported the school's closing,[89] while members of the black male elite led the drive to keep Ware High open. The opposition to the closing was led by propertied, middle-class, mixed-race families who filed a suit against the school board that reached the Supreme Court. The litigants named in the suit were J. W. Cumming, James S. Harper, and John C. Ladeveze.[90] Laney's deposition on the side of the school board further aroused suspicion among the plaintiffs' families, who suggested that Laney colluded with the school board. The circumstantial evidence paints a cloudy, but unsubstantiated picture of Laney's activism.[91] Her motives, if suspicions are true, have been attributed to jealousy and a desire to recruit Ware students to the privately funded Haines.[92]

When the Supreme Court ruling in *Cumming et al. v. the Richmond County Board of Education* was handed down in favor of the school board, it was a devastating blow to the black community. The 1899 ruling stated, in part, "States have the power to regulate the Negro in the enjoyment of his civil and social rights in accordance with tradition and custom, and unless his rights are greatly abused, he has no cause of complaint. The state need not provide for his education unless it sees fit."[93] The ruling followed the better known *Plessy v. Ferguson* Supreme Court ruling of 1896 that institutionalized "separate but equal" Jim Crow laws and piled on yet another legal obstacle in the struggle for equal education for black students. It demoralized the black leadership in the city,[94] and the plaintiffs either ceased their activism or left the state; some began passing for white.[95] The closing of the public high school left black Augustans with Haines Institute as the sole option for schooling beyond the elementary level.[96]

Laney clearly favored private mission schools whose survival did not depend upon the whim or interests of the white power structure. One can imagine that her strong belief in maintaining both high standards and black control affected her attitude toward the fate of Ware. The departure of Principal Wright undoubtedly further dampened her enthusiasm for the school's prospects. Laney's strong belief that blacks should control their own schools even got her name published in a Presbyterian yearbook as "part of the movement to put southern Negro institutions under Negro leadership."[97] Nevertheless, blaming Laney for Ware's demise diverts attention from state-sanctioned white supremacy, along with class and gender issues. As the most visible, active, black woman in Augusta, Laney did not conform to the accepted role of women in the community. There also may have been discomfort with the dark-skinned Laney among some mixed-race male leaders because of her growing clout and increasing national profile as the founder of "probably the best private elementary and secondary school in the state."[98] Although accepted in her conventionality as a spinster-teacher, her visibility and activism challenged socially accepted gender roles for women during that era.

The closing of Ware High added to Laney's prominence in black education in Augusta.[99] Haines remained the only high school option for blacks in Augusta until the opening of the A. R. Johnson public high school in 1937, four years after Laney's death. During the intervening years she continued to voice her mistrust of public education and her belief in a mission-based educational system. In a speech delivered during a West Coast fundraising tour in 1903, she repeated her view that the uplifting mandate needed by the black race was best received "through the schools and churches of various denominations."[100] But Laney, showing some flexibility and perhaps anticipating the changing landscape, also acknowledged a need for private and public schools to work together.

## A ROLE MODEL FOR WOMEN

Despite the changing times, Laney's views—about schooling, and women being the most effective activists and "civilizers"—were set during her formative years. They may have been influenced by inspiring stories of older women activists whose protests against race and gender restrictions gained wide attention. These women included Mary Ann Shadd Cary (1823–1893), the black woman abolitionist, journalist, lawyer, and women's rights advocate who defied gender restrictions by attempting to vote and protesting the treatment of blacks in the United States by becoming an outspoken champion of black migration to Canada.[101] There was also the well-publicized protest of white women's rights activist Susan B. Anthony. In June 1873, the month Laney graduated from Atlanta University, Anthony was being tried in Canandaigua, New York, charged with violating the law by voting in a local election. The story received national coverage, including on the front page of the *Atlanta Constitution*.[102] We do not know for sure how much the "race woman" Laney knew about Shadd Cary, nor whether the politically attuned activist followed press accounts of Anthony's defiance and the judgment against her. In the three newspapers she read each day, such examples of female assertiveness within a public sphere dominated by men, such women were models of nineteenth-century activism that Laney exhibited in her own life.

Whether emboldened by such examples or by her own biography and sense of justice, Laney's activism also got her arrested and hauled into court. It happened when she protested the callous treatment of her students by two white physicians who came to Haines to vaccinate the children against smallpox. Their methods frightened the children, and Laney asked the doctors to leave the campus. The men became incensed that she would question their professional judgment and they had Laney arrested. She was charged with violating a city ordinance of impeding vaccinations and resisting arrest. In the court case that ensued, both she and her lawyer were fined. Her lawyer was fined because he continually referred to his black female client as "Miss Laney." In yet another confirmation of the racism and sexism that existed, the presiding judge took the time to scold her for an "unwomanly remonstrance."[103]

There were several other reports of Laney standing up for her students even when there was an issue with local law enforcement. Oral recollections of incidents between law enforcement and Laney vary, including a story about her having hidden a black man erroneously accused of shooting a white man from a lynch mob in her girls' dormitory until he was cleared of the crime.[104]

Her effectiveness in standing up for the causes she cared about can be gleaned from a news account accompanying one of her lecture tours: "The lectures by Miss Laney have been a success from every point of view. She is well educated and as a public speaker she has few equals in this country. In picturing the condition of the race in the South, she often brought tears to the eyes of those who seldom weep."[105] The article continued to praise Laney for her staunch opposition to segregation: "[A]t all points of race contact in the North [—] in hotels, at the baptismal pool, in cemeteries, everywhere,"[106] she continued to vigorously insist that blacks be treated with dignity.

Concurrently, the spinster who turned away from the expected feminine fate of romantic suitors and marriage nevertheless extolled the virtues of married life, calling it, "the beginning of the home [and] a matter of great importance."[107] Invoking Scriptures, Laney called motherhood the "crown of womanhood," anointed by God. Children, she said are "our most important question." Yet perhaps feeling that the two roles would make for divided duty, Laney committed herself to a career as an activist-educator and to a symbolic, empowered motherhood. She insisted upon gender equality in educating children and chastised those who would instruct girls in character formation but allow boys to "sow wild oats." In the rousing closing lines of her Hampton speech, she invoked the dual themes of upholding tradition while seeking change that characterized her life. Laney asked the women to return to their churches and literary societies to "study our children by the search-light of the *new* psychology, [italics added] and with the spirit of the true and loving mother." Blending old and new ideas was a Laney trademark. It showed her to be a traditionalist with a progressive outlook. For example, her introduction of the kindergarten concept (discussed in the next chapter) in Augusta, for example, was an innovative application of her traditional views about the importance of women's role in molding young children.

In Laney's view, ignorance was the most vital threat to the black race. It had kept blacks from reaching the heights of civilization. That required the best education possible to change the circumstances brought on by centuries of enslavement and its aftermath. This "burden" became Lucy Laney's life's work. She believed in the biblical directive of shared suffering and that sacrificing oneself for others is the highest Christian calling: "Bear ye one another's burdens, and thus fulfill the law," she quoted from Scripture. The "self-sacrificing" narrative found expression in Laney's work and in the regional and national black women's club movement that she joined. It achieved great organizational reach after the founding of the National Association of Colored Women in 1896. The "burden" that she exhorted women to assume was thus a biblical calling as well as a practical necessity. Adopting a Christian value system based upon moral living and the pursuit of education was her way of subverting the rampant racist ideology that condemned blacks to inferior schools, homes, and low self-esteem.

In recovering details of her life, we find an activist-educator who clung to traditional ideas in order to imbue them with new and useful possibilities for the future of her people. On matters related to women, the notion of the Victorian mother as the "angel in the house" only partly reflects her views about women. While her ideas about motherhood and female duty seem outdated and burdensome to the modern reader, they did not keep her from encouraging women to "reach every hopeful field of wage-earning . . . and every intellectual arena."[108] Nor was she deterred from opposing racism and attempting to secure civil and human rights for blacks. With this mix of traditionalism and future-oriented thinking, she inspired other women, especially younger educators. Education, she believed, provided a footpath to attaining those rights and an equality based upon merit and accomplishment rather than appeals to white beneficence. Her preference for private rather than public education may have been one of the issues that led to a charge of collusion with the school board to close the black public high school. However, it was the Supreme Court of the United States and its judicial activism, tainted by a racist ideology, that caused the demise of Ware High School. All this shows that Lucy Laney cannot be easily confined and categorized because—as scholars now understand about Victorian women in general—she displayed a complexity that was not always acknowledged.[109] We do know that Laney remained a resourceful and innovative presence at

**Figure 2.1.** Lucy Craft Laney, founder and principal, Haines Institute, Augusta, GA. Photo courtesy of Moorland-Spingarn Research Center, Howard University, Washington, D.C.

Haines Institute for nearly half a century and, by way of that success, inserted herself into the national dialogue about race and gender. Her strongest argument was that blacks must take charge of their own institutions, especially their homes and schools, neither of which could be accomplished without women's leadership. Laney was described by Janie Porter Barrett as "working quietly," and had to be touted by others. But Laney's work for the causes that she championed was seen and heard by many.

The next chapter discusses how Laney's ideas were put into practice in building Haines Institute and transforming both the physical and cultural environment, while evolving into what some considered "the best secondary school" in the state.

## NOTES

1. Lucy Craft Laney Museum website, http://www.lucycraftlaneymuseum.com; Lucy C. Laney High School website, http://laney.rcboe.org/home.aspx. The museum is located in Laney's restored home. The Lucy C. Laney High School is located on Walker-Laney Boulevard in Augusta (10 September 2010).

2. Georgia Women of Achievement website, http://www.georgiawomen.org/honorees/laneylc/index.htm (10 September 2010).

3. "Lucy Laney's Death Brings Messages of Sympathy," *Augusta Chronicle*, 5 November 1933; "Thousands Attend Funeral Services for Lucy C. Laney," *Augusta Chronicle*, 29 October 1933.

4. "Lucy Laney's Death Brings Many Messages of Sympathy," *Augusta Chronicle* (5 November 1933): 5(A).

5. *Augusta Chronicle*, 5 November 1933.

6. *Augusta Chronicle*, 5 November 1933.

7. Mary Magdalene Marshall, "Tell Them We're Rising: Black Intellectuals and Lucy Craft Laney in Post Civil War Augusta, Georgia" (PhD diss., Drew University, 1998), 122.

8. A. C. Griggs, "Notes: Lucy Craft Laney," *Journal of Negro History*, vol. 1, no. 19 (June 1934), 97–102.

9. Lucille Laney Ellis Floyd, interview with the author, Augusta, Ga., 25 April 2003.

10. Several Lucy Laney memorials have sprouted in her home state as well as other locations, including the proposed Lucy Craft Laney neighborhood project in Minneapolis http://lucylaney.mpls.k12.mn.us (August 5, 2010).

11. Margaret Louise Laney interviewed by Jean Blount, "Miss Lucy Laney and Early 20th Century Education," *Oral Memoirs of Augusta's Citizens*, vol. 3. Augusta Regional Library (6 February 1975), 6.

12. This is the date cited in early documents, including the Presbyterian Historical Society archive and on her tombstone in Augusta, although the year 1855 is listed in other sources.

13. Lucy Craft Laney vertical file, Presbyterian Historical Society Archive, n.d.

14. Griggs, "Notes: Lucy Craft Laney," 97.

15. Following a monetary gift from Steven Ballard, the school was renamed in his honor, http://www.amistadresearchcenter.org/archon/?p=creators/creator&id=95 (6 March 2012).

16. Mary Jackson McCrorey, "Lucy Laney," *The Crisis* 41, no. 6 (June 1934): 161.

17. Clarence Bacote, *The Story of Atlanta University: A Century of Progress, 1865–1965* (Princeton: Princeton University Press, 1969), 34.

18. James D. Anderson, *The Education of Blacks in the South, 1860–1935* (Chapel Hill, N.C.: University of North Carolina Press, 1988), 31. The illiteracy rate among blacks in the South was 95 percent in 1860, 70 percent in 1880.

19. Anderson, *The Education of Blacks*, 4–32.

20. Robert J. Douglass, "Climbing Upward—She Lifted Others," *Abbott's Monthly* (June 1931): 32.

21. Marjorie E. W. Smith, "Putting First Things First," Board of Missions of the Presbyterian Church, reprinted in *Haines Journal* (April 1934): 8.

22. Elizabeth Ross Haynes, *The Black Boy of Atlanta* (Boston: House of Edinboro, 1952), 37.

23. Douglass, "Climbing Upward," 32.

24. Lucy Laney, "Address Before the Women's Meeting," paper delivered at the Second Atlanta University Conference, 1897, reprinted in Atlanta University Publications, ed. W. E. B. Du Bois (New York: Octagon Books, 1968), 55–57.

25. "Miss Laney's Address," reprinted in *Haines Journal*, no. 1 (1903), n.p.

26. "Miss Laney's Address."

27. The Georgia cities where Laney chose to work all had cultural and educational distinctions that did not exist in the rural areas of the state. Even the relatively small Milledgeville boasted a historical and cultural distinction as the former state capital and home to a military college, state penitentiary, and hospital, as well as being in the path of the famous march of General Sherman's Union Army that ransacked the city's stately capitol building, but left it standing, http://www.georgiaencyclopedia.org/nge/Article.jsp?id=h-769 (16 July 2009).

28. Edward J. Cashin, *The Quest: A History of Public Education in Richmond County, Georgia* (Augusta, Ga.: Richmond County Board of Education, 1985), 9.

29. "Miss Laney's Address," 1903.

30. Anne Kendall, "Lucy Craft Laney" (research paper), Lucy Laney File (Atlanta University Center Library, 1972): 1–10.

31. Laney suffered from several ailments, including nephritis, a serious kidney condition, that were all made worse by her constant travelling to raise funds for Haines, as well as her teaching and administrative duties.

32. Haines Institute, "Golden Jubilee," program booklet, 1934, Lucy Craft Laney vertical file, Reese Library, Augusta College and Richmond County Historical Society.

33. Hattie McDaniel, "Letters to Mother," 1916–1922, Hattie Perry vertical file, Amistad Research Center, Tulane University.

34. Harold G. Fleming, "Victorian Reformer," *Southern Changes* 11, no. 5 (1989): 18–19.

35. Jacqueline Ann Rouse, *Lugenia Burns Hope*, 5.

36. Lucy C. Laney, "Address Before the Women's Meeting," Atlanta University Conference 1897 (New York: Arno Press, 1968), 57.

37. Laney, "Burden."

38. Daniel Scott Smith, "Family Limitation, Sexual Control, and Domestic Feminism in Victorian America," *Feminist Studies* 1, no. 3/4 (Winter–Spring 1973): 40–57.

39. Laney, "Burden," 341–44.

40. Laney, "Burden," 341–44.

41. Laney, "Burden," 341–44.

42. Evelyn Brooks Higginbotham, "African-American Women's History and the Metalanguage of Race," *Signs* 17, no. 2 (Winter 1992): 251–74.

43. Carol Allen, *Black Women Intellectuals: Strategies of Nation, Family, and Neighborhood in the Works of Pauline Hopkins, Jessie Fauset, and Marita Bonner* (New York: Garland Publishing, 1998), 4.

44. Kevin Gaines, *Uplifting the Race: Black Leadership, Politics, and Culture in the Twentieth Century* (Durham: University of North Carolina Press, 1996), 128–52.

45. Linda Perkins, "The Cult of True Womanhood in the Education of Black Women," *Journal of Social Issues* 39 (Fall 1983): 17–28.

46. Lucy Laney, "Burden."

47. Mary White Ovington, *Portraits in Color* (New York: Viking Press, 1927), 62.

48. Catherine Owens Peare, *Mary McLeod Bethune* (New York: Vanguard Press, 1951), 76.

49. Audrey Thomas McCluskey, "Most Sacrificing Service," in *Women of the American South: A Multicultural Reader*, ed. Christie Anne Farnham (New York: New York University Press, 1997), 189–203.

50. Rouse, *Lugenia Burns Hope*, 6.

51. Janie Porter Barrett to William Harmon Foundation, Lucy Laney Correspondence in Harmon Collection, Manuscript Division, Library of Congress, Lucy Craft Laney file.

52. *Haines Journal*, Founders Day (13 April 1934), Lucy Laney file, Reese Library, Augusta College; Marshall, "Tell Them We're Rising," 111.

53. Booker T. Washington, *The Story of the Negro: The Rise of the Race from Slavery*, vol. 2 (New York: Doubleday, page 1909, reprinted by Negro Universities Press, 1969), 308.

54. W. E. B. Du Bois, *Crisis* 13, no. 6 (April 1917): 269. Du Bois may have aimed his derisive comment at Charles T. Walker, a prominent Augusta educator and devoted follower of Booker T. Washington.

55. McCluskey and Smith, *Building a Better World*, 50.

56. Audrey T. McCluskey, "'We Specialize in the Wholly Impossible': Black Women School Founders and Their Mission," *Signs: Journal of Women in Culture and Society* 22, no. 2 (Winter 1997): 403–26.

57. Anderson, *Education of Blacks*, 88.

58. Bacote, *Story of Atlanta University*, 15–16.

59. Bacote, *Story of Atlanta University*, 15–16.

60. Anderson, *Education of Blacks*, 34.

61. George A. Towns, "The Source of the Traditions of Atlanta University," *Phylon* 3, no. 2 (1942): 118–19.

62. Anderson, *Education of Blacks*, 328.

63. Anderson, *Education of Blacks*, 328.

64. Bacote, *Story of Atlanta University*, 2.

65. *Atlanta Constitution*, 26 June 1873, n.p.

66. *Atlanta Constitution*, 26 June 1873, n.p.

67. W. E. B. Du Bois, *The Souls of Black Folk* (Chicago: A. C. McClurg, 1903), 121–39

68. Lucy C. Laney, "General Conditions of Mortality," in the Atlanta University Papers Series, ed. W. E. B. Du Bois (Atlanta: Atlanta University, 1896): 35–37.

69. Lucy C. Laney, "Address Before the Women's Meeting," Second Annual Atlanta University Conference Proceedings, 1897 (New York: Arno Press, 1968), 56.

70. Britt Edward Cottingham, "The Burden of the Educated Colored Woman: Lucy Laney and the Haines Institute, 1886–1933," (master's thesis, Georgia State University, 1995), 79.

71. Frances E.W. Harper, *Iola Leroy; or, Shadows Uplifted* (Philadelphia: Garrigues Brothers, 1893), 147.

72. Harper, *Iola Leroy*, 152.

73. Laney, "Burden," 341–44.

74. John Dittmer, *Black Georgia in the Progressive Era, 1900–1920* (Chicago: University of Illinois Press, 1977), 5.

75. Du Bois, *Souls of Black Folk*, 111.

76. Dittmer, *Black Georgia*, 199.

77. Anderson, *Education of Blacks*, 7.

78. Dittmer, *Black Georgia*, 146.

79. Edward Cashin, *The Quest: A History of Public Education in Richmond County, Georgia* (Augusta: Richmond Board of Education, 1985), 34.

80. Dittmer, *Black Georgia*, xi.

81. Margaret Louise Laney, "Miss Lucy Laney and Early 20th Century Education," *Oral Memoirs of Augusta Citizens,* Vol. 3, Augusta Oral History Project (6 February 1967), 14.

82. June O. Patton, "Augusta's Black Community and the Struggle for Ware High School," in *New Perspectives on Black Educational History,* eds. Vincent P. Franklin and James D. Anderson (Chapel Hill: University of North Carolina Press, 1978), 46.

83. Edward J. Cashin, "Paternalism in Augusta: The Impact of the Plantation Ethic upon an Urban Society," in *Paternalism in a Southern City: Race, Religion, and Gender in Augusta, Georgia,* eds. Edward J. Cashin and Glenn T. Eskew (Athens: University of Georgia Press, 2001), 22.

84. Lloyd Preston and Stephens C. Terrell, *Blacks in Augusta: A Chronology, 1741–1977* (Augusta, Ga.: Preston Publications, 1977), 25.

85. Cottingham, "Burden of the Educated Colored Woman," 91.

86. Rouse, *Lugenia Burns Hope,* 10.

87. J. Morgan Kousser, "Separate But *Not* Equal: The Supreme Court's First Decision on Discrimination in Schools," *Social Science Working Paper,* no. 204 (March 1978): 7.

88. Gloria T. Williams-Way, "Lucy Craft Laney—'The Mother of the Children of the People,'" (PhD diss., University of South Carolina, 1998), 309.

89. Kousser, "Separate But *Not* Equal," F-14.

90. Kousser, "Separate But *Not* Equal," 21.

91. Kousser, "Separate But *Not* Equal," F-15.

92. The circumstantial evidence of Laney's collusion, other than not signing the petition to keep Ware High open, comes via oral history and hearsay in the Harper family, plaintiffs in *Cumming.* According to J. Morgan Kousser: "Mrs. Mary Harper Ingram reported to me that during the 1930s, Channing H. Tobias told Mrs. Ingram's mother . . . that he has never forgiven Lucy Laney for going to the School Board and asking them to abolish Ware and give the money to primary schools." Kousser, "Separate But *Not* Equal," F-15.

93. Transcripts of Records, U.S. Supreme Court Briefs, 1899, Case #164 (*Cumming*) vol. 12, 32.

94. Cashin, "Paternalism in Augusta," 36; Patton, "Augusta's Black Community," 55–56.

95. Kent Anderson Leslie, "No Middle Ground: Elite African Americans in Augusta and the Coming of Jim Crow," in *Paternalism in a Southern City,* 124.

96. Patton, "Augusta's Black Community," 55.

97. Andrew Murray, *Presbyterians and the Negro: A History* (Philadelphia: Presbyterian Historical Society, 1966), 186.

98. Dittmer, *Black Georgia,* 149.

99. Kousser,"Separate But *Not* Equal," F-15.

100. *Pacific Coast Appeal,* 1903.

101. Shirley J. Yee, "Finding a Place: Mary Ann Shadd Cary and the Dilemmas of Black Migration to Canada, 1850–1870," *Frontiers: A Journal of Women Studies* 18, no. 3 (1997): 1–16.

102. "Trial of Susan B. Anthony," *Atlanta Constitution,* 22 June 1873, 1.

103. Dittmer, *Black Georgia,* 150; "Lucy Laney," Kendall paper, vertical file, Atlanta University Center Library, n.d., 9–10.

104. Dittmer, 150.

105. "Miss Lucy Laney," *Pacific Coast Appeal,* San Francisco, 4 July 1903, 1.

106. "Miss Lucy Laney."

107. Lucy Laney, "Burden."

108. Lucy Laney, "Burden."

109. Anne Hogan and Andrew Bradstock, *Women of Faith in Victorian Culture: Reassessing the Angel in the House* (New York: St. Martin's Press, 1998), 5.

# THREE

## "The Best Secondary School in Georgia"

### Building the Haines Institute Culture

*How was it that in black untutored eyes*
*You sensed that dawning gleam, the light of hope?*
—Frank Garvin Yerby, Haines, class of 1933

The "quiet work" in building her school that Janie Porter Barrett attributes to Lucy Laney seems to have paid off. In 1916, a government-issued report on the status of black private high schools described Haines with these words: "The wise administration of the principal has won for the school the confidence of both white and colored people."[1] The report also documented its steady growth from a primary school to a combined elementary and secondary school with an enrollment of 860 students. Of that number, females outnumbered male students by 571 to 289. The report also described the teaching staff of twenty-two, four males and eighteen females, as "well prepared and doing thorough work."[2] The expanded curriculum showed that Laney's academic-oriented courses dwarfed the industrial-related offerings. The secondary-level requirements included four years of English and mathematics and three years of history. Students could choose from among Latin, Greek, French, or German for their foreign language and take electives in psychology, sociology, and civics. Yet, this success with a classical-leaning curriculum was not enough to satisfy industrial education advocates such as Tommy Jesse Jones, a former teacher at Tuskegee Institute who later worked for the Phelps-Stokes Fund, one of the philanthropic funds that favored industrial education for blacks. In citing the cooking and sewing classes for

37

girls and the manual training and gardening for boys, he concluded that industrial courses at Haines were "inadequate."[3]

Although Jones attributed the inadequacy to a lack of funding, not ideology, his report showed a bias that favored industrial education. Laney did not intend for industrial courses to dominate her school, and the disparity was likely part of Laney's stated intention to provide an education to "develop all sides of the pupil's life"[4] in an environment that was academically rigorous and mission-oriented. This situation raises important questions: What factors influenced Laney's calculations about what she could accomplish in Augusta, considering the harsh social and political situation for blacks in post-Reconstruction Georgia and the rising tide of industrial education? How was her vision for a different type of school articulated through the physical environment and social and cultural setting that she created at Haines? Given sparse resources, how did Laney manage to keep Haines afloat and, indeed, growing, for more than half a century? While full and incontrovertible documentation of Laney's work is lacking because of a loss of institutional records in a fire at the school, the evidence that does exist offers interesting insights into her ideas, strategies, and goals. Building upon her efforts discussed in the last chapter, we find Lucy Laney re-authorizing history and reimagining the environment in and around her school as part of her larger vision for permanence, control, and transformation.

## EARLY YEARS

Augusta's reputation as a city where blacks were on the move made it a compelling choice for Laney to build her school, but this decision was not without risks. The city was home to thriving black institutions, including Springfield Baptist Church, founded between 1773 and 1787, and the incorporated community of Springfield Village.[5] Additionally, over 300 industrious free blacks were employed in business and trades as bakers, tailors, piano tuners, blacksmiths, and general store owners.[6]

However, one aspect of Augusta's culture that was not so inviting to blacks was its alignment with the politics of the Confederacy in perpetuating white supremacy, paternalism, and outright hostility towards people of African descent. Augusta in the late 1890s was described as a place where "discrimination, segregation, and ostracism increased," and blacks were denied political rights, privileges, and agen[cy].[7] Haines Normal and Industrial Institute was sustained in that contrasting duality of circumstances, and came to be considered a community resource by blacks and even some white Augustans who were often antagonistic toward black advancement. The uniqueness of Haines was evident. Augusta had other outstanding black educational institutions including Paine Institute (later Paine College), chartered in 1883 by the Methodist Church, and presided over by a white male; Walker Baptist Institute, founded in 1898 by Rev. Charles T. Walker, a political ally of Booker T. Washington and an advocate for Washington's brand of industrial education; and Ware High School, an exemplar of high academic standards, until its forced closure was upheld by the Supreme Court in *Cumming v. the Richmond County Board of Education* in 1899. In this environment, Haines Institute rose to equal prominence and was the only school in Augusta founded and presided over by a black woman. The school elicited pride among blacks but also exposed sexism as shown by the reluctance of the Presbyterians to support Laney at first. There was also the early criticism she received from some black males who thought that an unmarried woman should not be in charge of such an operation.[8]

In deciding to open her school in 1886 in Augusta, rather than in the other Georgia cities where she had lived—Macon, Atlanta, Savannah, and Milledgeville—Laney also heeded the advice of allies such as Richard H. Allen, secretary of the Board of Missions for Freedmen of the Presbyterian Assembly. Allen convinced Laney to seek support from the General Assembly of the Presbyterian Church. With the request granted belatedly, sponsorship by the Presbyterians provided a significant boost to the fledgling school.[9] Laney also had the support of vocal black leaders such as Rev. William J. White, who self-identified as black (although he looked white), and several others in the black community. The friendly relationship between Laney and White was documented by a brief news item in the *Savannah Tribune* in June of 1889 noting the second graduation exercises at Haines. It stated that at the request of founder and principal Miss Lucy C. Laney, Rev. W. J. White presented the diplomas to the eight members of the graduating class and heartily congratulated both students and teachers.[10] The *Tribune* article also noted the excellent essay presented by one of the graduates, Miss Florida Desverney, on the subject of "Unity." The graduation exercises continued for three nights and the graduates "covered themselves with glory," the writer concluded.[11] The first graduation had taken place a year earlier, when the original five young women—Fannie Belcher, Josephine Belcher, Florence A. Lewis, Annie E. Scott, and Louisa A. Smythe completed their studies.[12]

Although the gender of the members of the second class of graduates, except for the speaker, is not mentioned, Laney always envisioned an institution that would dispel notions of black inferiority, especially pervasive myths about black women being incapable of teaching black children. In her Hampton Institute speech in 1899, Laney urged black women to become teachers and take up the "burden" of uplifting the race, while condemning published remarks attributed to white Southern women saying that black women suitable to teach could not be found.[13] While Laney's Victorian views entrusted educated black women with a greater responsibility for teaching and nurturing children, her teaching staff at

Haines comprised both women and men who were well educated and held to the same standard of excellence—as was the co-ed student body.

From its beginning in 1883 in a rented lecture hall of the Christ Presbyterian Church, with five students in attendance, Laney's ambitions for the school were evident. Yet she endured many setbacks in the early years that really tested her mettle. Aside from money woes, there were floods, cramped quarters, frequent moves, fire, and illnesses among faculty and students. One of the many early tragedies that hit Haines was a devastating typhoid fever epidemic that sickened several students and took the life of Laney's first teaching assistant, Cora Freeman of Framington, Massachusetts.[14] Despite such hardships, Laney made strides towards the permanence and control she sought for the school. She immediately realized that the need was too great to admit only girls, as she had once hoped to do, and soon the school's enrollment was up to 75 girls and boys, with no growing room. In the second year, the enrollment ballooned to 234. She moved into a larger house with a barn that provided additional classroom space. With the charter secured in 1886, and the Presbyterian Board of Missions now a sponsor,[15] Laney sent a progress report to the board in 1893 assuring them that their support was reaping dividends and creating a large corps of trained teachers, although she made it clear that more work was necessary:

> Already in the public schools of this city, in sight of our building, four of our girls are employed teachers. We are through our students yearly reaching a large number of persons. Through our forty student teachers with schools now under their care that average 35 scholars each, we are reaching 1400 children . . . [we] reach indirectly about 1800 young people; but, oh, large as this number seems, it is small when we think of the many hundreds to whom scarcely a ray of light has yet come![16]

What comes across in Laney's report to the board is the delicate diplomacy that she mastered to remain in good standing in a southern city by cultivating white allies on both sides of the Mason-Dixon line. She took advantage of Augusta's strategic location as either a destination or a stopover for wealthy white northerners en route to their winter vacation homes in Florida or on the Georgia coast. Although she developed a routine where the student choral group would assemble on cue to entertain the visitors, there was an absence of the usual deference expected of blacks who interacted with potential white donors:

> A very large number of northern travelers passing have called upon us. Gen. Saylor of Boston was loud in his commendation. Among the many who have called on us in the past few months were a number of southern women, some paying a second visit during the month, bringing other friends. None of these ladies were ever before in a Colored school. They expressed themselves as well pleased, and have since

showed their good will by little courtesies. I reasonably expect from these sources in the future something of moral support.[17]

Laney's indirect solicitations, without outwardly bragging or begging, showed confidence and deliberateness and speak to her diplomacy and management skills. She was able to draw praise from visitors who may have held different views about the kind of schools black children should attend. Her personal appeal allowed her to move forward without undue scrutiny. An article written by journalist Robert J. Douglass, who visited Haines in the early 1930s, provided insight into her methods and her character: "Haines school might have been richly endowed were she a beggar, but Miss Laney would never beg. If men [and women] of means who visit could not see the needs or the cause without [her] constantly reminding them, then they need not expect to be urged to support it."[18]

## THE BUILT ENVIRONMENT

Laney's emphasis on the children's need for decent surroundings was especially appealing to white women donors. A telling example of Laney's broad outreach was the support she received from Mrs. Anson Phelps-Stokes of the family that established the previously mentioned philanthropic fund founded in 1911 to support mainly industrial education. Still, Mrs. Phelps-Stokes made a personal donation to Haines that enabled Laney to acquire a block of land to initiate the growth and physical transformation that she envisioned. With this purchase of land, the permanent campus began to take shape. Mrs. Phelps-Stokes also contributed a "costly and beautiful organ" that allowed Laney to organize a school orchestra.[19]

In an early report to the Presbyterian Board, the handicaps Laney faced were as clear as her transformative intent:

> We are sadly in need of a comfortable schoolhouse, not only to meet the demands of the increasing number of applicants, but to improve classification and a comfortable shelter. A comfortable room, besides being indispensible [sic] to health, with suitable furniture and appurtenances, has much to do with the discipline and progress of the school. . . . This is especially true when the children come from . . . such poor homes (it pains me to say) not homes, but wretched hovels. We are striving to teach them to care for, to love, and make their home pleasant. We can have no success in this unless we can make the school surroundings pleasant, or at least decent.[20]

The campus continued to expand, and new structures were built during Haines's first decades. For a school with itinerant beginnings, the support of the Presbyterian Board of Missions for Freedmen opened up other revenue streams and was a major step in securing funds from like-minded donors.[21] However, as historians have noted, Presbyterians and other northern liberal friends of the Negro did not divest themselves of paternalism and the belief that blacks needed whites to help them manage.[22] Added to that was the male chauvinism of the board and some elements of the black community that underestimated what Laney could undertake and accomplish. It was, however, the confidence in Laney shown by women philanthropists that helped her to shape the physical environment. In addition to namesake Francina Haines's initial bequest that made it possible for the school to continue operating and the gift of Mrs. Phelps-Stokes that enabled a land purchase, Marshall Hall, the first brick structure to be erected, was built with a $10,000 donation to memorialize the mother of Mrs. Emma Marshall Bell.[23] This handsome, four-story building was in the heart of the black community that housed the girls' dormitory, dining room, library, and classrooms. Located at the intersection of two busy streets, the building certainly added stature and visibility to Haines and was an anchor for the whole community as well as an affirmation of what the community, working together, could accomplish. The arched entryway, balcony, and landscaped grounds resembled buildings at Laney's alma mater, Atlanta University. The next building was erected in 1906. It, too, was made possible by a woman's philanthropy. Mrs. McGregor, of Detroit, who wanted to contribute to a school founded by a woman, donated $15,000 for the construction of McGregor Hall. The multistory colonial-style red brick structure boasted a front view with rows of windows on each floor and a crest of windows in the center to mark the entrance. The building served as home to the administrative offices and the high school department. Laney's brother, Dr. Frank Laney, a teacher at Haines, helped his sister supervise the construction projects.[24] But Lucy Laney often surprised her students and others with her knowledge of the intricacies of the buildings. She was said to know where "every nail was" because she was present when it was hammered in.[25] Such attention to detail with each building bespoke her goal of having Haines be ranked with the best anywhere, and not viewed as merely a "good Negro school."[26] In 1924, another female supporter, a Mrs. Wheeler of New York City, made possible the construction of the Cauley-Wheeler building named in honor of her nurse. This building was used to house the primary grades.[27]

Shaping the school's physical environment was a continual transformative process that included not only new buildings, but also new programs and staff, and accounted for almost every aspect of student and faculty life. This included standards of deportment, cleanliness, and participation in extracurricular activity. Laney's emphasis on cleanliness and tidiness offered spiritual clarity. She believed that "cleanliness is next to Godliness." This view was shared by other black clubwomen of the period and can be attributed to their Victorian sense of order and discipline as well as a reflection of what many black leaders thought was needed to undo the generations of damage that enslavement had wreaked upon the black race, especially its women. The physical environment as a reflection of orderliness, immovability, and legitimacy was what Laney sought for her school and for the black community at large.

The Haines campus, an amalgam of impressive brick structures and smaller wooden buildings and cottages, became a testament to Laney's sense of a neat and orderly environment. For example, tree trunks were "white washed." This was a practice made popular in the American South and in Latin America that involves applying white paint or lime-water mixture to tree trunks to "give a clean, manicured appearance."[28] Laney could be seen wearing an apron and sweeping the campus yard with a broom—apparently unconcerned that this activity, engaged in by peasant women in Africa and many other parts of the developing world, including the South, was looked down upon by Augusta's black elite as "undignified"[29] for a woman of her status. Laney considered this a super-ficial attribute of femininity. Her view was consistent with a line in one of her speeches that "no[one] is judged by the superficial information af-forded by his clothes" and adds to the impression that Laney looked beyond appearances in deciding what was worthwhile and appropriate. Laney did rely upon some established gender roles, such as the Victorian reification of maternity and domestic duty. Yet she simultaneously defied others—such as taking a public stance against the mistreatment of her students, and advocating for women's suffrage[30] at a time when the fe-male norm was submissiveness. This led to a response in a black news-paper that criticized Laney for demonstrating a lack of gentility.[31]

## STAFFING THE TRANSFORMATION

In selecting the staff that would help fulfill her mission, perhaps the most important hire was Mary Jackson, later Jackson McCrorey, after leaving Haines in 1916 to marry Dr. H. L. McCrorey, president of Johnson C. Smith College in Charlotte. Jackson arrived in 1895 and stayed two decades, becoming associate principal during the period of great expan-sion. An Atlanta University alumna who continued graduate study at Harvard and the University of Chicago, Jackson was responsible for teacher training, or the normal department. She was an active presenter at teachers' conferences and a fundraiser for Haines, and she wrote occa-sional newspaper columns about education. Equal to Laney in intellect and passion for race uplift, Jackson was entrusted with running the school during Laney's frequent fundraising trips. To illustrate their close-ness, when W. E. B. Du Bois invited Laney to be one of the fifty black leaders to participate in the conference at Joel Spingarn's Amenia Farm to chart the future of black America in 1916, Laney wrote back and asked if Jackson could also attend. There is no record of Jackson's attendance, but the request demonstrates how much Laney valued the presence of "Mamie," as Jackson was called by friends. It was during Jackson's tenure that Haines developed "a comprehensive education program" that included a college preparatory curriculum that paved the way for junior college certification by 1931.[32] According to reports, Laney was very upset when Jackson left to get married.[33] Laney endorsed the Victorian notion of "self-sacrifice" as it pertained to women who forgo traditional female pursuits in service of a cause, such as black education. In fact, the term "self-sacrificing" was used among the women themselves in referring to their work.[34] Jackson was replaced by Lincoln University graduate A. C. Griggs in 1921. After Laney's death, and a brief stint as acting principal by her niece, Louise Laney, an Atlanta University graduate, Griggs became permanent principal in 1935 and stayed until the school closed in 1949. The ability to attract dedicated teachers enabled the school to grow and develop its secondary program and even to attain junior college status, while several of the teachers who apprenticed with Laney went on to distinguish themselves after leaving Haines, including school founders Mary McLeod Bethune and Janie Porter Barrett (1865–1948).[35] With disciples like Bethune and Barrett extolling Laney's virtues and the growing number of Haines graduates who were graduating from college and entering the professions, becoming teachers, physicians, lawyers, and dentists, its founder became a nearly iconic national figure. Lucy Laney Leagues sprouted up in several cities in the country. Organized in 1905 by friends and graduates of Haines for the express purpose of "helping the school," they became a national network of local chapters with a full slate of officers and an executive committee.[36] The Lucy Laney League of New York, which by 1916 had almost 100 members, was composed of enthusiastic supporters of the school and its programs, even holding a fundraising event at the world-famous Madison Square Garden.[37]

Kindergarten, introduced in Augusta in 1890, was just one of Laney's innovations that fostered the growth and rapid development of Haines. Laney hired Irene Smallwood, a teacher from Buffalo, New York, to run the program. The concept was quickly imitated, as Laney used her knowledge of Friedrich Frobel's (1782–1852) work to spread the gospel of early childhood education, touting it in her 1899 Hampton speech, in which she notably said: ". . . the kindergarten and primary school is the salvation of the race."[38] A nursing program, headed by a Canadian woman, J. S. Bolden, followed in 1892. Haines also took over the management of Lamar Hospital on Gwinnet Street, an arrangement that lasted until it was destroyed by fire in 1912.[39] According to the Jubilee program booklet, Haines also led the way in requiring school uniforms, developing an orchestra, as mentioned earlier, and supporting sports teams. The faculty member responsible for athletics programs was himself a Haines graduate, John M. Tutt, of the class of 1902. His exemplary preparation at Haines allowed him to enter the sophomore class at Lincoln University, which along with Atlanta University enthusiastically recruited Haines students. Tutt returned to his alma mater to teach mathematics, and in 1908 became director of athletics, implementing Laney's belief in training the mind along with the body. His profile in the Jubilee program counts him among the school's "most brilliant graduates." Mrs. Wille Mae McNatt-Oliver is also listed in the program booklet as another exemplary Haines graduate who received degrees from Cheney State University in Pennsylvania and the School of Social Work at Columbia University, and who returned to Haines to become head of the primary division. The school's teaching staff as a whole, many of them Haines graduates, reflected Laney's focus on offering the best preparation possible.

There were several colleges and universities represented among her staff, including well-established black colleges and universities such as Howard, Lincoln, Fisk, and Atlanta University, as well as white institutions including Cornell, Columbia, Oberlin, Harvard, and the University of Chicago, where Laney herself took summer courses. Haines's teaching corps comprised agents of knowledge, cultural exposure, and transformation, and served the school and its students as exemplars of achievement and social purpose. Laney expected students not only to apply themselves in the classroom, but also to adhere to a moral code that prohibited smoking, drinking, dancing, and even movie-going. Students were encouraged to go to church and to help people in the neighborhood by delivering food to the elderly and participating in neighborhood clean-up days. Margaret Louise Laney said that her aunt made it mandatory for students to do certain things so "they would learn how to act." An example Laney's niece remembered was having girls set formal dining tables and having the whole table practice using a finger bowl. "We were reminded," said Margaret Laney, "that [the bowl] was not for drinking."[40]

## CURRICULUM AND SCHOOL CULTURE

Haines recruited some of the best teachers available, which resulted in the expansion of the curriculum as well as enrollment. Teachers were not well paid; they sometimes complained about overdue wages and on occasion had their pay supplemented from Laney's own pocket. Nevertheless, most teachers seemed to feel that they were a part of something special at Haines. One teacher, Hattie McDaniel, a Cornell graduate who taught French (not the Academy Award winning actress), expressed conflicting feelings in a letter to her mother in 1917: "I think I would be quite happy if I could only get . . . some pay. Haven't had a bit since I have been here, so you can imagine how broke I am."[41] Despite the financial straits and uncertainty about teacher pay, the school maintained a positive public image. A visitor to the campus described Haines as "a large boarding school, furnishing home accommodations."[42] By 1931, Haines was being called "the best secondary school in Georgia."[43] The classical curriculum had been augmented by instruction in practical arts courses designed to provide a respectable career for students who did not attend college. Mechanical arts, rapid calculation, cosmetology, shorthand and bookkeeping were among the innovative courses that Haines offered in practical skills.[44] The emphasis, however, remained on academic courses, including innovative courses such as Negro history, which Laney viewed as a way to illustrate black achievement to the students and to amplify their own prospects. Margaret Louise Laney, discussing the curriculum in a 1975 interview, surprised the interviewer with her description of the college-level courses taught at Haines:

> M. L. Laney: [W]e had Latin, Greek, French, and German. We had mathematics; we had two years of algebra, one year of plane geometry and one year of trigonometry.
>
> Interviewer: Was this during a time when it was considered a junior college?
>
> MLL: Oh, no. It was just plain old high school.
>
> Interviewer: Just plain old high school. Uhmm.[45]

Lucy Laney explained her reasoning for preparing students well for the next level of their education: "You can't afford to put medicine upon Haines' training—you have got to go to college first, and medicine [medical school] after—no dentist without a knowledge of Greek or physician without Latin can make it. You have got to dig down and take the required courses."[46] She also explained her progressive views about liberal education, calling it "a perpetual motion affair." According to Laney, "What is today won't be tomorrow and the man who stops educating himself after he closes his school books . . . lags behind the times, and gets out of step with the world."[47]

Yet her progressive views about education yielded to her more traditional views about student conduct. "We labor to bring about a high moral sentiment,"[48] Laney wrote to her Presbyterian Mission supporters. The rules and regulations were published in the Haines Bulletin and covered academic, social, and religious matters such as these examples:

> "Failure in two subjects renders the student ineligible to take part in any public entertainment; to be a leader of any student organization, [or] to represent the Institution. . . . Good order, diligence in study, neatness, cleanliness, and industry are required of all.—All students are required to attend daily prayers, [and] religious services on the Lord's day.—Visiting or receiving visitors on the Sabbath is discou-

raged.—Every applicant must present evidence of good moral character."[49]

Laney, influenced by the "cult of true womanhood," was invested in the ideal of pure and virtuous women and their dutiful roles. The teaching staff was expected to execute the rules "with fairness" and to encourage the development of traits that Laney believed were indicators of the well-educated person. Aside from "book learning," those traits included having compassion and concern for the less fortunate and using those acquired skills to uplift them; being informed about and interested in history (including black history) and culture; having knowledge of the world around and beyond one's own door; and having good deportment. These were all characteristics of Laney herself, who read several newspapers each day and had mastered two foreign languages, Greek and Latin.

School culture at Haines focused upon participation in wholesome activities. These included attendance at musical concerts, cultural events, and exposure to the arts. Among the actors, poets, musical artists, inspirational speakers, and scholars who visited Haines were actor Richard Harrison, poet Langston Hughes, contralto Marian Anderson, and violinist Robert J. Douglass, grandson of Frederick Douglass. Laney's younger friend and protégé, school founder Nannie Helen Burroughs, and scholar W. E. B. Du Bois were also among Haines's distinguished visitors. In fact Nannie Helen Burroughs gave the commencement speech on two different occasions, in 1919 and 1922, drawing rave reviews. Hattie McDaniel, the French teacher, deemed the 1919 address "one of the finest in the history of the school."[50] In order to emphasize race pride and the importance of black history, Haines students were also active participants in Emancipation Day, an annual, citywide celebration of black progress that was organized by Rev. Charles T. Walker on January 1. During this festive occasion, sports and physical activity were encouraged for boy and girl students alike. Margaret Laney, who attended her aunt's school in its heyday, bemoaned the fact that children today don't know "how to walk." She remembered how each day began with physical activity—a march called to order by a bugle call. The "girls could drill as well as the boys," she said. Margaret Laney went on to explain that all the athletic events occurred during the day because mothers did not want their daughters to be out at night. On Friday nights, though, girls were allowed to attend parties held at someone's house. There were also sanctioned hayrides, picnics, and lawn parties.[51] Another example of the culture that Laney created was that everyone took a music class, and most students learned to play an instrument, guided by a Fisk University graduate who was the music teacher during that time.

J. Lawrence Cook was a student who transferred to Haines in 1914 from Snow Hill, a peer school that was founded by Tuskegee graduate

William J. Edwards in 1893 and that followed the Tuskegee-Hampton model of industrial education. Cook compared the two schools:

> How much better meals were at Haines than they had been at Snow Hill! There were two dining rooms; the tables had white table cloths and were neatly set. Instead of each plate being already served with food that had turned cold, hot serving dishes were brought to the table . . . older students at the head of each table to help serve and to keep order. . . . [A] serving dish . . . was replenished on request. . . Unlike Snow Hill, we had modern plumbing. . . .[52]

As the physical environment was transformed at Haines, the social and cultural aspects of campus life also changed to reflect Laney's broader purpose of race uplift. She was adamant in her belief that blacks were capable and equal to whites in educational potential and in every other regard. Her extant speeches and writings confirm her belief that racism and discrimination increased and intensified because blacks were viewed as uneducated and lacking in morality and culture. Laney, a devout Christian moralist and Victorian, wanted to correct that image and endorsed the activities of the Woman's Christian Temperance Union, an organization founded by white women in 1874 to crusade against the effects of alcohol on the American family. Another example of her exacting moralism is provided by A. C. Griggs, future principal of Haines, who reported that Laney took a particular dislike to some of the habits of the larger black community and launched her own crusades against them Griggs told of an activity called "Egypt Walking" which he described as "a sacrilegious and unbecoming religious ceremony" engaged in by elements of Augusta's black community on New Year's Eve. According to Griggs, Laney stamped it out with one bold stroke.[53]

Laney's strong views about culture were enacted at Haines through classical and spiritual music concerts, and the singing of hymns and black spirituals. She sought to preserve what she considered the more uplifting aspects of black cultural heritage by calling upon black writers to create short stories about black life in the Sea Islands of Georgia, with its unique historical origins.[54]

In the early decades of the twentieth century, Haines enjoyed national press coverage and recruited students from several states to its boarding program. Journalists and other curious observers visited Haines to see Laney's accomplishments. President-elect William Howard Taft, who had expressed the view that blacks were not suited for higher education, visited Haines in 1908. He had attended the 25th anniversary celebration at Tuskegee, and stopped at Haines before leaving the South. After touring the campus and giving an address in McGregor Hall, Taft praised Laney and showed his astonishment at what he witnessed with these words: ". . . that a colored woman could have established this great [institution] of learning and brought it to its present state speaks volumes for her capacity." He later said that he would always carry "the memory of the woman who created all of this."[55] With such recognition, the school continued to grow and transform itself and the community around it. With its offerings of frequent concerts and athletic competitions, and social service outreach that engaged both students and faculty, while Laney continued to be a public voice speaking on behalf of the blacks in the community, Haines became not just "Miss Laney's School," but the people's school.

Laney's well-prepared students could expect favorable consideration from higher learning institutions such as Lincoln, Howard, and Atlanta Universities. For example, Edward T. Ware, who succeeded his father, Asa Edmund Ware, as president of Atlanta University, set up a partial scholarship for Haines's top graduate and advocated for Haines to other potential donors.[56] William Hallock Johnson, president of Lincoln University, wrote an article about Laney titled "A Friend to Boys and Girls." Upon her death, Johnson delivered an address at the memorial service sponsored by the Lucy Laney League of Philadelphia.[57]

In Laney's waning years, the environment that she so caringly and dutifully constructed came under threat by compounding factors that were far beyond her control. For one, Laney was slowed by age and ailment, and was reported to get around slowly, dragging one foot.[58] Her duties were increasingly handled by A. C. Griggs, Haines's vice principal. Secondly, donations fell off due to the economic woes of the Great Depression. As a result, in 1933 the Presbyterian Board notified the school that it wanted to merge Haines with another school in Keysville, Georgia, and change its name to the Laney-Boggs Institute. Griggs kept the news from the ailing Laney, fearing that "the shock would prove fatal to her."[59] Griggs attempted to gather support to pressure the board to reverse its decision, but that effort failed. Lucy Laney died the same year, never knowing about Haines's pending fate.

After Laney's death, Haines alumni mounted a valiant effort to keep the school operating and raised $5,000 for teachers' salaries. Despite such concerted action, the school could not be sustained. With the opening of Augusta's first public high school for blacks since the closing of Ware High in the 1890s, Haines was deprived of tuition from black parents, whose taxes also supported Augusta's white high schools, which their children could not even attend. Opening in 1937, the new two-year A. R. Johnson High School finally gave those parents a public option for their children. Nevertheless, Haines, whose physical environment remained intact and whose curriculum still offered solid college preparation, soldiered on for twelve more years. An article in *The Crisis*, titled "The Spirit of Lucy Laney Marches On," noted that Haines had the distinction of being the only school to continue operating after losing its institutional support from the Presbyterians. The article, citing an advertisement for Haines in the same issue, listed Haines's tuition at $20 per year with a

$116 annual boarding fee.[60] The article also noted that the four-year cur-
riculum of Haines was of a high quality that contrasted significantly with
the two-year program at the new A. R. Johnson public high school for
blacks in Augusta. Announcing the launch of a $100,000 fundraising cam-
paign drive by the fiercely loyal Haines alumni, the article concluded that
"although Miss Laney has passed away, the principles and ideals she
instilled are being continued by those who now have succeeded her."[61]
The loyal alumni, with obvious appreciation for and exaltation of Laney,
reveled in her memory. One of those alumni was the best-selling romance
novelist Frank Yerby, whose works included *The Foxes of Harrow* (1946),
which was made into an Academy Award-winning Hollywood movie
directed by John Stahl. Yerby paid tribute to Laney in a poem published
in the Jubilee anniversary program booklet of 1936, excerpted above. It
ends with these elegiac lines: "[We] know well that through our veins
your vision runs/And these your myriad host of stalwart sons/Shall bear
your dream unto eternity."[62]

In Lucy Laney's lifetime, Haines became more than a school. It was
the embodiment of her vision of black achievement. Edward T. Ware
considered it one of the two best high schools in the state, and in 1932
Robert J. Douglass dubbed it "the best secondary school in Georgia."[63]
During its peak years, Haines became, along with Paine College, founded
in 1883, a symbol of black achievement, prestige, and transformation in
Augusta and beyond.

Born before emancipation, Laney lived through both the hopeful period of Reconstruction and the deathly repression that characterized the
post-Reconstruction era that institutionalized Jim Crow segregation in
the American South. Yet Laney, girded by her faith, imagined what
Haines should look like and become, and how it should help transform
the community. In making her dream a reality, in addition to being a
visionary, she had to be a good manager, adept in dealing with the vagar-
ies of white power while withstanding both racial and personal setbacks.
Her progressive educational outlook was framed by a mix of Puritan and
Victorian moral sensibilities that prescribed traditional gender roles. Yet,
because her sense of Christian duty was devoid of a "holier than thou
attitude," people who knew her considered Laney "broadminded." What
she was able to accomplish at Haines challenged preconceptions of black
women, and of the race itself. Unlike her mentees, the upcoming generation of black women school founders—including Mary Bethune, Charlotte Hawkins Brown, and Nannie Helen Burroughs—Laney did not live
to see the ascendancy of black political and civil rights. Nevertheless, the
work that she undertook in building the Haines Institute culture into one
that symbolized self-respect, achievement, and the radical notion of human equality for African-Americans, most surely helped to prepare the
way.

**Figure 3.1. Marshall Hall. First permanent building, Haines Institute. Courtesy of Georgia Archives, Vanishing Georgia Collection.**

## NOTES

1. Tommy Jesse Jones, *Study of Private and High Schools for Blacks* (Washington, D.C.: U.S. Printing Office, 1901), appendix 11.
2. Jones, *Private and High Schools*, appendix 11.
3. Jones, *Private and High Schools*, appendix 11.
4. Griggs, "Lucy Craft Laney," 98.
5. Springfield Baptist Church, http://historicspringfieldbaptistchurch.org/index.php?s=au&nid=108502 ( 5 July 2010).
6. Marshall, "Tell Them We're Rising," 49.
7. Glenn T. Eskew, "Black Elitism and the Failure of Paternalism in Postbellum Georgia: The Case of Bishop Lucius Henry Holsey," *Journal of Southern History* 58, no. 4 (Nov. 1992): 656; 637 –66.
8. Ovington, *Portraits in Color*, 59.
9. Lucy Laney file, Presbyterian Historical Society, Philadelphia, n.d.
10. "Haines Normal School," *Savannah Tribune* (15 June 1889).
11. "Haines Normal School."
12. "History of Haines Normal and Industrial School," Jubilee Program Booklet (1936), Lucy C. Laney vertical file, Moorland-Spingarn Research Center, Howard University, Washington, D.C.
13. Lucy C. Laney, "Burden."
14. A. C. Griggs, "Lucy Craft Laney," 98.
15. A. C. Griggs, "Lucy Craft Laney," 98.
16. Lucy Laney, "Progress Report," in Gerda Lerner, ed., *Black Women in White America: A Documentary History* (New York: Vintage Books, 1973), 122 –23.
17. Laney, "Progress Report," 122 –23.
18. Douglass, "Climbing Upward," 32 –34.

19. Marshall, "Tell Them We're Rising," 94.

20. "A Progress Report from the Founder of the Haines School," *Church at Home and Abroad* (August 1893), reprinted in *Black Women in White America: A Documentary History*, ed. Gerda Lerner (New York: Vintage Books, 1973), 122 –23.

21. Griggs, "Lucy Craft Laney," 98.

22. James M. McPherson, "White Liberals and Black Power in Negro Education, 1865–1915," *American Historical Review* 75, no. 5 (June 1970): 1374.

23. "History of Haines Normal and Industrial School," Jubilee Program Booklet, 1936.

24. Anne Kendall, "Lucy C. Laney," research paper in Laney biographical file, Woodruff Library, Atlanta University Center (May 1972), 1 –10.

25. Kendall, "Lucy C. Laney."

26. Kendall, "Lucy C. Laney."

27. Griggs, "Lucy Craft Laney," 99.

28. Richard Campanella, *Bienville's Dilemma: A Historical Geography of New Orleans* (Lafayette, La.: Center for Louisiana Studies, 2008), 298.

29. Ovington, *Portraits in Color*, 57.

30. Laney took a leadership role in organizing the local branch of the NAACP and led a drive to register black women to vote; she also worked to integrate the YWCA. She was arrested for standing firm against what she considered insensitive treatment of her students by two white doctors who came to the school to vaccinate them. Cottingham, "Burden of the Educated Colored Woman," 90 –91.

31. "Letter to the Editor," *Atlanta Independent* (16 December 1907), 1.

32. Cottingham, "Burden of the Educated Colored Woman," 52; Marshall, "Tell Them We're Rising," 114.

33. Mary Jackson McCrorey, "Lucy Craft Laney," *The Crisis* 41, no. 1 (June 1934): 161; Ovington, *Portraits in Color*, 57.

34. Mary McLeod Bethune, letter to Nannie Helen Burroughs, December 29, 1934, Burroughs Papers, Library of Congress, Manuscript Division, box 3.

35. Social reformer and educator Janie Porter Barrett founded a settlement house for black women and, in 1915, the Virginia Industrial School for Wayward Negro Girls in rural Virginia. The Hampton Institute graduate was also the founding president of the Virginia Federation of Colored Women's Clubs. The Virginia Historical Society, http://www.vahistorical.org/sva2003/barrett.htm (9 May 2010).

36. "The Lucy Laney League" (29 March 1924), Lucy Craft Laney vertical file, manuscript division, Library of Congress.

37. "Lucy Laney League."

38. Lucy C. Laney, "Burden,"341 –44.

39. Kendall, 1 –10

40. Margaret Louise Laney, "Oral Interviews with Augusta Citizens," Oral History Project, Augusta Regional Library, (6 February 1975), 11.

41. Marshall, "Tell Them We're Rising, 127.

42. Douglass, "Climbing Upward," 34

43. M. A. Majors, *Noted Negro Women: Triumphs and Activities* (Chicago: Donohue and Henneberry, 1891, reprinted by Books for Libraries Press, 1971), 325.

44. Douglass, "Climbing Upward," 34.

45. Margaret Louise Laney, "Oral Interviews with Augusta Citizens," 111.

46. Douglass, "Climbing Upward," 34

47. Douglass, "Climbing Upward," 34.

48. "Haines Institute Report to Presbyterian Church," 1888.

49. "Regulations," *Haines Journal*, 1935: n.p.

50. Marshall, "Tell Them We're Rising," 123.

51. Margaret Louise Laney, 1975, 8.

52. J. Lawrence Cook, *An Autobiography of the Early Years, 1899 –1922* , edited and annotated by his son Jean Lawrence Cook, M.D. (1972), http:/doctorjazz.co.uk/page16.html (30 August 2005).

53. Griggs, "Lucy Craft Laney," 100.

54. William Hartshon, ed., *An Era of Progress and Promise, 1863 –1910* (Boston: Priscilla Publishing Co, 1910), 300.

55. William Hallock Johnson, "A Friend of Boys and Girls," *Women and Missions*, Lucy Craft Laney file, Library of Congress manuscript collection , n.d.

56. Edward T. Ware to Lucy Laney, (7 February 1910), Edward Twichell Ware Records, Woodruff Library, Atlanta University Center.

57. William Hallock Johnson, "An Address at the Memorial Service of the Philadelphia Chapter of the Laney League," (November 26, 1933), the Lucia Chapter of the Lucy Laney League, Lucy C. Laney file Presbyterian Historical Society, Philadelphia, n.p.

58. Griggs to Francis Grimke (11 May 1933), in *The Works of Francis J. Grimke*, vol 4, ed. Carter G. Woodson (Washington , D.C.: Associated Publishers, 1942), 483.

59. "Haines Institute: "The Spirit of Lucy Laney Marches On," *The Crisis* 47, no. 8 (August 1940): 342.

60. "Spirit of Lucy Laney," *Crisis*, 342.

61. "Tributes to the Founder," Haines Institute Golden Jubilee Program, Moorland-Spingarn Research Center (April 1936), 37.

62. "Tributes to the Founder," Frank Garvin Yerby, "Lucy Laney" poem, 37.

63. Douglass, "Climbing Upward," 32.

# FOUR

## "Ringing Up a School"

### Mary McLeod Bethune's Impact on Daytona Beach

*The river glistening like silver in the sun, the palmettos and evergreen oaks hung with moss, the low rolling hills—incredibly beautiful! She strolled back to Colored Town and stood in the midst of the human exploitation. Deep down inside of her a voice seemed to say, "This is the spot. This is the place for your school".[1]*

The above passage describes Mary McLeod Bethune's reaction to her first visit to Daytona. Heeding advice from a minister in tiny Palatka, Florida, where she had started a small school, she set out to scout for another location in the state. Her dramatic decision to build her school amidst idyllic beauty and pressing need is retold in a popular 1951 biography of Bethune for young adults by Catherine Owens Peare. The passage, quoted above, from this idealized biography that had Bethune's blessing, may be true or reimagined. Yet it does point to the overarching theme of inspiration and faith that guided Bethune's venture in building her school with meager to nonexistent resources. It also provides an intro-duction to the disparate nature of life in Daytona Beach—incredible beauty in the midst of human exploitation. That dual reality in Daytona prompted the missionary-minded Bethune to remember her mentor Lucy Laney's response to her disappointment at being denied a missionary post in Africa. Laney, under whom she had a teaching apprenticeship in Augusta in 1895, told Bethune that "Africans in America need Christ and school as much as they do in Africa."[2] That advice to Bethune, recounted in several different sources, was the starting point of much of what she was to accomplish in the next fifty years of her life. Bethune often praised Laney and acknowledged the instrumental role she played in her deci-sion to focus on the plight of black girls.

Historians have acknowledged the founder of the school that began with the myth-provoking "hope, a prayer and $1.50" and maintained itself for over a century to grow into the co-ed Bethune-Cookman University (formerly College) as one of this country's most important educators. Mary McLeod Bethune is the only black woman and possibly the only woman to found a grammar school and have it become an accredited university. But Bethune is equally recognized as a trailblazer in other arenas. This includes the black women's club movement, in which she served as president of the first national black women's organization, the National Association of Colored Women, organized in 1896, for two consecutive two year-terms, from 1924–1928. Then, in 1935, she launched the National Council of Negro Women in order to exercise more political clout in national politics, especially in Washington, D.C. The rising visibility of her work with women led to an administrative appointment in one of President Franklin Delano Roosevelt's "New Deal" programs. From 1936 to 1944, Bethune served as director of the Division of Negro Affairs in the National Youth Administration, which was charged with the daunting task of combating the massive Depression-era youth unemployment. Although her residence in Washington and her frequent travels in service to her country, her school, the NAACP, and other organizations to which she belonged kept her away for long periods, Daytona Beach remained her home and the starting point of her prodigious and well-documented public life.[3] We know less about her work in Daytona and the early days of building her school, and how she navigated the politics of the white moneyed class of Northerners, the local white establishment, black religious and civil society, and the struggling black newcomers who worked in the service industry and doing the backbreaking work of day laborers.

Bethune came to Daytona Beach as a young, audaciously hopeful African American woman, determined to bring education to impoverished black girls and to aid the families of these workers. Her intent was in step with the efforts of national black leaders such as Booker T. Washington. Bethune's early emphasis on domestic science and vocational skills suited to the existing labor market reveals Washington's influence on her. Although as the school expanded, she broadened her view of the purpose of education toward W. E. B. Du Bois's ideas about education as empowerment, she once stated that the Tuskegee Institute president's writings were "a second Bible to me." When she opened her school in Daytona, she followed his exhortation to blacks to "cast down your buckets" where you are.[4]

Her work in Florida also places Bethune within the broad spectrum of the racial uplift ideology that so engaged educated African Americans during the early 1900s. For black women of the middle class, the fervor to uplift the masses was infused with a desire to improve the image of their sex. Bethune and her counterparts in the growing black women's club

movement—women's club president Mary Church Terrell, school founders Nannie Burroughs and Charlotte Hawkins Brown, and others—
wanted to acquit black women of the scurrilous charge of immorality that
resulted from blaming them for their own sexual exploitation during
slavery. Taking her cue from role models that included Emma Wilson,
her first teacher in her native Mayesville, South Carolina, and Haines
Institute founder Lucy Laney, Bethune sought to provide black girls with
"usable" skills for work and a wholesome, productive life that would
help them meet financial obligations to themselves and their families
while refuting the harmful charges.

When she moved to Daytona in 1904, at the age of twenty-nine to
open the Daytona Educational and Industrial Training School for Negro
Girls, she vowed to do "the greatest good for the greatest number."[5]
Having failed to get the response she wanted to her earlier efforts in
Palatka, the economic promise that the Daytona Beach area offered was
very attractive to her. The lack of financial resources in Palatka made her
aware that more than passion and commitment were required to build a
school. Bethune, the "pragmatic idealist," was only beginning to exploit
her persuasive charm and charisma in service of her goals. The flock of
wealthy Northerners who would spend their winters in the little village
where "the tepid and saline waters make bathing a luxury at any season"
were among America's richest families.[5] Their large beachfront homes in
Daytona Beach and the nearby town of Ormond would surely require
skilled domestic help. Bethune was confident enough to expect their support in building her school. This consideration was very important in her
plans.

A new railroad, the Florida East Coast Railway, added to the lure of
Daytona. Henry Flagler had extended a railroad line through Daytona
south to Miami and Key West that promised economic prosperity. That
prospect also lured new black workers and their families to the area.
Although blacks had lived in the area since Daytona was incorporated in
1876 and had established a community that included business owners
and two churches, the new arrivals markedly increased the numbers.
"Those children need a real school, and I have come to serve them,"
Bethune declared with her natural flair for the dramatic.[6] Conditions in
the area ignited her passion for uplift: "I found dense ignorance and
meager educational facilities and racial prejudice of the most violent
type,"[7] she said.

As a native of South Carolina, Bethune had witnessed the psychologi-
cal and physical devastation of racial violence near her home in Mayesville. She had also lived in Concord, North Carolina, where she attended
the all-female Scotia Seminary, a school that prepared black girls to be
teachers and skilled service workers. Her formal education ended after a
two-year stint at the evangelical Moody Bible Institute in Chicago, where
she, along with one African male, constituted the entire black student

population. Her experience among whites convinced her that there were alternatives to racial hatred and violence. This confluence of circumstances boosted Bethune's enthusiasm to start a school in the heart of this vibrant and promising southern city.

At the turn of the century, when Bethune arrived in Daytona, the black population lived in a closely confined section of town devoid of street lights, sidewalks, and basic sanitation facilities.[8] Schooling for black children was rudimentary and haphazard. Throughout the state, public support for black schools lagged far behind support for white schools. Black students received fewer instructional hours, and the condition of most black schools was described in the 1912 state of Florida biennial report on public instruction as "dilapidated." Black teachers earned less than white teachers, and only about 60 percent of black children ever enrolled in school. The state spent $11.50 a year for the education of each white child but only $2.64 per black child.[9] In counties with black schools, the curriculum stressed manual or industrial education, reputedly for its value in producing a dependable and pliant work force.[10] In 1904, Daytona Beach had no viable school system for blacks.

There was one kindergarten that had been started by a black woman with the support of white clubwomen. According to letters from Dora Maley, support from white clubwomen like her was also instrumental in Bethune's success. Maley, a prominent local citizen and member of the exclusive Palmetto Women's Club, reported that she was the first to assist Bethune by "emptying out the contents of [her] change purse" after a chance meeting in a grocery store.[11] Maley was so impressed with Bethune's plans to start a school that she took the news to her fellow club members. She also convinced her brother-in-law to allow Bethune to use, rent-free, one of the shacks that he owned in the black section of town.[12] Bethune wooed other members of the white establishment in Daytona by asking influential citizens to serve on her board of trustees. Her efforts were generally met with a favorable response from local officials. The mayor of Daytona, in a 1931 letter, praised Bethune's work as "outstanding" and urged "public spirited men and women" to assist her.[13] The Ku Klux Klan took exception, however, and marched on her school in 1920.[14]

Despite the presence of the Klan and strict segregation, Daytona had a reputation for being relatively tolerant on race issues. Unlike in many towns in the deep South, the early white settlers of Volusia County were mostly Northerners—many from states with strong abolitionist traditions, such as Ohio and New York—who brought with them more moderate racial views. The city founder, Matthius Day, Jr., was a transplanted Ohioan.[15] Many formerly enslaved people also settled in the area, attracted by the promise of free homesteads in exchange for work at a lumber company that had ties with the Freedmen's Bureau. When the company failed, a significant number of blacks stayed in the area, working in a variety of jobs, including farming and semiskilled labor. Resourceful and ambitious, some of the black settlers were also Civil War veterans.

Yet Daytona was no oasis of positive race relations. By the early 1900s there was an influx of native white Southerners who brought with them a more virulent form of racism. Blacks were banned from the beaches, and racial laws now entered the city codes. Although African Americans labored as service workers for the new, sprawling tourist-linked oceanfront developments, well into the 1950s laws required black servants to be "back to the West side of the [Halifax] River by sunset."[16]

The developing tourist industry and new railroad encouraged continuing immigration of both white and black laborers at the turn of the century. Competition for jobs increased, causing further racial polarization. Daytona grew steadily, from a population of 1,690 in 1900 to over 3,500 ten years later.[17] Blacks comprised over 50 percent of that number. Whites responded to this changing demography by fortifying racial boundaries. When Bethune arrived in 1904, segregation was an entrenched reality. Nevertheless, the city managed to develop a progressive image. Blacks could vote in Daytona, while many other southern cities were erecting elaborate schemes of disfranchisement.

Bethune's efforts to found the institution that was to become Bethune-Cookman College thus took place in a distinctive community, the nature of which is suggested by a variety of anecdotes about the school's origin.[18] In addition to several versions of the story about the $1.50 that Bethune reportedly used to launch her dream, folklore has it that a local minister gave Bethune an old fire engine bell and told her to "go ring up you a school."[19] This version bestowed a spiritual as well as communal blessing on her endeavor. Another version holds that Bethune approached John Williams, a carpenter and one of the few black property owners in the area, with her plan to turn his small two-story frame house into a school. At first he was reluctant: "I'm not thinking about turning my house into a school house!" By the time Bethune finished her talk about being partners in a "new adventure for our people," Williams supposedly agreed to rent the house to her for eleven dollars per month.[20]

The first class of six students—five girls aged six through twelve and Bethune's five-year-old son Albertus—began classes on October 4, 1904. Bethune welcomed each girl with a cheerful greeting: "Come in, little girl, we've been expecting you. I hope you'll be happy with us."[21] The original name of the school, the Daytona Literary and Industrial Institute, denoted the dual purpose that Bethune envisioned: to teach both academic and practical skills to black girls. The long title was soon shortened by community residents, who—similar to how Augusta's black population adopted Haines Institute by shortening its name to "Miss Laney's School"— simply called it "the School" or "the Bethune School." Bethune charged tuition of fifty cents per week for those who could pay. The families of those who could not offered food and services in exchange for tuition. She accepted chickens, eggs, and produce as payment.[22] Extant school records dating from 1906 show that Bethune used a ledger to record all income and expenses. In the tuition column many students appeared in a non-pay status.[23] With this flexible policy, enrollment tripled within months.

Bethune's zeal to succeed was legendary: "We burned logs and used charred splinters as pencils, and mashed elderberries for ink. I begged strangers for a broom, a lamp, a bit of cretonne to put around the packing case which served as my desk. I haunted the city dump and trash piles behind hotels, retrieving discarded linen and kitchenware, cracked dishes, broken chairs, pieces of old lumber. Everything was scoured and mended. This was part of the training—to salvage, to reconstruct, to make bricks without straw."[24] She envisioned a setting in which students and teachers worked side by side building a purposeful, self-sufficient community. Together they made almost all of their essentials, including brooms, rugs, mattresses, and writing materials.[25]

The school soon outgrew its cramped space, and Bethune looked to buy land to erect a larger building. The only property that she could afford was a garbage dump called "Hell's Hole." To the deeply religious Bethune, this was her inspiration, "to plunge into creating something from nothing."[26] She bought the land for $250, giving the owner $5 down in small change, which she had raised by selling homemade ice cream and sweet potato pies. When she delivered the payment wrapped in a handkerchief, Bethune probably recalled a recurring dream in which Booker T. Washington handed her a diamond, also wrapped in a hand- kerchief, and told her to "go build [you] a school."[27] The actual building began before she knew where she would get the money to finish it. When it was completed, the four-story, forty-by-forty-foot frame house was ap- propriately named "Faith Hall." It had been built almost entirely with surplus supplies and volunteer labor.[28]

Bethune initially was responsible for every aspect of the school's oper- ation. She taught all the grade levels and managed the school and all of its outreach and fundraising projects. With increased enrollment, several new teachers joined the staff and were paid between fifteen and thirty dollars a month plus board. Bethune, realizing that her chief assets were her administrative and fundraising skills, sought out experienced teach- ers: "I have a vision. I need strong women to help me realize it."[29]

One such woman was Frances Keyser, a graduate of Hunter College in New York City and supervisor of the White Rose Mission for delin- quent girls in the city. In 1909 she arrived in Daytona Beach and took over the entire educational program of the school, freeing Bethune to concentrate on administrative and fundraising matters. A recipient of the first prize in French at Hunter and a skilled literary critic (to whom the noted poet Paul Laurence Dunbar submitted his poems for pre-publica- tion critique), Keyser's educational programs earned the school its good reputation and state accreditation. Frances Keyser's importance to Bethune is comparable to Mary Jackson's importance to Lucy Laney at Haines. They were both well-educated and accomplished women who used their good management skills to develop and enhance the curricula and put the schools on firm foundations. Bethune also hired Portia Smiley, a graduate of Hampton Institute and the Pratt Institute of New York, to supervise the domestic science program. Smiley, who had practical nursing skills, was described as "an artist" in domestic science and crafts.[30]

Because of her ability to articulate her vision to others, Bethune attracted a contingent of highly qualified and very dedicated black women teachers who often accepted lower pay in order to join the Bethune "family." With such teachers the school developed a curriculum that reflected the dual traditions of vocationalism and liberalism in black education. Many of the teachers whom Bethune recruited spent their entire careers with her and remained on in the campus community after they retired. Marion Speight, whom I interviewed in 1991, was one of them.

The Daytona Educational and Industrial Training School became the clearest articulation of Bethune's educational philosophy. She followed Booker T. Washington's lead in stressing vocational, or what was then called industrial, education, but her expanding curriculum also reflected her beliefs about the uplifting role of black women as embodiments of morality, service, and self-reliance. At the opening of the school, she announced: "This is a new kind of school. I'm going to teach my girls crafts and homemaking. I'm going to teach them to earn a living. They will be trained in head, hand, and heart. Their heads to think, their hands to work, and their hearts to have faith."[31]

Initially, the curriculum offered courses in the domestic sciences. These included sewing, cooking, handicrafts, music, poultry raising, rug weaving, chair caning, and broom making. Academic subjects, such as reading, writing, and mathematics, were also taught, along with mandatory Bible study. Early criticism from some blacks in the community who felt that teaching housekeeping and domestic science prepared the girls for a menial, segregated labor force dissipated as the curriculum expanded to offer more business and liberal arts courses. As school enrollment increased, Bethune became a leading spokesperson for black political and economic opportunities in Daytona Beach and throughout the segregated South. In an unusually blunt and stinging indictment of the evils of segregation in the late 1920s, Bethune argued that these practices also hurt whites:

> The South has definitely committed itself to the task of keeping the Negro in his place. That place by all accepted teaching and belief is and must be for all time an inferior one. To keep [Negroes] inferior they must be huddled in segregated ghettoes without drainage, light, pave-

ment, or modern sanitary convenience. They must be denied justice and the right to make a decent living. They must be insulted and bullied and mobbed, discriminated against in public places and denied access to parks and recreational centers. In dollars and cents the cost of this system is tremendous to the commonwealth which sponsors it.[32]

In Bethune's view, the reality of these conditions made it necessary for black females to support themselves while they simultaneously strove toward better opportunities. Education, she believed, had a dual purpose—survival and uplift. In the early 1900s industrial education and domestic science meant self-sufficiency, but academic and cultural education were also necessary. In her view the two were "concomitant to a better way of living."[33] Her education at Scotia Seminary had impressed her with the possibilities for merging both the academic and vocational aspects of learning and for forging a disciplined community of teachers and students working together for the common good. "Of what use . . . is an educational system," Bethune asked, "that does not have its roots in the life and needs of the people?"[34] From her vantage point those needs centered on the ability to earn a living and help maintain a family. Black females in particular had a "special need" for education and training because of their pivotal economic and social roles in the family. Bethune, who subscribed to the Victorian view of women as agents for moral change, targeted girls because they would be able to instill the notion of moral and spiritual uplift in their families while also helping to sustain them with their earnings. The "wasteful habits" present in many black homes weighed heavily on black girls. One study of living standards in Negro homes reported:

> Sanitary provisions are wholly lacking in many rural homes. Dug wells are used and are often left open and unprotected. Women carry the water long distances. Habits of living are not such as to insure good health. Preventable sickness abounds; old fashioned superstitions are still followed. . . . Infant mortality is very high. . . . There is but little variety in the diet . . . nor is the food prepared with care—cooking is frequently badly done, starches are too often underdone, and frying is the method of cooking most universally employed. Wasteful habits in handling food prevail. Meals are irregularly served, members of a family being allowed to eat whenever and wherever they please.[35]

Her curriculum represented a response both to these conditions and to middle-class mores, such as eating meals at a set time. A national report issued in 1923 put the burden of counteracting "the evil effects of present conditions" on the shoulders of women.[36] The report concluded that "it is imperative that Negro girls be trained in good health habits, in wise expenditure of money, in economical use of products . . . [and taught how] to exercise good taste in dress and house furnishings, [that] they may help to make the home both healthful and attractive and to bring the family to a more efficient and happy life."[37]

Bethune, like other black women educators of her day, touted the value of this type of instruction for black girls as the best way to improve the family. She once stated, "The education of the Negro girl must embrace a larger appreciation for good citizenship in the home. Our girls must be taught cleanliness, beauty and thoughtfulness and their application in making home life possible. For the proper home life provides the proper atmosphere for life everywhere else."[38] In addition to improving the general welfare and stability of the black home, this brand of middle-class conformity emerged as a prerequisite for the full participation of black women in public life and for their recognition as worthy women.

The outreach programs of the school, patterned after those at Hampton, and especially at Haines Institute, provided the black community with tangible benefits. Bethune borrowed other ideas from Haines, including the visiting black artists and speakers and Laney's initial interest in educating black girls. These ideas, including the working farm that both Laney and Washington pioneered, were all carried through by Bethune. There were workshops for the area's farmers that introduced them to modern farming methods, public bazaars to display and sell student projects, and a community center and reading room. Beginning in 1911, Bethune took her staff and students to area turpentine (lumber) camps to offer both Sunday school classes and lessons in hygiene, health, and sanitary food preparation. Bethune, like Lucy Laney, believed that workers' shanties were breeding grounds for "drunkenness, ribaldry and immorality."[39] Both the black and white communities praised her missionary work in the camps. The following year, 1912, she enlisted one of her trustees to donate the funds to build a YMCA near the campus, which could be used as a recreational outlet for area youth. She also established a summer school and playground for black children in the city.

Also in 1912 she spearheaded the fundraising and building of the first hospital for black people south of St. Augustine.[40] McLeod Hospital, like most of her other endeavors, grew out of a pressing necessity. When one of her students became critically ill with appendicitis, she begged a white physician to admit her to the all-white hospital. Bethune later appeared at the door of the hospital, but a nurse ordered her to the back. "I thrust her aside and found my little girl segregated in a corner of the porch behind the kitchen. Even my toes clenched with rage," she later recalled.[41] This encounter led to a fund drive that built a hospital and started a training program for nurses at the school.

For her hospital project Bethune secured donations from industrialist Andrew Carnegie and other affluent whites who vacationed or resided in Daytona. To the best of their ability, members of the Daytona black community also supported the hospital. The result was a "well-appointed" twenty-six-bed hospital and a nurse training program that maintained an interracial staff of doctors and medical personnel. [42]

After a thirteen-month training course, nurses went into the city to provide health services to the black community. Between 1917 and 1918 nurses visited 230 patients. Another 530 patients received treatment at the dispensary, a large number of whom could not pay the nominal fee. [43] The elderly, sick children, and young mothers were specially targeted for health services. The hospital remained in operation for twenty years, until August 1, 1930, when the county hospital system absorbed the hospital. [44] In 1912, Bethune started an outreach program for black children in a nearby turpentine camp. The children had little opportunity for any type of schooling, and Bethune hoped to improve unhealthy conditions in the camps by conducting special mission services on the campgrounds.

The school also operated a profitable farm that supplied needed food and sold any surplus to the public. The farm became an important source of revenue. A visitor to the school observed a "splendid patch" of strawberries and asked if they were for the students or to sell. Bethune's reply was to the point: "We never eat a quart when we can get fifty cents for them." [45]

Having limited financial resources, Bethune clearly needed community support from blacks as well as whites for her ambitious programs. From all indications, black support helped her during the early years. Bethune was welcomed at two black churches and allowed to take up special collections for the school. Similar to Haines Institute in Augusta, "The School" became a source of pride for community members, and they supported it through frequent fundraising activities. Chicken supper sales were a favorite and frequent fundraising event. Supporters often identified specific needs for these occasions, such as paying a teacher's salary or meeting an overdue bill. [46] The list of volunteers from the community continued to grow. Construction workers, fundraisers, ministers who taught the Bible course, and others gave hundreds of volunteer hours to the school. Community members were also the principal consumers for the school's developing commercial enterprises, such as farm produce, home crafts, and clothes from the dressmaking department.

Bethune enlisted prominent white and black residents to serve on her board of trustees, and she maximized these connections by also establishing an advisory board that included the wives of many wealthy winter residents. These women were very effective in raising money and sponsoring special programs and projects on behalf of the school. Bethune's frequent speaking engagements to upper-class white women's groups, such as the Palmetto Club, appealed to their sense of noblesse oblige because she emphasized the virtues of cleanliness, hard work, and moral living, which many whites thought the black populace lacked. Bethune, who viewed alcohol as a threat to family life and black progress, founded a campus chapter of the Women's Christian Temperance Union (WCTU).

Many of the school's Sunday afternoon programs ended with the WCTU pledge sung in unison by the girls: "God helping me, I promise not to buy, sell, drink, or give alcoholic liquors while I live."[47]

Among blacks, Bethune's stock continued to rise. Her support for the development of black-owned businesses and the granting of contracts for work at the school to black firms and workers added to her stature. In speeches to black groups, she urged them to patronize black-owned establishments.[48] She encouraged blacks to vote in county elections, which precipitated a 1920 visit from the Ku Klux Klan. The Klan attempted to silence Bethune and to intimidate potential black voters by marching onto campus in full regalia. In response, she met them at the front of the campus "with arms folded and head held high." The frustrated marchers soon left, and the next morning Bethune led a group of blacks to the polls. Polling officials forced the blacks to wait in line the entire day in hopes that they would get tired and go home. Bethune reported, "They kept us waiting all day, but we voted."[49]

The ballot, to Bethune, was a means of fostering change. In 1948 she, along with the new president of Bethune-Cookman College, urged the faculty and students to get involved in the campaign of George Engram, a black businessman running for a seat on the city council. Although he lost the election to a white politician, this activism inspired other efforts by blacks to organize for economic and political improvements.[50]

Many white moderates supported Bethune and her work, particularly the school. She admitted that she did her "best missionary work among the prominent winter visitors to Florida."[51] Bethune scanned the society pages of the newspaper for notices of newly arrived visitors in Daytona and invited them to visit the school. She recruited her board of trustees in a similar manner. The board included James N. Gamble of Procter and Gamble, who became board president and a lifelong supporter; John D. Rockefeller, founder of Standard Oil, and Samuel White, founder of the White Sewing Machine company.[52] Access to wealthy Northerners such as Rockefeller and Gamble added to her clout among the white city fathers.

From the beginning, one of her most effective methods of garnering supporters was to distribute leaflets to visitors describing the school's goals. Drawing upon her skills as a missionary, she stood on street corners in the business district and stopped anyone inclined to listen to her message. Soon after the school was founded, she began making fundraising trips to the North, speaking to both black and white groups. In 1909 she attended a National Association of Colored Women's (NACW) convention in Hampton, Virginia, where she asked permission to address the delegates.[53] Bethune made such an impression that the clubwomen took up a collection for her school. Fifteen years later she became its president. Her desire to do more for black women motivated the founding of the National Council of Negro Women in 1935. As an attempt to unite black

women within and across their organizational affiliations, its agenda included gaining better wages and working conditions, equal educational
opportunities for black women, and greater political and economic
strength for black women via the ballot box.

Within a few years of her arrival in Daytona, Bethune had become an
important catalyst for racial tolerance in the community. Her Sunday
afternoon chapel programs were described as an oasis of integration. The
chapel was the only place in town where seating was not segregated
according to race. She diplomatically guided whites to their seats, ex-
claiming how pleased she was to have them present. Before they realized
it, they were sitting next to blacks.

Bethune's involvement in economic ventures with black businessmen,
her advocacy of black business ownership, as well as her charm offensive
among whites, prompted comparisons with Booker T. Washington. The
most notable example of her entrepreneurial spirit was Bethune-Volusia,
Inc., which was founded in 1948 and spearheaded by Bethune and businessman George Engram. Their intent was to "establish a Negro beach
community . . . owned and controlled by blacks and available to them for
construction of homes and recreational facilities."[54] The project allowed
blacks to use the beaches, many for the first time.

Bethune's success in Daytona was due to her ability to gather support
from large numbers of whites and blacks. More outward and direct in her
cultivation of important friends for the school than the quiet Laney, Bethune's message of self-help and education appealed, for different reasons, to both groups. Blacks understood her message to mean economic
and social empowerment through education and hard work. Most whites
did not perceive a threat to their hegemony in helping blacks achieve the
kind of practical education and moral values that Bethune espoused.
These attitudes helped to ease troubled race relations. Eleanor Roosevelt's visit to the campus in 1940, however, made some city fathers ner-
vous. The First Lady's decision to stay in Bethune's residence on campus
rather than at one of the expensive whites-only hotels confirmed among
them her reputation for "race-mixing." Bethune helped to avert a potentially ugly situation when she arranged for a state police escort after city
police refused to accompany Mrs. Roosevelt to the college. Unfortunately, the visit had no effect on segregation laws in the city. Daytona continued to segregate until well after the passage of the Civil Rights Act of
1964.[55]

Daytona's reputation for racial tolerance was a factor in 1946 when
Brooklyn Dodger owner Branch Rickey selected the city for Jackie Robinson's debut in the first integrated major league baseball game in modern
history on March 17, 1946. Rickey asked black politician Joe Harris and

Figure 4.1.   Mary McLeod Bethune (1875-1955), founder and president, Bethune-Cookman College. Photo courtesy of Moorland- Spingarn Research Center, Howard University, Washington, D.C.

Bethune to serve as Robinson's hosts. Although city officials promised their "wholehearted cooperation," Robinson's scheduled appearance outraged many whites. Black people throughout the area, including Bethune, enthusiastically supported the black ballplayer. Ultimately, favorable national attention to Robinson's debut created goodwill between both races in Daytona.[56]

The city was the launching pad for Bethune's growing national prominence as a spokeswoman for racial justice and education. By becoming increasingly involved in the national debate on race and education, she expanded her contacts and was able to enlist the support of a national constituency of prominent Americans. The school that she founded, although never sufficiently endowed, survived and even prospered. She also earned a reputation as a consensus builder by voicing the concerns of a diverse constituency—the black underclass and blacks with middle-class aspirations—and courting the moderate segment of the white citizenry. Her emphasis on practical skills and moral development helped to diffuse any notion of a radical agenda, and that appealed to a large segment of middle-class blacks as well as white liberals and conservatives. America soon took notice. Her friendship with Eleanor Roosevelt led to a friendship with President Roosevelt and the title of "presidential adviser" on racial matters. Bethune's ascendancy to national prominence showcased her skills as an administrator and diplomat—a woman whose interracial reformist tactics and programs were in step with national opinion-makers in black and white America. There were other black leaders who articulated more militant and innovative views, but it was Bethune's ability to appeal to people from various factions and ideological positions that ensured her legacy as an institution builder. Christopher Linsin is correct in noting that Bethune's rare mix of "deference, flattery, and political pragmatism" equipped her to deal with whites of different political stripes.[57] Her photograph on the cover of *Time* magazine in 1950 was further confirmation that what she started in Daytona Beach had become a celebratory American story.

The white establishment in Daytona was sometimes uncomfortable with the attention that followed Bethune, especially when it focused the spotlight on their segregationist practices. Her adept use of the press served her well in advancing a broad agenda for better

**Figure 4.2.   Mary McLeod Bethune and students of the Daytona Literary and Industrial School for Negro Girls, circa 1910s.**

race relations and forced the beautiful and placid playground of business titans to expose its darker side. White Daytonans must have joined blacks in feeling pride, however reluctantly, in the fact that their most celebrated citizen—a black woman—had rung up a school in their midst and, in doing so, bestowed a stature on their community far greater than the town founders could have imagined. Today, there are statues and plaques that honor Bethune in Daytona Beach, and her school, now a university, is still an important part of the city over one hundred years later. Another telling testament to the change she helped to bring about in Daytona Beach is the Jackie Robinson Ballpark,[58] where the Bethune-Cookman Wildcats baseball team and the city's Daytona Cubs minor league team both play their home games.

## NOTES

Note: An earlier, shorter version of this paper was published in the *Florida Historical Quarterly* 73, no. 2 (Oct. 1994), 200–217.

1. Catherine Owens Peare, *Mary McLeod Bethune* (New York: Vanguard, 1951), 85, 77.

2. Mary McLeod Bethune, "Faith That Moved a Dump Heap," *Who: The Magazine about People* (June 1941), also in Mary McLeod Bethune papers, Amistad Research Center, Dillard University, New Orleans, hereafter ARC.

3. Bethune's varied career as an educator, administrator, and advocate for women is detailed in the following sources: Audrey Thomas McCluskey and Elaine M. Smith, eds., *Mary McLeod Bethune: Building a Better World: Essays and Selected Documents* (Bloomington: Indiana University Press, 1999); B. Joyce Ross, "Mary McLeod Bethune and the Administration of the National Youth Administration: A Case Study of Power Relationships in the Black Cabinet of Franklin Delano Roosevelt," *Journal of Negro History* 40 (January 1975): 1–28; Elaine M. Smith, "Mary McLeod Bethune and the National Youth Administration," in *Clio Was a Woman: Studies in the History of American Women*, ed. Mabel E. Deutrich and Virginia C. Purdy (Washington, D.C.: Howard University Press, 1980), 149–77; Elizabeth Lindsay Davis, *Lifting a s They Climb* (New York: G. K. Hall, 1996); Paula Giddings, *When and Where I Enter: The Impact of Black Women on Race and Sex i n America* (New York: William Morrow, 1984), 197–215; Carol O. Perkins, "The Pragmatic Idealism of Mary McLeod Bethune," *Sage* (Fall 1988): 30–35. Audrey Thomas McCluskey, "Representing the Race: Mary McLeod Bethune and the Press," *Western Journal of Black Studies* 23, no. 4 (Winter 1999), 236–45. Also, Mary McLeod Bethune Papers, ARC; *The Mary McLeod Bethune Papers: The Bethune-Cookman College Collection* (Bethesda, Md.: University Publications of America, 1995); Joyce Ann Hanson, *Mary McLeod Bethune and Black Women's Political Activism* (Columbia, Mo.: University of Missouri Press, 2003), 206–14.

4. This sentence is a key line in Washington's famous Atlanta Compromise speech of 1895, which called for black self-help as a way to encourage racial harmony in the racially polarized South, http://historymatters.gmu.edu/d/88 (5 September 2009).

5. Bethune, "Faith That Moved a Dump Heap," 34.

6. Helen W. Ludlow, "Bethune School," *The Southern Workman* 41 (March 1912): 144.

7. Interview with Mary McLeod Bethune, n.d., Mary McLeod Bethune Papers, Bethune-Cookman College Archives, Daytona Beach, Fla. (published as *The Mary McLeod Bethune Papers: Bethune-Cookman College Collection* (Bethesda, Md.: University Publications of America, 1995, hereafter BCCC).

8. Bethune, "Faith That Moved a Dump Heap," 34; Ludlow, "Bethune School," 144.

9. State of Florida, Biennial Report of the Superintendent of Public Instruction (Tallahassee, 1912), 22.

10. August Meier, "The Vogue of Industrial Education," *The Midwest Journal*, no. 7, (Spring 1955): 250.

11. Dora E. Maley to unknown, March 17, 1955, letter on the occasion of the fiftieth anniversary of Bethune-Cookman College, Mary McLeod Bethune file, Halifax Historical Society, Daytona Beach, Fla.

12. This version of events is contradicted by Bethune, who stated in an undated interview that a man named John Williams owned the house she occupied. See Bethune interview, n.d., BCCC.

13. B. B. Baguette to B. N. Loving (Bethune's personal secretary), November 24, 1931, ARC.

14. "Personal Impressions of a Great Woman by One of Her Students," undated manuscript, BCCC.

15. T. E. Fitzgerald, *Volusia County, Past and Present* (Daytona Beach, Fla., 1937), 99–100.

16. Untitled, uncatalogued manuscript, BCCC

17. Fitzgerald, *Volusia County*, 191.

18. In 1923, under the auspices of the Methodist Episcopal Church, the Bethune school merged with Cookman Institute of Jacksonville to become the co-educational Bethune-Cookman Collegiate Institute. The Cookman Institute was founded in 1872 and named for Alfred Cookman, a white minister from New Jersey. See Sheila Y. Flemming, "Bethune-Cookman College," in *Black Women in America: An Historical Encyclopedia*, ed., Darlene Clark Hine (Brooklyn: Carlson Publishing, 1993), vol. 1, 127–28.

19. Untitled, undated document, BCCC.

20. Interview with Bethune, n.d. BCCC; Rackham Holt, *Mary McLeod Bethune: A Biography* (New York: Doubleday, 1964), 58.

21. Holt, *Mary McLeod Bethune*, 59.

22. Bethune, "Faith That Moved a Dump Heap," 34.

23. Record Book of the Bethune School, 1906, BCCC.

24. Bethune, "Faith that Moved a Dump Heap," 35.

25. Florence L. Roane, "A Cultural History of Professional Teacher Training at Bethune-Cookman College," (PhD diss., Boston University, 1985), 44.

26. Roane, "Professional Teacher Training," 44.

27. Interview of Bethune by Charles S. Johnson, n.d., Oral History Project on Black Leaders, BCCC.

28. Interview of Bethune, n.d., BCCC.

29. Holt, *Mary McLeod Bethune*, 102.

30. Holt, *Mary McLeod Bethune*, 108.

31. Walter Russell Bowie, *Women of Light* (New York: Harper and Rowe, 1963), 123.

32. Mary McLeod Bethune, "The High Cost of Keeping the Negro Inferior," Bethune Papers, ARC.

33. Mary McLeod Bethune, "Present-Day Task for Women in the Field of Business," Bethune Papers, ARC.

34. Ludlow, "Bethune School," 153.

35. Carrie Alberta Lyford, *A Study of Home-Economics Education in Teacher-Training Institutions for Negroes* (Washington, D.C.: Federal Board of Vocational Education, 1923, reprint ed., 1969), 3.

36. Lyford, *Study of Home-Economics Education*, 6.

37. Lyford, *Study of Home-Economics Education*, 6.

38. Mary McLeod Bethune, "A Philosophy of Education for Negro Girls," Bethune Papers, ARC.

39. Peare, *Mary McLeod Bethune*, 112.

40. Clara Stillman, "A Tourist in Florida," *The Crisis* (February 22, 1924): 173.

41. Lerner, *Black Women in White America*, 142.

42. Peare, *Mary McLeod Bethune*, 115.

43. Clement Richardson, ed., *The National Cyclopedia of the Colored Race*, vol. 1 (Montgomery, Ala.: National Publishing Co., 1919), 379.

44. Sadie Iola Daniel and Hallie Quinn, *Women Builders*, rev. ed. (Washington, D.C.: G. K. Hall, 1997), 100.

45. Benjamin Brawley, *Negro Builders and Heroes* (Chapel Hill: University of North Carolina Press, 1974), 286.

46. "Personal Impressions of a Great Woman by One of Her Students."

47. Ludlow, "Bethune School," 147.

48. Holt, *Mary McLeod Bethune*, 269.

49. "Personal Impressions of a Great Woman by One of Her Students."

50. Peare, *Mary McLeod Bethune*, 137.

51. *Daytona Beach Evening News* (7 June 1988).

52. Lerner, *Black Women in White America*, 140.

53. Giddings, *When and Where I Enter*, 200.

54. Holt, *Mary McLeod Bethune*, 269; *Daytona Evening News* (28 August 1949).

55. J. Irving E. Scott, *The Education of Blacks in Florida* (Philadelphia, 1974), 108.

56. Jules Tygiel, *Baseball's Great Experiment: Jackie Robinson and his Legacy* (New York: Oxford University Press, 1983), 104–105.

57. Christopher E. Linsin, "Something More Than a Creed: Mary McLeod Bethune's Aim of Integrated Autonomy as Director of Negro Affairs," *Florida Historical Quarterly* 76, no. 1 (Summer 1997): 38.

58. The Jackie Robinson Ball Park http://www.ballparkreviews.com/daytona/daytona.htm (20 May 2011).

# FIVE

## "Show Some Daylight Between You"

*Charlotte Hawkins Brown and the Schooling Experience
of Memorial Palmer Institute Graduates, 1948–1958*

> *It was because my parents wanted the best for me. Maybe it is just history
> now, but I think we lost something special when Palmer closed.*
> — Alma Grace Moreland Motley, PMI, 1946–1948

When Palmer Memorial Institute (PMI) closed in 1971, it also marked the closing of an era not to be repeated in the history of African American education. In its sixty-nine years of existence, between 1,000 and 2,000 students matriculated on its campus. Founded in 1902 in rural North Carolina by Charlotte Hawkins Brown (1883–1961) and outliving her by a decade, the school became an exemplar of black middle-class aspirations in early to mid-twentieth century America. By the 1940s, the North Carolina-born and Massachusetts-bred Brown had transformed PMI from its early beginnings as one of the American Missionary Association-sponsored schools charged with bringing basic literacy along with agricultural and industrial training to poor rural blacks to what *Ebony* magazine called in 1947 a "Finishing School" and a culture factory.

Palmer focused upon the social graces and offered a college preparatory curriculum that sent over 95 percent of its graduates to college.[1] In its pre-high school (called sub freshmen) and high school grades, the private boarding school attracted a national demographic that was made up largely of the sons and daughters of black teachers, doctors, business people, and other middle and upper class professionals who eagerly paid the $500 tuition (cost in 1947) to give their children a leg up in racially enclaved America.

Brown had lofty goals for her school and its students. It may have been an act of camouflaged subversion for a black school in the rural South to offer liberal arts, student travel, and cultural events, and to espouse attitudes of human equality based upon performance, not race. Yet Brown's charismatic personality and tireless promotion of social and moral correctness focused public attention where she wanted it, while ingeniously appealing to the different expectations of both races. Whites saw and applauded PMI's well-mannered black youth who kept their place in the social order. Black middle class parents envisioned the promise of racial and educational parity for their children. Brown purposely kept the enrollment relatively small so she could hand pick each of her students. By the late 1940s, Palmer enrolled no more than 240 students in all grades from eight through twelve.[2] The transformed school was built upon what Brown called a "triangle of achievement," which she enumerated as being: "educationally efficient, culturally secure, and religiously sincere."[3] PMI's location near the highway on a wide, gentle slope of 400 acres of fertile farmland, gave Brown an ideal site not only to grow most of the food that would supply the dining hall,[4] but also to personally groom the student body in her particular approach to achieving racial equality. In the half century that Charlotte Hawkins Brown was at the helm, PMI experienced growing national prestige, as well as significant setbacks and financial fissures. Yet her constancy and dedication to the school and the principles she established are what students who attended PMI in those years remember best and share in the interviews below.

In the waning years of her presidency, Brown oversaw the appointment of her successor, Wilhelmina Crosson, in 1952. Crosson closely adhered to her mentor's exactitude in running the school, but Brown's continued presence and oversight of the finances made asserting her own authority problematic. Still, Brown remained a forceful presence on the campus well beyond her retirement years. Despite health issues, including diabetes and increased forgetfulness,[5] she gave lengthy lectures and chapel talks that sometimes disrupted the regular class schedule. PMI was Brown's self-described "baby," and she was not inclined to relinquish it easily. In the words of a well-worn cliché and verified by her former students, it was her way or that aforementioned "highway"— interstate 85/40, which was within walking distance from campus.

The "Twig-Bender of Sedalia" was the name a biographer gave Brown. An associate, Richard Wharton, a PMI board member whose family had been among the school's longtime white supporters, described Brown as "a person with a lot of energy, outspoken . . . charming . . . not someone having met that you would forget."[6] What was student life like on the campus that this charismatic woman had created and nourished? In the decade before the Civil Rights Movement was in full swing, life on the PMI campus also provided a window into how segments of the black middle class responded to the separate and unequal state of segregated

American education. PMI confirmed their belief that, despite the obstacles, full citizenship and success were within their reach and could be earned through a particular kind of education. Brown, in an undated speech to the Commission on Interracial Cooperation in Atlanta, personifies that thinking:

> [I]n order for the Negro to get even half the recognition which he may deserve, he must be even more gracious than others, more cultured, more considerate, more observant of the little courtesies and social finesse if he would gain a decent place in the sun.[7]

Mastering the social graces, then, became a defining feature of PMI that distinguished it from other private black boarding schools of that era.[8] Her little red book, *The Correct Thing to Do, to Say, to Wear: A Ready Reference for the School Administrator, the Busy Teacher, the Office Girl, the Society Matron and the Discriminating Person* (1941), was required reading for all students. It is said that among the more eager students, sections of its well-thumbed pages could be recited from memory, like Bible verses. There were other items on the required gender-specific list that all accepted students received before entering. For boys, the number (and color) of shirts, jackets, types of ties, underwear, shoes, and stockings were specified. For girls the mandate included "white middies and dark blue skirts, . . . at least one voile or organdie dress, modestly and prettily made"[9] were among the must-haves for the daily rituals of life at PMI.

Although the attention that Brown paid to "being correct" was criticized by some blacks as a slavish attempt to imitate whites, especially white women, Brown's motives appear to be more complex. As a founding member and president of the North Carolina State Federation of Colored Women's Clubs, and vice president of the National Association of Colored Women Clubs, she was allied with women who dedicated themselves to the work of elevating black womanhood and removing the stigma of slavery. In several speeches to both white and black audiences, Brown chastised white women for looking the other way as white men violated black women. She also warned black women that Emancipation did not free them in the same way it freed black men, and that their conduct would determine the future of the race.[10] Her belief in the power of black women to elevate themselves and their race reflects a version of Victorian ideals of womanhood that was shared by her contemporaries, including school founders Mary McLeod Bethune and Nannie Helen Burroughs, as well as the scholarly Anna Julia Cooper, whose classic treatise *A Voice from the South* (1892) argued that a "regenerative" and "vital" black womanhood would uplift the entire race.[11] In a speech to a "packed house" in Buffalo, New York, in 1930, Brown explained why the black woman should not imitate the "vices" of white woman—including smoking, drinking, and carousing. She spoke directly to the young women in the audience, showing her view of their latent power:

> Young women, you can face the future only as you accept the respon-
> sibility resting upon your shoulders. . . . I beg you to stop and think.
> The Negro man will be just what the Negro woman makes him. The
> truly powerful Negro woman has not yet arrived. But . . . someday this
> old world is going to reel and rock like a drunken man and the Negro
> woman is destined to lead women of other races into a fuller and freer
> atmosphere of love and of the things that are beautiful . . . and helpful
> in our desire to solve the great question [of race]. [12]

Brown viewed black women as potentially the most powerful force in
solving the racial divide, and that helps to contextualize her insistence
upon cultivating the social graces among her young charges. It also ex-
plains the stricter scrutiny that she paid to the behavior of female students who, she believed, had to overcome the stigma that began when
their foremothers were enslaved and forced into sexual relationships.

After Brown's death in 1961, and Crosson's retirement in 1966, PMI
experienced administrative upheaval and mounting financial challenges.
Although the school still attracted enough students to be viable, the un-
tested leadership and a drifting mandate, combined with the coming of a
more restive, civil rights-minded student body that scoffed at the repressive rules and regulations, hastened Palmer's end. Student protests
against those regulations began in the late 1960s, and culminated in the
burning down of the Alice Freeman Palmer building, the heart (and soul)
of the campus in 1971. The trustees, fearing a black power surge, abruptly
closed the school, despite its record enrollment. [13]

Taken together, her own words and the recollections of former students provide an addition to the historical record of Brown and daily life
and culture at Palmer during her tenure. The former students who were
interviewed, in no particular order, over several months in 2011–2012,
attended PMI between 1941 and 1958, during its heyday. They represent
a range of professions—now mostly retired—in education, medicine, social service, and the military, among others. Their ages range from the
mid-seventies to mid-eighties. Most of the interviewees are members of
the PMI Alumni Association, which is charged with sustaining the legacy
of the school and of Dr. Brown. Their organization, along with friends
and advocates, not only was successful in helping to restore some campus buildings, but was also instrumental in having the original campus
become one of the 27 state historic sites that are maintained and adminis-
tered by the North Carolina Department of Cultural Resources. State
Senator William Martin of Greensboro introduced the 1983 bill to preserve     the     campus     site.     State     Representative
H. M "Mickey" Michaux, a former Palmerite, assisted the effort, as did
the late Maria Hill Gibbs. In 2011, the visitor count was 14,442, with
steady increases expected in the coming years. [14] The Charlotte Hawkins
Brown Museum, established in 1987 by the North Carolina General Assembly, became the state's first historic site to honor an African

American. It consists of several restored buildings, including Canary Cottage, the home where Brown lived and entertained visiting dignitaries, and other buildings that hold poignant memories and historical significance not only to former students, but also beyond the campus grounds. The PMI Alumni Association continues its work with a membership of over 100, and has held biennial reunions in different cities since the early 1990s. Similarly, the Charlotte Hawkins Brown Museum keeps her legacy alive through exhibits and programs, including youth-oriented events that focus on the social graces, using Brown's book, *The Correct Thing*, as a guide and reference.[15]

The interviews that follow were conducted by the author and edited for clarity and conciseness. They are presented in either third-person narration or first-person italics.

Alice Wyche Hurley (PMI 1947–1952) and Anthony "Tony" Hurley (PMI 1948–1952) of Columbia, South Carolina, met at Palmer and have been married for more than a half century. They have four adult children, all of whom are college graduates. They operate a family-owned funeral home in Columbia and are actively involved in the PMI Alumni Association.

Alice Wyche Hurley arrived at Palmer from Charlotte at the age of 14. The circumstances that prompted her enrollment were the death of her mother and her father's remarriage, coupled with the fact that her father, realizing how poorly funded the segregated public schools in Charlotte were, decided that PMI, with its emphasis on molding proper young ladies and gentlemen, would offer a better environment for his budding teenager. Tony Hurley's path to Palmer was paved by several family members who preceded him. He followed suit at the age of fourteen.

When Alice first arrived at Palmer, she was homesick and did not like it at all. She cried every day for two straight weeks. Finally, the dean of women told her that she was going to call her father and have him come take her home. "I knew my father would not like that, so I settled in and accepted it," she said. She noticed how the campus was divided by gender—the girls' dormitory was on one side of the campus, the boys' on the other. The dining hall was in the center of the campus, along with the classroom building. "Boys entered on one side of the dining hall, girls entered a door on the other side. Only seniors could enter the front door," Alice recalled. "There was a grand piano in the dining hall, and someone, usually a teacher or a selected student, would play. Before we ate, we all stood and repeated the grace in unison. At each meal we would practice table etiquette—with napkins in our laps, no arms on the table and quiet conversation." The meals were served family style, with a senior at the head of the table.

As far as academics were concerned, Alice feels that the education she got at Palmer was fine. "I remember taking two foreign languages, Latin and French. Some of my teachers were better than others; there was no uniform quality among the teachers. Overall, the social graces really were the big focus. That was very important to Dr. Brown," Alice said. She remembers how Brown would use the daily chapel talks to affirm not only the dos and don'ts of the social graces, but also to share anything else that was on her mind. Her extended talks would sometimes make them miss class. "In the balance between academics and social graces, social graces won the day," Alice concluded. Asked about her impression of Dr. Brown while on campus, Alice bluntly stated: "We would try to avoid her as much as possible. She could always find something [to comment on] too much lipstick, heels too high, you name it."

Speaking about the surrounding area, Tony mentioned that the town of Sedalia was not a town at all. "It was just a road," he said. There was one store on that road, but the girls were not allowed to go there. It was owned by a white family—the Paisleys. "The boys were allowed to go there and buy cigarettes that they would smoke behind the building, not the girls!" The student-run campus Tea House was open to both sexes. "You could buy snacks and sodas," he recalled. The rules were strict, especially for the girls. It was not as bad for boys. Nevertheless, they sometimes broke them. But both boys and girls knew they could be sent home if they were caught. Since girls were not allowed off campus except for special occasions and were always chaperoned, the campus was the center of the social life that included roller skating and dances. Tony remembered that Dr. Brown would sometimes chaperone the dances and would patrol the dance floor to remind the couples to "keep some daylight between you."

"There was a Congregational Church nearby and we would sometimes attend, but most of our spiritual instruction took place in daily chapel. Otherwise, there was not much involvement in the community," Alice continued. "Boys could go to a local barber's house and get haircuts on Saturday, while girls took to the basement of the dormitory to get their hair done by a hairdresser who came from Greensboro."

While Alice doesn't remember black history being formally taught, black history as a concept was all round them, she said. Important black leaders often visited the campus—including Benjamin E. Mays (president of Morehouse College) and Mary McLeod Bethune. In her chapel talks, Brown mentioned black Americans who she thought were making contributions to the race—and that included herself. "She considered herself equally accomplished and in the same category with her good friend Mary Bethune, although she thought that Bethune received more recognition. Dr. Brown was extremely competitive [with Bethune]."

The Hurleys have fond memories of meeting students from all over the country and even some foreign countries, such as Costa Rica, Cuba, and Liberia. There were sports activities such as basketball and football for boys. Girls participated in gym classes but had no organized sports.

There were also gender divisions in the chores that all students had to do: Boys did the farm work that supplied much of the food for the school, while girls, who outnumbered the boys, kept the campus clean.

As a member of the Sedalia Singers, a group modeled after the famed Fisk (University) Jubilee Singers, singing spirituals and a classical repertoire but no gospel, Alice, a soprano, had opportunities to travel to different cities on fundraising tours. She remembers missing the big trip to Boston, the center of fundraising for the Massachusetts-bred Brown, because she was considered too young. Although she did not recognize at the time just how important fundraising was to Palmer, she did notice how the campus prepared for white visitors from the North when they came to campus. "Everything on campus had to be spick and span. We cleaned for days," she recalled. She also recalled how often Brown would talk to the girls about how they should conduct themselves around the opposite sex. The twice (briefly)-married Brown would say, "I am not meant for marriage." She was in a real sense, married to her school. "I used to think that the woman was crazy," said Alice, "but my father, who was a doctor, knew her and explained that she was a diabetic and some of her eccentricities might be due to her illness." Both Alice and Tony agree that Palmer was the kind of place that you learned to appreciate in retrospect. "It was strict, but we found ways to get around the rules," said Tony. "Yes, it was strict," echoed Alice, "but we felt protected."

Alma Grace Moreland Motley, a native of Charlottesville, Virginia, attended Palmer from 1946 to 1948. She also attended Bennett College in North Carolina and after marriage and motherhood graduated from Johnson C. Smith College, in the Tarheel state, in 1952. Her late husband was Rowe E. Motley, who was the first black county commissioner in Charlotte. She taught first and second grade for thirty years before retiring. Alma's account is in her own voice.

*Both my parents were teachers with master's degrees from Columbia University. My mother taught elementary grades and my father was principal of an elementary school. When I think back to why I attended Palmer even though my parents taught in the public schools, I remember that something happened with brother at school — I don't remember what — that made my dad transfer him to the school where he was principal and then also decided to send me to Palmer. I had no say in the matter. He simply announced, "I'm sending you to Palmer." I knew nothing about the school, really, except what friends said and some of my friends were already attending. My first impression of the school was positive. I liked living in the dormitory and being on my own. I don't remember anything negative — I was not even homesick. But when I first met Dr. Brown, I was already scared to death based on what others had said about her. We would get demerits for things like wearing too much lipstick. If you got too many demerits, you would be sent home. We all lived in fear of being sent home. She [Dr. Brown] would hold that over you. You could not chew gum, even. She was real strict.*

*She could not see well by the time I was there. But if she thought you had on too
much lipstick, she would still tell you take it off. It was a good experience for me
because I was sort of a tomboy. At home, I used to follow my brother around and
do whatever he did. When I went to Palmer, the experience helped to polish me
off as a young lady. Good etiquette was the norm, and we all had to practice it.
Dr. Brown, it seems, was always away in Boston—rubbing shoulders with rich
white people. I think she wanted to show that blacks would be socially accepted.
In terms of the education I received at Palmer, I think it was comparable to public
schools in my hometown. Since my parents were teachers, I knew the value of
education, and there were good teachers in the black schools at home. It was not
so much the quality of schooling at Palmer, because the education was comparable, but I think that many of the teachers at Palmer were there because they
couldn't get the opportunity to teach in public schools.*

*It has been over sixty years now, and I don't remember any of the teachers.
But I do remember the dietitian, Miss Burnside. She ran the dining room. She
would also accompany us on trips as our chaperone. She followed Dr. Brown's
ideas, and that had lot to do with shaping us as young ladies. She was always
friendly, and we actually had more contact with her than with Dr. Brown. Dr.
Brown also had members of the Sedalia community, such as the minister, to
accompany us on trips. There was always a chaperone for the girls and one for
the boys. My first trip to Boston was as a member of the dance troupe. We
performed there in 1948. We always performed using a classical music repertoire—never jazz. When we took trips, we were always told "people are watching
you, don't bring a bad mark on the school or your family."*

*Of course, that didn't occur to me when I was a teenager, 15-17 years old, but
as I look back, I think of how important my experience at Palmer was. I now
value it very much. That is why I stay involved in the alumni society. If you
attended Palmer, it was something special. You will always cherish that. For my
parents to pay to send me there, I was blessed, and they were proud to send me. It
was because my parents wanted the best for me. Maybe it is just history now, but
I think we lost something special when Palmer closed. We still need something
like that for some of our [black] students today.*

Robert Lipscombe is a native of native of New York City who now lives
in Denver. He graduated from Palmer in 1954, then served eight years in
the Air Force. He later earned a bachelor's degree from Metropolitan
State College in Denver and has had a varied professional life as a counselor, actor, and musician.

*My aunt, Florence G. Hillman, was a Palmer graduate who attended in the
1940s. I wanted to attend Palmer because I saw what it had done for my aunt.
My grandparents took me down there where I was interviewed by Miss Crosson
[Dr. Brown's assistant and future principal]. She knew my family and that they
wanted me at Palmer because education in New York [City] was inferior [for
blacks]. Students were not encouraged. I was told that I would never accomplish
anything. That was how it was in public schools for blacks in my West Harlem*

neighborhood. It was woeful—geared to basic instruction, but no more. By contrast, I was challenged at Palmer and I excelled academically. Palmer demanded that you function at the highest level possible. We were always kept busy. We had a two-and-a-half hour study period every day after class. After study time and free time, we were in bed at 10:30. When we were not studying, we were engaged in activities like chapel, band, or athletics. Teachers lived in the dorm with us and were always available. I was able to graduate with honors because of this kind of attention.

Before I arrived at Palmer I was filled with frustration and anger. That turned to self-confidence and a "do not get in my way or I will run over you attitude." Palmer made me see that black people were capable achievers. It made us students feel pride in our race. "Be who you are—don't be ashamed" was the message. The first time I learned about black people in an educational setting was at Palmer. In New York blacks were seen as having no intellect.

On Saturdays we could go into town for a couple of hours. It was always a planned activity with chaperones. When we left campus, we had to wear a shirt—tie was optional, but always a jacket. We had to have matching colors. Boys sat on one side of the bus, girls on the other. We were always in groups of twos and fours wherever we went. We treated each other with respect, especially young ladies—it made a lasting impression on me. What I appreciated most about Palmer was that it taught me to be able to handle myself in any situation. I learned the social graces—to converse [with] anyone, to travel, and wherever I am, I can handle myself.

After graduation I joined the U.S. Air Force and spent eight years there, earning the rank of staff sergeant. Military discipline was not a big deal to me because of my foundation at Palmer. I had learned how to be a leader as well as a follower. Later, I earned a bachelor's degree from Metropolitan State College in Denver in multimedia communication. I have had a rich and varied professional life. It has included being a counselor, being an actor in theater productions, including the Denver Shakespeare Festival, and playing multiple instruments in a jazz combo featuring jazz standards and original compositions.

As I reflect back on my time at Palmer, it makes me see how lacking schools are today. The education I received was 100 times better than what I would have received in public school. Palmer was the shining light of my educational life.

Olvin McBarnette, a native of New York City, studied at Palmer during the "war years," 1943–1945, and 1946–1947; he is among the oldest surviving graduates of Palmer Memorial Institute. He spent nineteen months in the U.S. Army, then returned to graduate in 1947. McBarnette's mother became an admirer of Charlotte Hawkins Brown after hearing her speak during fundraising trips to New York and reading about her in the newspapers. The West Indian immigrant parents decided to get their son "out of the streets of New York and down to Sedalia." They disagreed with the vocational tracking of black students that was prevalent in the city's schools. Olvin was fourteen at the time and had been earmarked to attend the vocational Commerce High School (now Brandeis High) in Manhattan. He was very apprehensive about being put on the train alone, heading south for the first time, but was joined on the train by students from Philadelphia and other northeastern cities who were also heading south to attend schools, including Palmer. When the students changed trains at Union Station in Washington, D.C., they got their first taste of Jim Crow—all the seating was segregated, and they were herded into the "colored" car for the trip to Greensboro, North Carolina. The nine students headed for Palmer then took a bus for the short trip to Sedalia. McBarnette's first thought upon arrival at Palmer was that he had entered "another world." The campus was tranquil and beautiful, but he and the other arriving students were apprehensive about meeting Dr. Brown. "It was total intimidation and fear. All of us were shaking," he said. Since his mother had made all the arrangements and bought all the items on the required list, he did not know what to expect. Yet he became acclimated very soon. It helped that he bonded with the other students who were all having the same experience. Part of the school culture included a mild form of hazing by the older boys. They would take the younger boys out into the woods for hikes late at night when all the adult supervisors were asleep. They tried to put fear into the boys, but he knew that he had to prove himself and not let the upper classmen take advantage of him. "I decided, 'Hey, I am from New York, I am going to make it here,'" he said. The older boys knew that they had to get all the younger boys back safely, so it was no big issue. They all later became good friends. "We functioned as a family. I don't think there was anyone on the campus who was an outsider. We all had the same experience and ate the same food," McBarnette said. If there were class differences, he did not know it. A number of students were on scholarship, but no one knew who they were. Some others were well off, like A'lelia Walker Perry, granddaughter of hair care magnate Madam C. J. Walker. The daughter of the founder of Apex Hair Company, Joan Spencer Washington, was also a Palmerite, as were Paul Robeson's nieces, but you would not know it. Everyone was the same as far as he could tell.

He remembers Dr. Brown as always being there, like a mother hen: "She always said something that made you feel like somebody. When you saw her coming, you would always try to straighten up, and walk taller." She knew every student by name and everything about each of her students and their parents, too. His mother used to write letters to Dr. Brown. He remembers one day Brown called him aside—for what reason, he does not remember—and said to him, "You are not going to bring that New York stuff down here!" He felt like she was always on top of him. Although she may not have *actually* singled him out—and he felt like she did—every other student felt singled out, too. Because of that, he never got into real trouble, but did get some demerits. He feared that he would be sent home, and some who did not follow her rules were sent packing. That fear forced the students to look out for each other. As far as the academic experience at Palmer, McBarnette felt that it was all about the atmosphere that she created. Dr. Brown expected everyone to excel. Her secret, he feels, was that she made you think you were academically better than you really were. She was very supportive of blacks in military service and took the Sedalia Singers to army camps near campus to entertain the soldiers, who were in segregated units. She gave them words of encouragement, and she supported McBarnette when he joined the Army. She also welcomed him back after discharge. "Come on back," she told him. Brown didn't lose too many kids, minus the few misbehaving students to whom the threat of expulsion became real. McBarnette feels that what made Charlotte Hawkins Brown special was that she knew how to talk to people regardless of their race or class. While blacks were being lynched in the South, she would go to white women's meetings and tell them to control their men and "stop the lynching!" "She shamed them, really," he said. Brown worked behind the scenes to get things done, such as having her students participate in programs at the all-white Guilford College nearby, even though segregation was in full force. McBarnette also remembers important people coming to campus who would be pointed out to them or would address them during chapel — such visitors as Walter White of the NAACP, First Lady Eleanor Roosevelt, and Brown's friend, Mary McLeod Bethune. "[Brown] was different from anyone you would ever meet, and that was what made Palmer different from other schools. She and Mary Bethune were such brave women," he added. After graduation from Palmer, McBarnette attended college at Long Island University. He also did graduate work at New York University and earned a master's degree at City College of New York. His career was in educational and social services and he often used some of Brown's techniques on his students. He is now retired and lives in Alexandria, Virginia.

Ida Daniel Dark, a native of Rocky Point, North Carolina, attended Palmer between 1954 and 1957. Her brother, John T. Daniel, preceded her at Palmer and paved the way. In her own words, Ida Dark recalls her Palmer experience:

*Both my parents were educators. My father was the principal at the Pender County Training School, and my mother taught elementary school. I spent my first eight school grades in public school. When my parents decided that I should attend Palmer, I arrived on campus, and immediately loved the school — everything about it. I loved the structure — the triangle of achievement that Dr. Brown emphasized as being educationally efficient, culturally secure, and religiously sincere. The setting was like [being] at home, but more social. Compared to public school, the classes were smaller. The teachers were very good. My Latin teacher also taught French and algebra. There were students from all over — Africa, Bermuda, Costa Rica, Haiti — all over, and I loved that, too.*

*Our social environment was very sheltered. Girls could not go beyond the flagpole (the flagpole was in front of the dining hall). Even in the classroom, boys sat on one side, girls on the other. Boys could call on girls only on Sunday at the girls' dormitory—for two hours. Girls and their male visitors would sit in the living room of the dorm. Everything was supervised.*

*As I remember it, a typical day began with the 6:30 rising bell. We made our beds, cleaned our rooms, recited Bible verses or similar activity before breakfast. Another bell would ring at 7:20. We had to be in the dining hall by 7:30. Dorms were close to the dining hall. There was a girls' dormitory and one boys' dormitory. One cottage for senior girls. The red book [an instruction book required for all students] had everything listed by time. We had thirty minutes for breakfast. Then we returned to our residence, where each one of us was assigned a specific duty in cleaning the dormitory. This was called a "duty sheet" and was posted every week by the dorm matron. I remember times when if you didn't have your bed made, they would come in the dining room and get you. That strictness made us find ways to take short cuts. Some of us learned to slide out of bed without disturbing the sheets. We were in class at 9, with a 45-minute lunch and recess break that was also sex segregated. On Fridays, we were allowed ten minutes to chat with boys. Then we were back to class until 3 p.m. From class we returned to the dorm, after which we could go the teahouse for snacks. There we could watch television shows like [the teenage dance show]* American Bandstand. *I worked in the teahouse, which was quite an honor. It was open daily from 3:30 to 4:30. Dinner was from 5 p.m. to 6 p.m., and we were again called by the bell. On Saturday, the teahouse stayed open a bit longer, but closed on Sunday. We had a supervised study hour after dinner back at the dorm, during which senior girls would watch over us. Study hour meant that there was no radio, no talking.*

*There was chapel everyday for one-half hour. We were lined up according to class and height and had to walk in tune with the music. A devotional hymn was sung, and we all had to recite a Bible verse, "Fret not thyself because of evildoers, neither be thou envious against the workers of iniquity"— Psalm 37 . We had to recite verses 1–11 in unison with two groups of readers. We learned lots of Bible passages, like "Wait patiently on the Lord." Lights were out at 9:00 p.m. for underclassmen. Upperclassmen, separated on first and second floors, had lights-out at 9:30. The dorm matron and senior girls' matron would do a room-by-room check.*

*We had lots of activities such as basketball and skating. We played cards on the weekends. We also had gym classes, of course. I sang in our choir, the Sedalia Singers. We had French club, cheerleading, concerts. We had orchestra and glee club, too. I remember when the noted pianist Philippa Schuyler performed at Palmer. Since I loved music, this was perfect for me.*

*I only met Dr. Brown after she had become emeritus. She would come to breakfast every morning and was very insistent that we follow school discipline—think positively about things. "You have to make it a good life for yourself," she would tell us. After graduation in 1957, I attended Hampton Institute and majored in music education, and was a music teacher in the Charlotte public* school system. I also lived and worked in New York and earned a Ph.D. in music at Columbia University.

John Scarborough is a funeral director in Durham, North Carolina. He attended three high schools, including Palmer. Both sides of his family had attended PMI, including aunts, uncles, and cousins. He enrolled in Palmer for his senior year. After he graduated in 1956, he attended Ohio University, then transferred to North Carolina Central University, then called North Carolina College for Negroes, graduating in 1960.

*I left Hillside High school in Durham due to a racial incident. Durham was very segregated, and it was the beginning of integration with a lot of fallout. You had to deal with the racist mentality. One day in downtown Durham, I saw this white man push a black woman to the side as they were both about to cross the street between two cars. When I saw this and instinctively raised my foot to kick the man, my mother grabbed me before I could. She then scolded me real good. She told me that what the white man did was wrong, but what I did was also wrong. Two wrongs don't make a right, she said. She told me that we would have a family discussion. My parents decided to send me away to school. I could get in real trouble in Durham in the 1950s for doing something like what I was about to do. I was thirteen years old at the time. I had just been promoted to 9th grade. A friend of the family had a daughter who attended Westtown Preparatory School in Pennsylvania. It was founded by Quakers in 1799 and was located a mile away from the all-black Chaney State University, just outside of Philadelphia. I took the entrance exam and was admitted. I stayed at Westtown through my junior year. I had a couple of racial incidents there, too. One time in the dining hall, a white boy called me a "nigger." I jumped over chairs and hit him. The administration, being Quaker, did not punish me. They understood that the boy was wrong, yet they also did not like any fighting—but I was not expelled.*

*I was one credit away from my senior year when I arrived at PMI. I also took an exam there before I enrolled that took two hours. They told me I passed. Although I was at PMI for only a year, I would not give a billion dollars for my experiences there. You see, I am not an ordinary person; Palmer made me realize that. On my first day at PMI, in 1955, I was standing with my hand on a young lady's shoulder. Ms. Crosson [Dr. Brown's successor] approached and said, "Young man, we do not touch young ladies." Meanwhile, someone touched me on my other shoulder and asked if I were new to campus. As I turned, I saw it was Dr. Brown. I said "Yes." She asked if my bags were unpacked. I said, "No." She then said, "You know the Greyhound bus that brought you here also runs both ways. Are you sure your bags are still unpacked?" I was given a reprieve. But I got the message. At first, I was amazed at the strictness. One day as I was thinking about it, I realized how great it really was. I came to understand my surroundings and what Dr. Brown and the teachers were trying to do.*

*Another encounter I had with Dr. Brown happened when I played basketball. I was captain of the team, and during one game, I came down wrong and fell on top of another player and broke a cartilage in my knee. I had to go to hospital and was placed in a leg cast. Days later, I was sitting in the dining room with my cast leg in the aisle. Students at the table muttered, "Uh-oh, here comes Dr. Brown." She stopped at the table and told me not to sit with my foot in the aisle. She then asked me what happened to my leg. When I told her, she invited me to sit at her table. I sat with Dr. Brown at her table for a week. What I remember about the conversations is that she asked me what I wanted to do in life, and we talked about my future. She also knew many of my family members who had attended Palmer. Meanwhile, I was thinking to myself, this is the person I have heard so much about, and now I am sitting at her dining table having dinner with her!*

*I have found artifacts that belonged to my grandfather, John Scarborough, who was a friend of Dr. Brown. One was a penny postcard from Booker T. Washington. He and my grandfather were also friends. The card said that he would be in Durham and looked forward to sitting on my grandfather's porch. I realized what a close community these [aspiring, educated blacks] were. I also found in my grandfather's belongings programs of events from Tuskegee [University]. Many of the programs had Dr. Brown listed as a speaker. James E. Shepard, who founded North Carolina Central (formerly North Carolina College for Negroes) in 1920, was also a friend of my grandfather's and Dr. Brown. I still have photographs of some of them.*

*There were two books that we treasured. One was the* Bible; *the second one was Dr. Brown's book,* The Correct Thing . . . *which was like our bible for conduct. Many years later, as my wife and I were being seated at a Durham restaurant, as we approached our table, I pulled out the chair for my wife. Everyone in this fine restaurant was looking at us. You could hear a pin drop. One white man at a nearby table said: "My father used to do that for my mother."*

*Another thing I remember about PMI is the amateur talent hour the students had. One time I recited a poem that I had been practicing a long time. It was a love poem that my friends teased me about. I recited it while a friend played the piano. I won first prize! That really impressed my girlfriend.*

*If you wanted to visit a girl in the girls' dormitory, you entered at visiting hours and introduced yourself to the matron. She would ask you who you came to see, and that person would be called down. Then you sat in the lobby with a chaperone nearby. I haven't kept in touch with many of my classmates. I wish I had. Many are now deceased. After a building was set on fire in the 1960s, things went downhill at Palmer. Students had become more radical. Some of the board members began to say that the school had lived out its time and was no longer needed. The school soon closed after that.*

Olga Black Fluker is a Blackville, Arkansas, native who attended Palmer from 1951 to 1954. After graduation, she attended Tennessee State University, majoring in history and minoring in sociology. Her professional career included teaching, social work, and working in community organization. She retired after several years as a pioneering administrator in continuing education at the University of Arkansas-Pine Bluff. She is married to Dr. John E. Fluker and is the mother of three adult children.

Olga Fluker arrived at Palmer Memorial Institute at the age of fifteen, soon after her parents read an article in *Ebony* magazine about the school. "That would be a good place for you to go," they said to her. That settled the matter, and Fluker did not resist. Her family was very influential in the town of Blackville. In fact, her grandfather and his relatives founded the town that bears the family name. The family lived on a huge farm, and Fluker attended the village's church and school, both originally built by her ancestors. The school—and most of the town—no longer exists, but it once housed grades one through nine. It was staffed by teachers recruited from black colleges and offered a good education. But her parents wanted Fluker to continue her education, especially her father, who thought that Palmer would help his "tomboyish" daughter to become a more refined young lady.

Fluker said her first impression of Palmer was that it was like living at home in many ways. The chores and duty work were what she was used to living on a farm. So were the family-style meals and living arrangements. The learning and practice of the social graces was a new experience. Everything was so organized, she said. It was a no-nonsense environment. The classes were basic, but they included foreign language instruction by native speakers. Fluker found it more academically challenging than her country school. It was a place where most of the students had similar backgrounds. It worked because they all were held to the same high standard—with no exceptions. "No one felt better than anyone else," Fluker recalled. She said there were no rebellions among the students during her years at Palmer. "If you didn't follow the rules, you were sent home," Fluker remembered. "It was as simple as that." As she recalls, the cost of attending PMI was about $800 to $900 a year. Although that cost included everything, it was more than what it cost to attend Tennessee State University. A special memory that Fluker has is the time she spent working for Dr. Brown. She and her friend cleaned Dr. Brown's house, a job that lasted until Fluker graduated. Brown talked to the girls about a lot of different subjects, but they mostly listened. "You did not talk back to her, unless she asked you a question." Fluker said. She also remembers the frequent illustrious guests that came to campus, such as college and university presidents Mary McLeod Bethune (Bethune-Cookman), Benjamin Mays [Morehouse], and Mordecai Johnson (Howard University).

Active in the PMI alumni organization, Fluker continues to look forward to the biennial reunions, which have been held since 2000 and draw about100 participants. "Before the reunions, most of us had not seen each other in over 50 years, but we rekindled our relationships immediately," Fluker explained. "It is like a conference; it includes a meet and greet. We have such a good time!"

Henry M. "Mickey" Michaux, Jr., is a lifelong Durham, North Carolina, resident. He matriculated at PMI from 1943 to 1948. He earned both his undergraduate degree and law degree from North Carolina Central University. Michaux was first elected to the North Carolina Legislature in 1972, serving for four years. He was reelected in 1983 and is one of the state's longest-serving legislators. He was instrumental in prodding the state to buy the PMI campus property, which is now the Charlotte Hawkins Brown Museum and Historic Site.

*My mother was a school teacher from Washington, D.C. My father was from the mountains of North Carolina. He became an entrepreneur, a real estate and insurance broker. They met when my mother came to Durham to teach school. They had two children—me and my younger brother. I attended the segregated public schools of Durham until seventh grade. My parents were planning to send me to a prep school up North when they heard about Palmer from parents of Palmer students. Dr. Brown had a great reputation among parents and in the community. Everyone knew about her and her school. [My parents] decided to send me there because of her great reputation and the fact that it was closer to home than their original choice. There were three students from Durham who went to Palmer the year I enrolled. My parents drove me from Durham, and by the time they drove away, I had already been made to feel right at home. Life at Palmer began with introductory sessions, called orientation. The first thing I remember was being given a copy of* The Correct Thing to Do, to Wear, to Say, *the book that she wrote about the social graces. My first meal was lunch, which was served family style. I don't remember specific things about that, but I do know that we always felt Dr. Brown's presence. I had a chance to leave but never did. In the dormitory, we met with the teachers and they reinforced the rules and what was expected of us.*

*We learned that as boys and young men we were to stand up when ladies entered the room. We were expected to walk ahead of young ladies when descending the stairs. In case they fell, a young man would be there to break their fall. If a rule was broken, you could expect to be called into Dr. Brown's office. Once, all the senior boys got expelled because of an incident that occurred on the bus. I was president of the junior class but wasn't on the bus at the time. I never learned exactly what happened, but it concerned one of the senior boys making an inappropriate remark to a female teacher who was a chaperone on the bus. Because of that one incident, all the senior boys were sent home. Dr. Brown called me into her office after the incident and told me that if something like that happened among the junior boys, she would not send all the junior boys home, but she would send me home. As president of the junior class, I was responsible for the others in my class. Dr. Brown was always about instilling a sense of responsibility into us. After two weeks, she readmitted the senior boys. Boy, did I feel relieved! Her psychology worked—from then on, I really felt responsible for all the other students in my class.*

Dr. Brown made me headwaiter, which was another big responsibility. My job was to make sure that all the other waiters did their jobs. The waiters had to wear white coats. As headwaiter, I did not have to wear the white coat. I thought she took a special interest in me. But as I reflect on it, she made all of us feel that way. I don't think she took a special interest in me. She was interested in every one of the 200 students there—she knew everyone by name and their background.

There was a definite dress code at PMI. Sundays we had to dress in coats and ties. Friday was casual. Breakfast and lunch were also casual. That meant for dinner boys had to wear coats and ties. Before you arrived on campus, the parents of admitted students received a letter telling them what items students should bring with them. I remember that it included a pair of skates [there was a skating rink on campus] as well as how much underwear and types of shirts and slacks you should have. Name labels had to be sewn into your clothes. The girls had a different list. The academic atmosphere was serious. The curriculum followed state guidelines. We were required to take a course called "Civics," but it really was black history. The teacher who taught the course, we called him "Mr. Coffee." He was short and had long arms. I know that Rev. Jesse Jackson popularized the saying, "I am somebody." But I heard it first from Dr. Brown. At one point Carter G. Woodson [the father of black history and Black History Month] visited the campus. He gave a lecture that stayed with me. It was about black people and their great contributions to history. I took Latin for two years. I found out why they call it a dead language—it killed the Romans. At the time it was also killing me!

As far as campus activities, I played basketball. One of my teammates was Quentin North, from Miami.[16] He and George Lewis, also from Miami, were my roommates. I also ran the Tea House [and was]—chosen by Dr. Brown for that task.

There was a small black community in Sedalia. It included Rev. Brice and his musically inclined family. He was pastor of the local church and also our school chaplain. A World War I veteran who stood about 6'6" tall and was very slender, [Brice] made a memorable image on Armistice Day when he preached a sermon wearing his army uniform. His daughter was Carol Brice, who became a famous singer [She was a celebrated African American contralto who was born in Sedalia and attended PMI, Talladega College, and Julliard]. Rev. Brice once led the student body in learning and performing the Hallelujah Chorus [from Handel's Messiah]. Other members of the community worked at Palmer in various service-related jobs. During my senior year, singer Nat "King" Cole married Dr. Brown's niece, Maria. The couple spent the first week of their honeymoon on campus in Dr. Brown's Canary College. Another notable person at PMI during my time there was A. D. King, the younger brother of Dr. Martin Luther King, Jr. He is in one of the photographs published in the 1955 Ebony magazine story on Palmer. He was cutting up a lot and Dr. Brown didn't like it. The younger King's antics during the photograph session really ticked her off. He wasn't at PMI much longer. In 1956 Dr. King came to Durham to deliver a *speech and I got in touch with him because I knew his brother. After that, whenever Dr. King came to Durham, he stayed with my family—in my mother and father's house. I remember him telling me that blacks should get into politics. Dr. Brown also stressed giving back to the community. I think that is why I ran for political office. She would always invite black leaders to campus. Mordecai Johnson, president of Howard University, gave the graduation speech the year I graduated, and Benjamin Mays, president of Morehouse College, was an annual speaker. Theologian Howard Thurman also came to campus.*

*One thing about Dr. Brown, she would correct anyone who spoke out of ignorance, even powerful white people, like the governor. Whites in the South had a habit of pronouncing the word 'Negro,' as 'niggra.' If they said it in her presence she would stop them and give a lesson in pronunciation. She would say to the offender, "Repeat after me, "knee"—she would say as she pointed to her knee. Then she would ask, "What do trees do?" The offender would reply, "grow." "Now," she would say, "put them together and say it—'Negro.'" All of this did not mean much to me until much later. I still use the Palmer creed in my daily life. I recite it to students that I teach and mentor. I have been a lawyer for 45 years, and I have never forgotten. PMI provided an experience better than I could have gotten anywhere else. Some of us did not like everything about the place, but we learned to appreciate it later. Most important of all, she taught us to believe that we were somebody.*

Naomi Mannigault Holmes was born in Georgetown, South Carolina, where her parents were in the funeral business. Her older brother, as well as several members of her extended family, attended PMI. She attended from 1956 to 1958. Following graduation, she enrolled at Talladega College in Alabama and graduated in 1962. She has lived in Virginia Beach, Virginia, since 1953. Walter Mannigault, Holmes's father, was a personal friend of Charlotte Hawkins Brown. He and his wife, Maggie McLeod Mannigault, sent two of their three children to Palmer. The youngest of the three decided the school was not for her because, in her words, "there were too many rules," and there was no band. But Naomi's attraction to Palmer was more personal. Dr. Brown came to Georgetown to speak at the high school graduation, and Holmes was chosen to present Brown with a bouquet of roses. Holmes vividly remembers the occasion of meeting the famed educator because it took place at the Bethesda Baptist Church, as the black high school had no auditorium. Her family connection to Palmer—where her brother and first cousin Anthony Hurley [interviewed earlier] attended before her, swayed Holmes to attend. "My father tried to always give us opportunities to enrich our lives," said Holmes, and she considers Palmer an example of that enrichment.

The young woman's first actual visit to the campus was with her parents to pick up her brother. Holmes was struck by the beautiful campus. Her father had donated benches for the well-kept lawn, and she recalls the beauty and warmth that greeted them. Arriving at Palmer at age fourteen and graduating at age sixteen made Holmes younger than some of her classmates. Although she missed being home with her mother, the rules did not bother Holmes. Her mother had attended boarding school in Alabama and enjoyed her experience and warmed her daughter towards it. Although there were some students who did not want to be there and grumbled about the rules, most of the students, she remembered, wanted to be there.

Echoing what others have said about how teachers were always available to assist students, Holmes was satisfied with the academics at Palmer, but also notes that some areas were stronger than others, with math and foreign language being particularly strong. The major difference she observed between the public school that she had attended and Palmer was how well-mannered PMI students were. They always stood when an instructor entered the room. As Dr. Brown got older and her dementia increased, this protocol could be ripe for satire. Obviously forgetting where she had been, Brown would come in and out of a classroom, which caused students to stand up repeatedly.

Late in her tenure, Brown relinquished administrative authority to her assistant, Miss Crosson, but students were still very aware of the founder's presence. Although Brown was greatly respected, students did not appreciate her disrupting classes as she did.

Just before Holmes was about to graduate, Dr. Brown called her over and asked, "Young lady, where are you planning to go to college?" "I haven't decided. Either Hampton, Talladega, or Howard," Holmes replied. "Go to Talladega," Brown commanded. And that is where Holmes went. College was the expected next step for Palmerites. Holmes estimates that up to 99 percent of the graduates attended college. This was a time when students were becoming aware of the Civil Rights Movement, but Palmer students were not involved in it, although some of the invited campus speakers were. Vivian Carter Mason, a civil rights leader from Norfolk, Virginia, spoke at Holmes's graduation. Nearby Greensborough, where the always well-dressed PMI students went to shop, was also the epicenter of the student movement and lunch counter sit-ins were being launched there by North Carolina Central College students. Back home, her father and brother had become active in the movement and allowed the NAACP to meet at their funeral home. Upon reflection, Holmes said, "I think my father was disappointed that I was not involved more in the Civil Rights Movement."

"Palmer was able to succeed for so long because there were common values between the school and the parents," she reflected. The school's motto exemplified those values: [Being] socially secure, religiously sincere, and academically efficient, "was the aim," Holmes explained. A lengthy speech that she had to memorize and recite has stayed with her. It is from John D. Rockefeller's letter to his children. It included this line: *"I have to live with myself so I don't want to keep on the closet shelf, secret things about myself."* Palmer students even had a special hand-clap. All this served to keep them feeling connected—even today, this is true. She concludes by saying that she and her husband, a brigadier general, sent their three children to parochial school. Unfortunately, there was no Palmer for them to attend.

William "Bill" Brooks spent his entire high school career at Palmer. He entered in 1955 and graduated in the class of 1959. He is a native of Oxford, North Carolina, which is about seventy-seven miles from the Sedalia campus. He has one older brother, a retired dentist, but he is the only family member to attend Palmer. He is an Air Force veteran and a former business owner who now resides in Florida.

*I was not a very good student. My parents thought that a new environment would help me become a better student and prepare me for a good future. My father was a minister and my mother was a first-grade teacher. I don't know why they selected Palmer [for me], but it was a nationally recognized private school, and it was not far away. I was the first and only member of my family to attend Palmer, and I was simply told, "You are going to Palmer, no discussion." I had also attended Mary Potter, a private, church-established school for one year.* [There were several such private schools due to segregation and black parents wanting a better education for their children.]

*My first impression of the school was that it was like summer camp—or a boy scout camp. There were numerous kids my age who I bonded with. We had to live, sleep, and eat together. As far as the strict rules were concerned, my father had been a military person—he was one of the first black military officers and a[n] [army] chaplain. Compared to my very strict father, PMI was relaxed. Hazing was a general practice when I was attending. I was from this small town in North Carolina living in the dormitory with older guys from large cities. I was kind of small and wore glasses; I looked like I could be hazed. Mr. Dardo, my Spanish teacher—he also taught French—encouraged me to take boxing when I went to his door and whined about the hazing. Boxing gave me the self-confidence to stand up for myself.*

*Because the male teachers lived in the same dormitory with the guys, we had a counselor and a tutor available all the time. I had some favorites among the teachers. Dr. Alfredo Sharp, in particular, was a mentor. He taught Latin and was fluent in many languages and spoke with an accent, although he was African American. He excited my interest in learning languages and encouraged and motivated me to continue. Later, when I was in the Air Force and stationed in Spain, people thought that I was Spanish when I spoke. They didn't believe I was African American. I loved Spain. I still have my adopted mother there—in Zaragoza, Spain. She is 92 years old. I was in Spain for 18 months from 1962 to mid-1964. My willingness to learn a new culture and language is due to Mr. Sharpe. I wanted to go back to Palmer to speak to Dr. Sharp and thank him. But I never got to see him again to let him know how much he had taught me. At Palmer, all the instructors were interested in seeing you achieve. I remember Mr.*

*Steptoe who taught geometry. I am not good in math, but I received a B in geometry, my highest grade at Palmer.*

*I had very few encounters with Dr. Brown who had become emeritus during my stay. When I became headwaiter in the dining hall, I had to maintain Dr. Brown and Miss Crosson's table. We followed strict protocols in the dining hall. We had to arrive at a certain time. We all stood at our places until we sang the grace. Girls and boys entered separate doors. Then the waiters went to deliver the food. Everything was about training. What was the training for? To learn good etiquette, good table etiquette. Many of the students came from families where they didn't learn that. You were not to be belligerent. In fact, Dr. Brown had a statement at the bottom of the application that said, "Incorrigibles need not apply." Miss Crosson kept the same standards, but she, too, retired. Her replacement, a male, loosened the rules. The new principal began to accept everybody. Students rebelled against the rules. It was during his tenure when the students burned the Alice Freeman Palmer administration building down. Things had changed at PMI. With integration coming, well-to-do blacks could send their children elsewhere.*

*After graduation, I enlisted in the Air Force. My grades were not good enough for college so my father suggested that I enlist. I spent four and a half years in the Air Force. When I was stationed in Spain, I learned to speak fluent Spanish. After I left the service, I enrolled in Fayetteville State University [North Carolina] from 1964 to1969 and earned a business education degree. I also earned a master's degree in industrial relations from the University of New Haven. I returned for a visit to Palmer in 1964. I was then a student at Fayetteville State, but my mind was so much on Palmer Memorial Institute. I spent my formative years there. It was basically the same. During chapel, I was sitting in the back, but Miss Crosson [who was then principal] wanted to call me on stage with instructors. I declined, so she had me stand and speak about my experiences in the Air Force and in Spain and in college. I was asked to attend one of the Spanish classes and help teach it. I did, and helped to explain the difference between how the language is taught and how it is spoken.*

*I did begin to see the change over the four years that I was there. At first the upperclassmen would take personal interest in each student as a "little sister" or my "play kid." He or she would be your mentor. It was a very informal, but effective mentorship. It felt like a family. When you left Palmer or you travelled to another city you could call a Palmerite in that city and say that you were a Palmer graduate and they would come and pick you up! That was a given. You just called, I went. That also changed. That closeness died. Now, when you call and say you are a PMI graduate, they might say, "How are you? May I help you?"*

*Because of how I feel about PMI, I would still do it. Among the older graduates, this still goes on. But the alumni association is drifting—older people are dying off. The younger graduates don't have the same interests. PMI could not exist today. There are so many other opportunities. But I would send my children, if it still existed. But today the family connection is not there. Students are*

*much more lax in their behavior and their attitudes. But, if it still existed, I*
*would have sent my children to Palmer. Yes, I would.*

*I became a human resource manager, labor relations. After I retired and*
*moved to Brandon, Florida, I bought a franchise of Mailboxes, Inc., which are*
*now the UPS stores. I had always wanted to own my own business. After nine*
*years, I sold the business. I have two children. My son is an architect who*
*studied at the University of Notre Dame, and my daughter is a medical doctor*
*who graduated from Drew University. I am in my second marriage.*

Jeanne Lanier Rudd was a student at Palmer during the 1947–1948
school year. Her family lived in the community and her father was principal in the Sedalia public schools. After she graduated from North Carolina A&T University, both father and daughter worked at Palmer with
Dr. Brown. She served Palmer as assistant registrar and later as manager
of the state of North Carolina's Charlotte Hawkins Brown Museum at the
historical campus site.

Rudd, a native of Sedalia, was part of the group that worked tirelessly
to establish the state historical site that honors Dr. Brown. They lobbied
the North Carolina state legislature and worked with black legislators Bill
Martin and Mickey H. N. Michaux and PMI alumni to get the state funding and designation as an historical site. She then served as its director
from 1979 to1989. She has had a lifelong attachment to the founder and
the school. Her father, William Henry Lanier, graduated from Palmer
and was a protégé of Dr. Brown, who was instrumental in helping him to
attend Lincoln University. He returned to become a school principal and
later work as alumni director at PMI. When Rudd was fifteen, her mother
died. She then began attending Palmer. Rudd's older sister and brother
also attended for a brief time, but preferred a northern environment. She
lived off campus with her father. Dr. Brown wanted Rudd to live on
campus, but the sophomore hesitated because of the strict rules. She attended class, ate her meals there, then headed home. She later realized
that the rules were a good thing, because at that time in the rural South,
one scandal would have closed the school.

Dr. Brown and her family were close. "She even tried to dictate who
my widowed father should date," Rudd said. Brown was very direct, but
Rudd also thinks that people told lies about Brown, such as that she
didn't like dark-skinned people. "She was dark-skinned herself," ex-
claimed Rudd. Another myth was that she favored only the upper-class
black kids. "Everybody worked on campus, so you didn't know who was
rich or poor," Rudd said. Brown never embarrassed anyone and treated
everyone the same, regardless of his or her station in life. "If a janitor
came into classroom to change a light bulb, the students would stand and
greet him," Rudd said. Rudd indicates that Brown did not want to turn
her school into a reform school. So a member of the admissions committee would visit all applicants—go to the hometown and interview the
applicant, the neighbors, and the ministers. "She wanted to make sure

that a parent wasn't trying to get rid of a [problem] child," Rudd remembered.

What stands out in Rudd's mind about the school and its leader after all these years is that Brown taught her students that "they were somebody." "I now understand why she did what she did," Rudd said. "I appreciate the strictness, the manners, the fact that she taught us that 'we were somebody and to respect people regardless of their status in life.'"

For years both she and her husband worked on campus. He served as superintendent of the campus and grounds. Things started changing, Rudd said, when the "wrong" students were admitted after Brown's death. "The Alice Freeman-Palmer classroom building was burned down by a group of rebellious students in 1969. Brown would not allow the students to mess around. She would call a student's parent and ask them to meet her/him at the train station. At the time of the fire, Charles Bundridge was president. Miss. Crosson had returned to Boston," Rudd remembered. Nobody was charged with setting the fire. Rudd was still assistant registrar at that time. Students continued to the end of the year and there was a wait list for admission the next year, but the board decided to close the school. "We did not understand why. We are in need of PMI today," Rudd said. "It was not integration that closed PMI; parents were calling saying that they wanted their child to attend." In retrospect, Rudd believes that Dr. Brown was able to do so much because of the contacts she had, in addition to the help that Miss Crosson, her hand-picked successor, provided."[Miss Crosson] was wonderful," Rudd said. "We could still use some of Dr. Brown's scruples today. She was not old-fashioned—she was before her time," Rudd concluded.

She was happy to work for the Charlotte Hawkins Brown Museum because it let people know how a young woman was able to bring her dream to fruition. Rudd started a program at the museum called "It's About Time" that retells Brown's story and more about North Carolina history. She also instituted a black heritage program and connected the museum's activities to other state historic sites. The memorial to Brown officially became the Charlotte Hawkins Brown Museum at Historic Palmer Memorial Institute. It is the only memorial dedicated to an African American or a woman in North Carolina. There was no opposition of which Rudd was aware. There was, at first, slow traffic to the site because people did not know it was there. That began to change with new programs, more advertising and events such as an African American festival, holiday open houses, etc., and some of the original buildings were restored. The facility is now used for special programs and events, including family reunions and holiday gatherings. It has become a community-oriented site. Ms. Rudd thinks that Dr. Brown would be very pleased.

**Figure 5.1.    Charlotte Hawkins Brown, founder and principal, Palmer Memorial Institute. Photo courtesy of Moorland-Spingarn Research Center, Howard University.**

Figure 5.2.    Senior Prom at Palmer Memorial Institute. Photo courtesy of personal collection of William Brooks, class of 1959.

**Figure 5.3.   Charlotte Hawkins Brown and Wilhelmina Crossen of Palmer Memorial Institute. Photo courtesy of NC Dept. of Cultural Resources.**

NOTES

1. "A Finishing School," *Ebony* Magazine (October, 1947): 22–27.
2. "A Finishing School."

3. Palmer Memorial Institute Catalogue, 1930–1931, in Charlotte Hawkins Brown Papers, Manuscript Division, Library of Congress, reel 1.

4. Constance Hill Marteena, *The Lengthening Shadow of a Woman: A Biography of Charlotte Hawkins Brown* (Hicksville, N.Y.: Exposition Press, 1977), 65.

5. Charles W. Wadelington and Richard F. Knapp, *Charlotte Hawkins Brown and Palmer Memorial Institute* (Chapel Hill: University of North Carolina, 1999). 190.

6. Wadelington and Knapp, 201.

7. Charlotte Hawkins Brown, "The Negro and the Social Graces," Joel Spingarn Papers, Moorland-Spingarn Research Center, Box 94-3, folder 51.

8. Black boarding schools of early 1900s included the Piney Woods School, founded in 1909, in Mississippi; Snow Hill Normal and Industrial Institute, founded in 1893, in Alabama; and Boggs Academy, founded in 1906, in Georgia.

9. Charlotte Hawkins Brown Papers, Manuscript Division, Library of Congress, "Palmer Memorial Institute Catalogue," reel one, 17.

10. Charlotte Hawkins Brown, "Negro Woman Not Freed by Emancipation," The Buffalo *Progressive Herald* (15 March, 1930), Charlotte Hawkins Brown Papers, reel one.

11. Anna Julie Cooper, *A Voice from the South* [1892], New York Oxford University Press, 1988, 24–25.

12. Charlotte Hawkins Brown, "The Negro Woman Not Freed by Emancipation."

13. Tera Hunter, "The Correct thing: Charlotte Hawkins Brown and the Palmer Institute," *Southern Exposure* (September/October 1983), 43.

14. The visitor count was provided by Ms. Frachale Scott, site manager, Charlotte Hawkins Brown Museum, Sedalia, N.C.

15. A description of current activities at the Charlotte Hawkins Brown Museum was provided by Ms. Frachale Scott, site manager.

16. The late Quentin North was the author's high school history teacher at Booker T. Washington Jr.-Sr. High in Miami, Florida. He was the author's favorite, teacher—the person who ignited her interest in majoring in history in college.

# SIX

## "Telling Some Mighty Truths"

### Nannie Helen Burroughs, Activist Educator and Social Critic

*When we all know justice*
*What a day of rejoicing that will be.*
*When we all have justice,*
*We'll live in peace and harmony.*

—Nannie Helen Burroughs

Nannie Helen Burroughs (1879–1961) was perhaps the most colorful, uncompromising, and certainly the most prolific and gifted writer among the four activist women school founders and activists discussed in this study. Burroughs served as corresponding secretary and later as president of the largest national organization of black women—the one million strong National Baptist Woman's Convention, formed as an auxiliary to the male-led National Baptist Convention that merged with another organization in 1895.[1] Burroughs was a defining presence in the women's missionary-oriented organization from its beginnings in 1900 in Richmond, Virginia, until her death in 1961. She instituted many innovative programs in the black Baptist Church, including the annual Women's Day program that has today become a mainstay in congregations across the nation. She also started Christian women's retreats, church pageants and plays, and other activities that focused on women and youth. Her one-act play, *The Slabtown Convention* (1909), was a humorous take on missionary work—and a fundraising bonanza in black Baptist churches for many years. Under the auspices of the Woman's Convention in 1909, Burroughs founded and served as president of the National Training School for Women and Girls in Washington, D.C. In making her plea to the Baptist women to sponsor the school and purchase the six-acre hilltop site, Burroughs declared that it "must be national, not Baptist—something all Colored women can do for all Colored girls." Burroughs wanted the school to be a beacon of light for black women, insisting that it be built in the nation's capital. "Everyone comes here," she said, viewing the limelight of the capital city as an asset in raising the school's national, even international, profile.[2] This decision was not supported by her friend, Booker T. Washington, who advised against it because of his belief that blacks stood a better chance of success in the South, especially in rural communities where they could become landowners and farmers. Nevertheless, the Woman's Convention moved forward and became the first black women's organization to found and run its own school.

This fact set the black Baptist women and their school apart from schools supported by white male-led Christian organizations. This included the American Missionary Association, which established several black schools and colleges in the South after Reconstruction. Offering vocational training for black women and girls, it attracted students from many different parts of the United States, the Caribbean, and Africa. Burroughs adopted the motto "We specialize in the wholly impossible"[3] to signal her intention to reach those who had been denied the opportunity for education and advancement. It was her mission to prepare students for the existing job market and to be economically self-sufficient. "Two-thirds of the Colored women must work with their hands for a living, and it is indeed an oversight not to prepare this army of breadwinners to do their work well,"[4] she said. This outlook led to the installation of vocational courses not normally associated with the segregated sphere of women's work, such as printing, shoe repair, and barbering.[5] The school also offered the more traditional domestic science curriculum along with liberal arts courses.

Burroughs' vocational emphasis was inspired in part by Booker T. Washington and the example of manual training and self-help that he established after founding Tuskegee Institute in Alabama. Because of that connection and their friendship, Burroughs was often dubbed "the female Booker T. Washington."[6] As corresponding secretary of the Woman's Convention, she invited Washington to speak at the first annual meeting, the 1901 Woman's Convention in Birmingham, Alabama. However, Washington's much-anticipated speech was interrupted by a stampede brought on by an enthusiastic shout of "Fight!" that was misunderstood as "Fire!" That notable incident did not deter Washington, who returned to speak at the Woman's Convention every year until his death in 1915.[7] Despite Burroughs's alignment with Washington in his stance on industrial education and race self-help, she did not agree with his views on women.[8] Unlike Washington, Burroughs was a strong feminist and champion of women's suffrage, financial independence, and equality.[9] An outspoken public figure, she openly criticized those male leaders she considered errant in their views or actions. She eschewed some of the gender conventions of her era, including marriage. Like sister school founders Lucy Laney, Mary Bethune, and Charlotte Hawkins Brown, Burroughs chose to dedicate herself to activism and building her institution over pursuing a traditional family life. Her papers at the Library of Congress include copious correspondence, but they show little evidence of a personal life that was separate from her organizational and institutional work.

Burroughs was an activist educator who fought fiercely to sustain her school in the face of financial woes and challenges to her leadership by the male hierarchy of the Baptist Convention. Her leadership of the school and her role in the Woman's Convention, as well as newspaper columns, speeches, and writings, made Burroughs a national figure who effectively inserted herself into the male-centered discourse on race advancement. Her work paralleled that of well-known contemporaries and older black women leaders such as Mary Church Terrell (1863–1954), Mary McLeod Bethune (1875–1955), and Anna Julia Cooper (1858–1960). In fact, Cooper was one of Burroughs's teachers at the M Street high school in Washington, D.C. An article titled "True Womanhood" that appeared in the *Washington Bee* in 1906 described the young activist as "the most gifted speaker in the United States. Her equal cannot be found upon the rostrum. She is doing more to mold sentiment among the thinking people than any speaker in public life. Many of her hearers may not agree with her, but nevertheless, she is telling some mighty truths.[10]

Those truths were manifested in Burroughs' success as the builder of an institution that until recently survived as the Nannie Burroughs School, Inc., a private, pre-kindergarten through sixth-grade Christian day school.[11] The school still occupies the original six-acre hilltop site purchased in 1906 by the Women's Convention.[12] Through her writings and speeches, Burroughs created a lasting legacy of activism focusing on serious topics of the day, as well as providing ample doses of wit and humor that may have made her message more palatable to audiences. She used her platform not only to promote the interests of the school, but also to engage in a broad range of race and gender issues, both religious and secular, in her unique way.

To further compare her to her sister school founders, Burroughs was as political as Mary McLeod Bethune but less diplomatic in her manner. While Burroughs insisted that "good Christians [must] have good manners," she was less concerned with the "social graces" than was Charlotte Hawkins Brown. Burroughs was as committed to her religious beliefs and core values as the very serious Lucy Laney but was more confrontational in espousing them. Burroughs stood out among the four women for delivering social critiques that were pointed and direct and left little room for diplomatic ambiguity.

Nannie Helen Burroughs was born in Orange, Virginia, on May 2, 1878, the older of two daughters of John Burroughs and Jennie Poindexter, both of whom were formerly enslaved. With Burroughs's maternal and paternal grandfathers, the family became sizable landowners following the Civil War. John Burroughs, a farmer and preacher, died when Burroughs was a young girl, as did her baby sister. Nannie herself was stricken with typhoid fever at age seven and because of her health was forced to stay out of school for four years.[13] When she recovered, her mother, seeking better educational opportunities for her only child, moved to Washington, D.C. The move was good for Burroughs, as she made up two grades a year and graduated from the famed M Street High School. Renamed in honor of poet Paul Laurence Dunbar in 1916, M Street High earned a reputation for high achievement and for sending the majority of its graduates to college. For one thing, the city's segregationist hiring policies ironically supplied the school with a well-qualified teaching staff that included Oberlin graduate Mary Jane Patterson, who in 1862 became the first black woman to graduate from college. Another faculty member was Mary Church Terrell, also an Oberlin graduate and founding president of the National Association of Colored Women. Terrell was the first black woman to serve on the District of Columbia Board of Education. Oberlin graduate and noted author Anna Julia Cooper, who published the groundbreaking defense of black women *A Voice from the South* (1892) and earned a doctorate from the Sorbonne in her later years, served for a time as the school's principal.

Burroughs excelled in this environment. M Street's strong academic curriculum and its business and domestic science courses seemed to fuel the young women's desire for learning. Pursuing her love of the written word, she founded the Harriet Beecher Stowe Literary Society and graduated with honors in 1896.[14] Although only a high school diploma was required to be a public school teacher at the time, the ambitious and diligent Burroughs could not secure a position teaching in domestic science departments in the District of Columbia school system. She attributed the rejection to "politics" that favored the lighter-skinned black upper class. As a result of her experience, she vowed to one day start a school in Washington that "politics had nothing to do with and would give all sorts of girls a fair chance."[15] Subsequently, she left the city for a year and became an associate editor of *The Christian Banner*, a church-related periodical in Philadelphia. This marked the beginning of Burroughs's writing on Christian themes and to promote causes that were important to her. Burroughs soon moved back to Washington, D.C., where she passed a civil service exam to work as a government clerk. Despite passing the exam, she was told that they were not hiring blacks.

Burroughs made ends meet by working as a janitor and a bookkeeper for a while before she accepted a job as a stenographer and editorial secretary for the Foreign Mission Board of the National Baptist Convention in Louisville, Kentucky. There she organized a women's industrial club to serve moderately priced lunches to office workers in the Louisville business district. In the evenings, Burroughs taught typing, shorthand, and bookkeeping classes, as well as courses in domestic arts— millinery, sewing, cooking—to help women become more efficient in household management. For members of the women's industrial club, the classes cost ten cents per week. As the classes grew in popularity, Burroughs received financial backing to increase tuition and hire more teachers. This freed her to supervise and further develop the evening school.[16] Burroughs also became part owner of the office building in Louisville that housed the offices of several departments of the National Baptist Convention and then launched a successful business of her own promoting the "Negro Picture Calendar." This project showcased beautiful black homes and successful businesses and was a precursor to *Ebony* magazine.[17] With this background and experience, Burroughs combined her demonstrated talents as a teacher, organizer, and writer with her religious and social convictions to set the course of the next half-century of her activist life.

She stepped into the national spotlight in 1900 at the annual meeting of the National Baptist Convention in Richmond, Virginia. "How the Sisters are Hindered from Helping," was the title of the speech Burroughs gave criticizing the marginalization of women that placed them in supporting roles within the church and downplayed their leadership abilities. The resulting notoriety the speech created led not only to her election as corresponding secretary of the Woman's Convention, but to more speaking invitations as well. At the World's Baptist Congress in London, for example, Burroughs garnered favorable reviews from both the delegates and the press for her speech, "Women's Part in the World's Work." *The London Mirror* reported that "she was one of the most notable personages at the meeting."[18] Such eloquent oratory ignited her career as a public speaker, while her witty and candid writing style led to more freelance columns in several black newspapers, including the *Washington Afro-American* and the *Pittsburgh Courier*. Burroughs was also founding editor of *The Worker*, a missionary quarterly that the Woman's Convention first published in 1934.

The Woman's Convention remained a firm support base for Burroughs' school, strongly endorsing her idea of training black women and girls for missionary work as well as providing them with skills for "self-respecting careers."[19] The National Training School for Women and Girls began with seven students on October 19, 1909, and grew steadily. (The name was changed to the National Trade and Professional School in 1939.)

Burroughs's own background in domestic science influenced her belief that service-oriented jobs were in demand and would provide decent wages for those who could "professionalize" the existing race- and gen-

der-segregated job market.[20] As with other black women school founders, Burroughs's vocational focus did not limit the growth of liberal arts
courses such as English, history—including Negro history—foreign languages, higher mathematics, and science. Burroughs made this point in a
speech to the Woman's Convention: "We believe that an industrial and
classical education can be simultaneously attained, and it is our duty to
get both."[21] Similar to the other black women school founders, pragmatism—not strict educational ideology—shaped her curriculum. Even so,
it is reported that Burroughs was such a stickler for correct grammar that
she made two years of college-level English a graduation requirement for
all students.[22] Burroughs actually insisted upon being in charge of not
just the curriculum, but every aspect of the school's management—including finances, personnel, and development, which inevitably put her
at odds with the male leadership of the Southern Baptist Convention.

Regardless of her feelings about the governing body, the Scripture-
quoting Burroughs infused religion into every aspect of campus life. Indeed, the private Christian school became known as the "School of the
three Bs" which stood for "the Bible, the bath, and the broom." This,
paired with the focus on domestic science, were representations of Burroughs' belief in the elevating principles of a clean life, clean body, and
clean home for black women.[23] She believed that a spiritually rich education would create a strong Christian sisterhood among the students that
would allow them to deal with the obstacles of race, class, and gender
that they would surely face in society. Religion was a major part of Burroughs' public discourse and was a prominent theme in many of her
writings and speeches—some of which were stinging criticisms of the
black community, particularly its male leaders. In her public addresses
she spared neither white racists nor, for that matter, the president of the
United States. Her criticism of President Woodrow Wilson, whom she
accused of not doing enough to stop lynching, quickly led to her being
placed under government surveillance.[24]

Correspondence and speeches document Burroughs's rising stature as
an influential voice in public discourse, both locally and nationally, and
across two generations of black leadership. The voluminous papers of Dr.
Martin Luther King, Jr., for example, include his letter accepting Burroughs's invitation in 1958 to speak at the Women's Day program in
Chicago.[25] Actually, the insistent voice in many of her writings antici-
pates the oncoming civil rights and black power movements and indicates that acceptance of the status quo in race relations was quickly becoming a relic of a passing era. Her prolific writing often overflows into
several themes as well as into several genres. Burroughs wrote newspaper columns, letters, editorials, church plays and bulletins, essays, and
speeches to Christian organizations, as well as active correspondence
with notable individuals. Specific topics that emerge throughout her

body of work include women's rights, education, race uplift and race relations, and Christian activism.

The religious overtones of her subjects did not mute her forthright, sardonic writing style that was grounded in a secular social agenda. For example, Burroughs wrote a newspaper editorial urging blacks not to participate in white evangelist Billy Sunday's (1862–1935) planned month-long campaign in Washington in the winter of 1918. Sunday, the most popular and well-known travelling evangelist in the United States at the time,[26] proposed to deliver one of his sermons to a segregated black audience as he had done the year before in Atlanta, with the support of most of Atlanta's black clergy. Burroughs blasted the notion, calling it "religious Jim Crowism." Addressing Sunday directly, she chided him:

> You must be under the impression that the Colored people of this city want to hear you. This is not true. However . . . they may be willing to arrange for a "performance" at one of their own churches. . . . If the weather is favorable, but we cannot promise, even under favorable weather conditions . . . to have any intelligent Negroes see and hear you. Those who might attend would be just as ignorant as the Negroes in Atlanta who accommodated you.[27]

Criticizing errant blacks and holding white Christian leaders' feet to the fire by calling them out on their racism was Burroughs's specialty. She once refused to speak at the National Christian Mission, a nationwide touring division of the Federal Council of Churches, after the president of the white organization, Dr. R. L. Darby, wrote Burroughs asking to meet to discuss her upcoming speech in advance. He claimed she was not accustomed to speaking, in his words, "in this particular kind of meeting." She considered his remark an insulting attempt to censor her. Burroughs responded with an open letter to Darby that was published on February 1, 1911, in the *Pittsburgh Courier*, garnering the headline, "Nannie Burroughs Refuses to Speak on National Christian Mission":

> You speak of this "particular kind of meeting," Dr. Darby. As compared . . . with "the particular kind" of national and international meetings that I have been addressing in America and Europe for twenty five years, [your event] is only a little prayer meeting.

Burroughs was equally frank in her pamphlet "Making Your Christian Community," which she addressed to "intelligent white Southerners." Among the actions that she recommended to them was this straightforward advice: "Stop using the words 'nigger,' 'darkie,' and 'coon,' and stop telling 'nigger jokes.' They are not funny." She advised white Southerners to use courtesy titles like 'Mr.' 'Mrs.' and 'Miss' when speaking to blacks—a radical idea at the time—and to write their local newspaper and request that it publish photographs of black war veterans, or give money to those agencies that are helping black sharecroppers and wage earners. "Ask your librarian for books about blacks and praise your minister for preaching about brotherhood—or hint that it is about time that he did," she urged. Burroughs was optimistic about bridging the "great chasm" between the races, but cautioned that it would take concerted and meaningful efforts to forge individual friendships among like-minded individuals. She ended the essay by urging "intelligent" whites to subscribe to a Negro magazine or newspaper, because "as a white person in the South, you likely know very little about any Negroes except those who have worked for you in some menial position."[28]

She delivered a similar message in her speech, "How White and Colored Women Can Cooperate in Building a Christian Civilization," given in March of 1933 to the Women's Missionary Union of Virginia. She exhorted women of both races to unite to defeat their common enemies—ignorance, selfishness, and race prejudice. "A civilization like ours is not built on race; it is built on grace. It is not built on white; it is built on right," she concluded.[29] To the white nation as a whole, Burroughs issued a proclamation consisting of "Twelve Things White People Must Stop Doing to the Negro," including penalizing Negroes for not being white, teaching race prejudice to children, and putting up such barriers as discriminatory laws and practices.[30]

Burroughs applied the same bluntness in her criticism of black Americans. Her unflinching message to them was to get their own houses in order by making demands on their leaders and by doing more for themselves: "The Negro must unload the leeches and parasitic leaders who are absolutely eating the life out of the great struggling, desiring masses. . . . Chloroform your 'Uncle Toms.' Whether they are in the church as the preacher, in the school as the teacher, or in the ward as the politician—the quicker the better. They sold us for a mess of pottage. We got the mess but not the pottage."[31] Drawing upon her biblical dexterity, Burroughs equated the conditions of black Americans with that of the ancient Israelites. "We have not yet reached the Promised Land," she reminded her black audience. "Don't wait for deliverers," she admonished. "God said, 'Moses, my servant is dead, therefore, arise and go over Jordan.'" She continued, "There are no deliverers. We must get to the Promised Land ourselves." To Burroughs, that meant no turning back in the pursuit of justice.

Furthering this critique of her racial kin in an essay titled "The Negro Home," Burroughs implored blacks to "put first things first" and listed priorities that the race needed to focus upon, including their homes, their characters, and education. These were among the "twelve things" that she said blacks must do for themselves.[32] In her view, the race was emerging from a long ordeal of suffering, which increased the need to face the future with open eyes and guard against the temptation to "sacrifice essentials for frills."[33]

Burroughs' racial rhetoric also always encouraged blacks to be proud of their humanity and their race. She proudly asserted that "not all the Jim Crow [train] cars, or discrimination and prejudice could teach this 'mahogany blond' that she is inferior." In an article in the *Black Dispatch* newspaper, Burroughs asked a poignant question: "How Does It Feel to Be a Negro?" After enumerating a series of historical injustices against blacks and their righteous struggles to overcome them, she answered her question, saying how it feels to be black is to simply feel human.[34]

An eye-catching article under her byline in the Washington *Afro-American* in 1934 rebutted the author of a mournful poem written in response to a spate of lynchings that appeared a week earlier in the same newspaper. The poem had asked in rhyme:

> What will become of us—the Negro race; Must we be subject to every disgrace? Must we be victims of the white man's hate? What will become of us—sooner or late?

Burroughs took offense at the self-pitying tone and reminded the mournful poet that the United States, contrary to the notion of being a Christian nation, "is the most lawless and desperately wicked nation on the globe. It is no place for whiners." She retorted in prose:

> You are wasting your time begging the white race for mercy. In fact, the Negro does not need mercy. He needs common sense. Figuratively speaking, there are five classes of people: mud sills, doormats, stepping stones, hound dogs, and bull dogs. What will become of these five classes? . . . [T]he mud sills will be walked over; the stepping stones [and doormats] will be walked upon; the hound dogs will be kicked around; and the bull dogs will get what they go after. The poet did not seem to realize that the American Negro has enough weapons in his own possession right now, to use effectively, [and] serve notice on the world that he is taking himself seriously and means to fight his battles with the only weapons he has.[35]

Living in the nation's capital, Burroughs took every opportunity to involve herself in national political issues. She was a staunch member of the Republican Party and in 1928 urged blacks to support Herbert Hoover for president. She spelled out her reasons in an unpublished speech in which she called Hoover's Democratic opponent, Al Smith, a "showman, rather than a statesman," who was tainted by corruption. Her list of demands to the Republican Party for improving the condition of blacks, however, including the appointment of black women to major positions, showed that she expected concrete results to flow from her endorsement.[36] In 1944, Burroughs was among the signatories to a petition to the U.S. Senate authored by the biracial "Committee to Abolish the Poll Tax" in federal elections. Her friend Mary McLeod Bethune sent her the petition in support of Senate bill HR7 that stated: "Nothing is more essential to the functioning of our democracy than free use of the ballot without restrictions."[37]

The weapons of choice, according to Burroughs, were the ballot and the dollar. She reasoned that the white man fears the ballot and worships the dollar and insisted, therefore, that the wise use of both was the way to win the day for Negroes. Burroughs took particular umbrage at defeatist attitudes among blacks. In her column in the *Washington Tribune* on July 7, 1939, titled "Never Had a Chance," she upbraided two women she had overheard complaining that they "never had a chance." Her answer to them was that "people don't have chances, they take them!" Burroughs wanted that message to echo throughout black America and thus published her response in a black newspaper.

Yet as harshly as Burroughs criticized blacks for their foibles, she was always among the first to stand up for their rights to justice and for "an equal chance" in America. She was against all forms of segregation and persuasively argued that America was violating its principles by maintaining it. To her, there was no room for compromise when it came to granting blacks the same rights that other U.S. citizens took for granted.[38]

Nearly a decade later, after World War II hero General Dwight Eisenhower broke the Democratic Party's 28-year monopoly on the United States presidency, Burroughs still seemed to favor the Republicans, at least the Republican president. She wrote to her Baptist women constituents that she was among the United Church Women that President Eisenhower "came down" to address in Atlantic City, and she was impressed by his emphasis on community improvement. As in nearly all of her writings and speeches, Burroughs related how any issue or topic—in this instance, Eisenhower's call for community improvement—impacted the black community and what needed to be done about it.[39] She proceeded to spell out how unsuitable and unhealthy conditions in some black communities held back race progress. Then Burroughs asked the Woman's Convention to "have the boldness" to lead a community improvement campaign in their respective communities and encourage other black organizations to address "those serious and challenging problems."[40]

Burroughs' feminist sensibilities were evident in her activism. Always a stalwart in supporting women's rights, she was a strong advocate for women's suffrage. In the aftermath of the passage of the Nineteenth Amendment (1919) of the U.S. Constitution that granted the vote to women, Burroughs urged women to use it wisely and not take their new power and influence lightly. She was especially concerned about the racial divide between black and white women. To that end, she published an article in the *West Virginia Women's Voice*, cautioning them not to become factionalized over race. In her view, white women too often took black women's involvement or consent lightly by choosing a few token black women as leaders without consulting with or getting to know the real issues in the black community. Burroughs argued that black women must be allowed to select their own leaders. "Leave it to them" she insisted. "They can do it."[41]

Burroughs' view of herself as a spokeswoman for black women, especially those in the service professions, culminated in the founding in 1921 of the National Association of Wage Earners (NAWE). She served as president, with Mary McLeod Bethune elected vice president of the organization. As middle-class women, the members embraced the narrative of race uplift and self-improvement and felt it was their duty to disseminate it to their working class sisters and brothers. The stated goal of the short-lived NAWE was to raise the status of this large and important segment of the black female work force by providing training and working for better wages and living conditions. While Burroughs supported these goals, her more down-to-earth approach placed her closer to the grassroots type of management and to the working class women she hoped to serve. In a letter on the organization's letterhead, Burroughs' "organizational genius"[42] showed in the way she gently prodded Margaret Murray Washington, the third wife and widow of Booker T. Washington and an important ally, to adopt a more efficient and cost-effective process for uniform communication among the chapters and for spreading the organization to other locations within the black diaspora. Burroughs wrote to her elder, Mrs. Washington:

> Suppose each woman wants two hundred letterheads and two hundred envelopes, and we have six officers. You could get out twelve or fifteen hundred letterheads and envelopes much cheaper than we could individually. Of course, I think you ought to have your money in advance; not that we will not pay it, but the sum is too small to carry credit. Now, with reference to the representative to Haiti: I am sure you must have considered the matter very carefully before asking the women to put one hundred dollars in it. I do not know the person and, like in many other things . . . we trust your judgment. On the surface, it does not appeal to me as a very wise thing to do. If you were going [to Haiti] I would say O.K., but a hundred dollars is too much.[43]

Burroughs' organizational and management skills were at their best during the more than 50 years that she presided over what became the National Trade and Professional School. Her correspondence and other writings show both her skill at managing what could be described as a perpetually at-risk enterprise, and her indomitable spirit and attitude to protect and sustain the school. In her 1941 report to the school's board of trustees, Burroughs seemed to grasp its historic nature: "How a small Negro school without income could pull through five years of the worst depression in history and re-establish [itself is] going to make a thrilling story someday."[44] The numerous letters of desperation show what a task that was. A letter to supporters dated December 21, 1933, for instance, was written in the midst of the Christmas season. It expressed a sense of urgency steeped in Burroughs' dramatic style:

> My Dear Friends: Here we are! Cold! No coal! No money! Working— believing in our friends and in God. That's our story. I have tried my best to get along without writing you . . . because I know you are carrying a heavy burden and . . . have been so thoughtful. . . . But we are up against a stone wall. I have spent restless nights and anxious days, battling, believing, carrying on in spite of our distressing lack of funds, fuel, and food.[45]

Another sign of the distressing times that Burroughs plowed through, with her intent to use every available revenue source to generate income, was the letter she sent out soliciting soap wrappers that could be

**Figure 6.1.   Nannie Burroughs, founder and principal National Training School. Photo courtesy of Moorland-Spingarn Research Center, Howard University, Washington, D.C.**

**Figure 6.2. Girls Basketball team, National Training School for Negro Women and Girls. Photo courtesy of the Library of Congress.**

redeemed for cash. It announced that the school would receive $4,000 for every million coupons from Octagon soap.

In addition to financial woes, the school faced an attempt by the male-led National Baptist Convention to take over control of the school's charter. As noted in an unattributed article in the *Black Dispatch* that reads as though it could have been written by Burroughs herself, titled "You Can't Have My Baby," this power play by the National Baptist Convention failed. Citing the closure or sale of schools run by the convention as a reason to reject any takeover effort, the article further stated that men who once frowned upon the effort, when the school was first founded, now wanted to claim its success.

That success is part of the legacy of Nannie Helen Burroughs. It was effected by the armament of her many skills—writing, organizing, leading, speaking, and the possession of a sure-fire wit in the service of the "mighty truths" that she embraced and defended. Her belief in Christian brotherhood and sisterhood inspired her work and pursuit of justice. The lines from a song she wrote titled "Justice!" is a closing refrain, as noted above, that exemplifies her life and work:

> When we all know justice
> What a day of rejoicing that will be.

When we all have justice,
We'll live in peace and harmony.[46]

The city that she lived and worked in for most of her adult life acknowledged her legacy by naming the street that bypasses the present-day school Nannie Helen Burroughs Avenue. Nannie Helen Burroughs Day was proclaimed first by Mayor Walter E. Washington in 1975. Mayor Marion Barry continued the tradition of hosting an annual parade in her honor, which also served as part of a fundraising drive for the school.[47]

## NOTES

1. "History of the National Baptist Convention," http://www.nationalbaptist.com/about-us/our-history/index.html (8 March 2010).
2. Audrey Thomas McCluskey, "We Specialize in the Wholly Impossible: Black Women School Founders and their Mission," *Signs: Journal of Women and Culture in Society*, vol. 21, no. 1, 403–26 .
3. Audrey Thomas McCluskey, " We Specialize in the Wholly Impossible."
4. Undated school records, obtained from Alberta T. Ford of the Nannie Helen Burroughs School in Washington, D.C., May, 1995.
5. Biography of Nannie Helen Burroughs in school records folder [no author], NHB papers Library of Congress, Manuscript Division, Introduction, 6.
6. Sharon Harley, "Nannie Helen Burroughs: Black Goddess of Liberty," *Journal of Negro History* 81, no. 1–4 (Winter–Autumn, 1996): 62.
7. Evelyn Brooks Higginbotham, *Righteous Discontent: The Women's Movement in the Black Baptist Church*, 1880–1920 (Cambridge, Mass.: Harvard University Press, 1993), 159.
8. Booker T. Washington's views on women's rights are gleaned, in part, from some of his statements and letters, in particular his letter to Charles Monroe Lincoln (14 December 1908), which implied that women suffrage was not needed. Women's History Document sources, http://www.greenstone.org/greenstone3/nzdl (20 September 2012).
9. Harley, "Black Goddess of Liberty," 64.
10. "True Womanhood," *Washington Bee*, 17 November 1906.
11. The school closed in 2012.
12. Audrey Walker et al., *Nannie Helen Burroughs: A Register of Her Papers in the Library of Congress*, 1982, 3. The Nannie Helen Burroughs School, Inc., a private Christian day school located in northeast Washington, D.C., that Burroughs dubbed "the holy hill," is on the original site of the National Trade and Professional School. The school was renamed in 1964 to honor its founder, <http://nhburroughs.org/index.html (12 July 2012).
13. Clement Richardson, ed., *The National Cyclopedia of the Colored Race*, Vol. 1 (Montgomery, Ala.: National Publishing Co., 1919), 312.
14. National Trade and Professional School Records, 1–8, NHB Papers, LOC, n.d. Nannie Helen Burroughs School, Inc. 601 50th Street N.E., Washington, D.C. 20019, 1–8.
15. Sadie Iola Daniel and Hallie Quinn, *Women Builders*, rev. ed. (Washington, D.C.: G. K. Hall, 1997), 111–36.
16. National Trade and Professional School Records, 1–8, NHB Papers, LOC, n.d.
17. "Miss Nannie H. Burroughs," in *The National Cyclopedia of the Colored Race*, Vol. 1, ed. Clement Richardson (Montgomery, Ala.: National Publishing Co., 1919), 411.
18. "Miss Nannie H. Burroughs," in *National Cyclopedia*, 411.

19. Alberta T. Ford, undated school records , Nannie Helen Burroughs School, Washington, D.C.

20. Higginbotham, *Righteous Discontent*, 212.

21. Earl H. Harrison, "An Abbreviated Story of the Life of Nannie Helen Burroughs and the National Trade and Professional School," NHB papers, LOC [school records], 26.

22. Harrison, "An Abbreviated Story," 26.

23. William Pickens, *Nannie Burroughs and the School of the Three B's* (New York: 1921).

24. Higginbotham, *Righteous Discontent*, 225–26.

25. *The Papers of Martin Luther King, Jr., Vol. 4: Symbol of the Movement, January 1957–December 1958*, ed. Clayborne Carson et al. (Berkeley: University of California Press, 2000).

26. "African-Americans and Billy Sunday in Atlanta," African-American Religion: Documentary History Project, http://www3.amherst.edu/~aardoc/Atlanta_1.html (15 May 2011).

27. "Negroes Spurn Billy Sunday's Jim Crow Invitation," newspaper editorial, 13 January 1918, NHB papers LOC, Manuscript Division, box 46.

28. Nannie Helen Burroughs, *Making Your Community Christian* [pamphlet], "There Are Things to Do," third edition, n.d., Nannie H. Burroughs School, Washington, D.C., in NHB papers, Library of Congress.

29. Nannie Helen Burroughs, "How White and Colored Women Can Cooperate in Building a Christian Civilization," NHB papers, Library of Congress, Manuscript Division.

30. Aurelia R. Downey, *A Tale of Three Women: God's Call and Their Response*, (Baltimore, Md.: Brentwood Publishers, 1993), 32–33.

31. (A Celebrated Speech by a Celebrated Woman), "Unload the Leeches and Parasitic 'Toms' and Take Promised Land. . . ." Nannie Helen Burroughs Papers, Library of Congress, Box 46, n.d.

32. Downey, *Three Women*, 32.

33. Nannie H. Burroughs, "The Negro Home," *Outlook* 144 (September 1926): 84.

34. Nannie H. Burroughs, "How Does It Feel to Be A Negro?" *Black Dispatch*, 16 July 1938.

35. Nannie H. Burroughs, "Nannie Burroughs Says Hound Dogs Are Kicked, But Not Bulldogs," *Afro-American*, 17 February 1934, NHB papers.

36. Nannie Helen Burroughs, "Legitimate Ambitions of the Negro," *Missionary Review of the World* 45 (1922): 454–56.

37. The petition also argued that the bill should be passed as "a war measure" and supported by both parties, a tactic aimed at linking the legislation to support for the war effort. It did not work. Southern senators filibustered the bill. It took the passage of a constitutional amendment (the 24th Amendment to the U.S. Constitution, ratified in 1963) to rid the country of the poll tax in federal elections, which was a primary and effective means of suppressing the black vote, http://law.onecle.com/constitution/042.html (27 May 2011).

38. Nannie H. Burroughs, "What the Negro Wants Politically" [essay 1928], NHB papers, Box 46, Library of Congress, Manuscript Division. Following the election, President Hoover appointed Burroughs to a committee on Negro housing, as noted in the introduction to the NHB papers and in numerous letters about her work with the National League of Republican Colored Women.

39. Nannie Helen Burroughs, "On the National Front," unpublished speech, NHB papers, box 46, LOC, n.d.

40. Burroughs, "On the National Front."

41. Nannie H. Burroughs, "The Negro Woman and Suffrage," *The West Virginia Woman's Voice*, 15 June 1923, NHB Papers, LOC, box 46.

42. Higginbotham, *Righteous Discontent*, 158.

43. Nannie Helen Burroughs to Mrs. Booker T. Washington, Mary Church Terrell Papers, Box 102–12, Folder 239, Moorland-Spingarn Research Center, Howard University.

44. Report to the Trustees of the National Trade and Profession School, 25 September 1941, NHB Papers, box 309, LOC, Manuscript Division.

45. Nannie Helen Burroughs to "My Dear Friends," 21 December 1933, NHB Papers, box 309, LOC, Manuscript Division.

46. Nannie Helen Burroughs, "Justice! The Integration Song," NHB Papers, LOC, Manuscript Division.

47. Edward D. Sargent, "Nannie Helen Burroughs School: Keeping a High Profile," *Washington Post* (23 July 1981).

# SEVEN

## "The Masses and the Classes"

### Women's Friendships and Support Networks among School Founders

*"It is certainly good of you to offer to raise that money for a laundry, but Mrs. Bright, my whole mind is set on a new building, and if you are going to help us, do—for heaven's sake—help me raise the $15,000 to put up the kind of school building we need."* [1]

—Charlotte Hawkins Brown

Feminist historians have debated the value of women's separate sphere and social networks as either conferring an inferior status upon women by cutting them off from male-dominated power centers or, rather, providing them with the status and mobility needed to effect social change. [2] For black women school founders, it was not an either or proposition. It required a multiplicity of skills and political dexterity to maintain private schools for black students during one of the most tumultuous periods in American history—the late 1800s through the early decades of the twentieth century. It was necessary not only to navigate the undercurrents of the existing racist and sexist order, but also to find financial support and other resources in times of economic retrenchment and uncertainty. For Lucy Craft Laney, Mary McLeod Bethune, Charlotte Hawkins Brown, and Nannie Helen Burroughs, those skills were evident in their efforts to manage sometimes conflicting interests among donors and supporters while executing their own vision for maintaining and growing their schools. That meant hiring the right staff, selecting the best board of trustees, and generally doing more with less. Their faith in themselves, belief that God would make a way, and the strong sense among

**Figure 7.1.   Women attending interacial conference at Tuskegee Institute. Left to right: Fannie C. Williams, H. A. Hunt, C. Hawkins Brown, Mary McLeod Bethune, R. R. Moton, Nannie Burroughs, and H. L. McCrorey. Photo courtesy of the Southern Historical Collection, Wilson Library, University of North Carolina at Chapel Hill.**

them of a special bond of friendship and understanding of what each other was experiencing, anchored them. Collectively, they faced daunting odds. They had to make bricks from straw—build on a garbage dump, use charcoal for a writing instrument, rebuild after a fire, sell pies, and launch dollar and dime fundraising drives—just to survive.

In their long years at the helm of the schools discussed in these chapters, the founders depended upon several different funding sources, including the American Missionary Association, other church-related organizations, small amounts from community groups, and fleeting support from large foundations such as the Slater Fund, the Phelps-Stokes Fund, and the Rosenwald Fund.[3] With their fledgling schools always in need of cash and other types of assistance, every source of support was vital, even the small checks that the three younger women sent to each other. There was no gender distinction in soliciting or accepting contributions. In fact, each of them solicited prominent and influential men for their trustee boards—some from industry, others from the ministry and the professions, who along with women board members, provided valued service and support over the life of their institutions. Notably, James Gamble, chairman of Proctor and Gamble, was an early and steady supporter of Bethune. He served as chair of the interracial board of trustees of the Daytona Normal and Industrial School for Negro Girls. Charles W. Eliot, former president of Harvard, was one of several high profile white advisers Charlotte Hawkins Brown cultivated for Palmer Memorial Institute's board of trustees. The chair of the board was Galen L. Stone, a Massachusetts financier and philanthropist, who was PMI's largest donor. Nannie Helen Burroughs' National Training and Professional School for Negro Girls and Women had an oversight relationship with the National Baptist Convention, and her board of trustees reflected that organization's black male leadership. However, it was the Women's Auxiliary of the Baptist Convention, in whose name the school was launched, that could be counted upon for fundraising. Lucy Craft Laney sought out prominent black men in Augusta to join her Haines Institute board of trustees, in addition to women members.

The founders knew that because of their greater financial clout and involvement in public affairs, prominent men on their boards would provide access to important contacts and needed business expertise for their schools. It did not mean that in the life of these schools founded by black women, women would take a back seat. Indeed, women were a critical source of the early help that enabled the schools to stabilize and grow. Harnessing this core base of female support across the spectrum of race and class was, perhaps, the founders' most remarkable skill. Memorably, Francina Haines, a white Presbyterian woman, provided pioneering school founder Lucy Laney with initial financial support after the male hierarchy of that church turned her down (chapter 3). Nannie Burroughs established a legacy of black female leadership at her school that survives today. However, this chapter focuses on the networks of two of the founders, Charlotte Hawkins Brown and Mary McLeod Bethune. This is primarily because their lifelong friendship produced years of correspondence between them that sheds light upon the range and diversity of their networks and their relationship. The friends could sometimes be competitive with each other. Their letters also offer a glimpse into the interpersonal aspects of their guarded lives and show the political and cultural landscape in which they struggled to build and maintain their schools. Although the founders had different philosophical ideas about education, their shared purpose was to uplift the race by providing black youth with access to quality education. The networks of women that these charismatic founders developed were major contributors to the success they achieved.

## CHARLOTTE HAWKINS BROWN'S NETWORK

In 1901, at the age of eighteen, Charlotte Hawkins Brown returned to her home state of North Carolina at the behest of the American Missionary Association (AMA) to open a school in rural Guilford County. Her family's move from Henderson, North Carolina, to Cambridge, Massachusetts, when she was a child, had afforded her the greater opportunities for education that her mother believed would instill pride and confidence in her daughter. Brown attended Cambridge English High School, and through the intervention of the Wellesley College president, Alice Palmer, she also attended Salem State Teachers College. Palmer had been duly impressed after coming upon high school student Lottie (her given name) Hawkins in the park reading Virgil while working as a babysitter and pushing a baby carriage. Palmer became the first of her white women supporters, spreading the word about the enterprising young woman to many of her friends.[4]

Brown's initial goals at the AMA-sponsored Bethany School were aligned with the growing popularity of industrial education. The charter stated her intention to train black youth "in the skills of the artisan . . . [and to help them] contribute to the best citizenship of their communities."[5] The next year the AMA, citing dwindling resources, did not renew its support. The black community, determined to have a school for their children, implored Brown to stay and banded together to support the school by rotating the boarding of the teachers. In describing her first year of teaching in the little white church that served as both a church and school, Brown called it "a forlorn, forsaken place [but] the fifty or sixty boys and girls, barefoot, unkempt, heartened me with their bright questioning eyes . . . and [I] lost my very soul in trying to help them."[6] She did so by staying put in rural North Carolina, opening a new school in Sedalia, and writing letters to Northern friends seeking their support. Following Alice Palmer's death in 1902, the new school—with permission from George Herbert Palmer—was named in his wife's honor. The network of donors that had begun with Alice Palmer became a mainstay of support for Palmer Memorial Institute. Authors Charles W. Wadelington and Richard F. Knapp wrote a well-documented history of the school and its evolution from a rural educational outpost for poor blacks to the private college preparatory school that became a beacon for the children of some of America's wealthiest black families. When she began teaching, Brown considered herself to be following in the footsteps of Lucy Craft Laney, whose school she first learned about as a student in Massachusetts in 1897. There is no known surviving correspondence between the two women. However, according to Brown, after hearing about Laney's example, she determined to dedicate her own life to the calling of race uplift through education. Brown, like Laney, received initial support from white women, including the two women for whom the schools were named. Several buildings on both campuses are named for women donors. However, there were major differences between the two educators. The spinster, Lucy Laney, devoted her life to building and sustaining Haines Institute. With similar commitment to her school, Brown's two marriages, first to Harvard-educated Edward Brown and then to the dashing, much younger John Moses, were fleeting distractions.[7] While Laney's personal style was infused with the grassroots simplicity of her

Georgia roots, Brown's style and manner evoked her New England up-bringing and elite aspirations. Having left North Carolina at age four, she acquired the culture and the manners of the privileged white society of New England, including the accent and aesthetic tastes. Former PMI student Leslie Lacey wrote that Mrs. Brown's accent sounded more New England than those of the people he met in Boston.[8] Brown continued her close association with the area and attended Wellesley, the elite women's college, as a student and lecturer in 1927.[9] She moved steadily to transform PMI into an elite college preparatory boarding school for the children of the black middle class. Part of her self-reinvention included changing her name from "Lottie" to "Charlotte," which she felt sounded more in line with the names associated with Boston society.[10]

Facing the same great need and few resources that challenged other school founders, Brown again called upon her white "New England friends." Among the women donors were some of her close personal friends such as Carrie Stone, wife of Palmer Institute's largest donor, Galen L. Stone, as well as longtime supporters Daisy Bright, Helen Kimball, Frances Guthrie, and Mary R. Grinnell. These women gave Brown advice about running the school along with their financial support. Most of the advice tended to caution Brown against plans for expansion and development, or to limit what PMI taught black students. Frances Guthrie, for example, wrote to Brown suggesting that she should not try to teach her students beyond what their "natures are ready to receive," because they were not like her.[11] Whether Brown felt flattered or insulted by this soft racism, she certainly did not respond negatively. However, she did make a strong push for what she envisioned. An example is seen in her letter, quoted at the beginning of this chapter, to longtime supporter Daisy Bright of Washington, D.C. Brown stressed her idea for a proposed new building rather than the benefactor's proposal to help fund a new laundry. The letter shows the mixture of diplomacy, flattery, and directness that marked Brown's success as a fundraiser. It also illustrates another aspect of the black women founders' skills in growing their schools—the ability to maintain their vision for greater things in an environment that promoted less ambitious goals for their students and their schools. In a letter to Carrie Stone, Brown admits that she depended on others to "help me think." But she adds, "I don't want anybody to do all of my thinking for me." Brown seems to have taken some advice, but simply ignored the advice that she did not like, rather than contest it.

In addition to her New England friends, she was able to cultivate friendships among Southern white women also. They were often the wives of prominent men, such as Lula McIver, wife of Charles Duncan McIver,[12] president of the State Normal and Industrial School for Girls in Greensboro. Mrs. McIver was intrigued by Brown and became a supporter. Brown felt compelled to dedicate her book, *Mammy: An Appeal to the Heart of the South* (1919), to Mrs. McIver, viewing her as an exemplar of the kindness that some of the better class of white people showed to loyal servants like "Mammy." Some black leaders accused Brown of accommodating racial stereotypes with such a book. Yet in her outreach to white America, she made friends among Southern white women and was invited to speak at their clubs, presenting herself as an "interpreter" of black American aspirations. Brown's interpretation of Lucy Laney's exhortation to educated black women to bear the burden of race uplift by ministering to the educational and spiritual needs of "black babies," was her insistence that only educated women like herself could rightfully speak for black women. She told the white club members that black women "were not seeking social intermingling but social justice." Blacks, she said, wanted three things: education for their children, respect for their womanhood, and cooperation with white women—the ones who employed black working mothers to care for their children while their own children's needs were left unmet. [13]

Undoubtedly, the strongest financial support that PMI received was from white Northerners, male and female. Still, Brown's close relationship to Northern white women was matched by her very active involvement with black women groups, especially clubwomen. They provided her with spiritual, moral, and some financial support and were united with her in their mutual efforts to improve the status and image of black women. Brown's particular investment in that cause was reflected in the way she ran her school. Girls at PMI had stricter rules than boys. According to Alice Hurley, a 1952 graduate who met her future husband, Anthony Hurley, at PMI, girls were not allowed to leave the campus, but boys were. [14] By all indications, Brown really cared about her students, but she was strict and especially watchful and protective of female students. As Alice Hurley recalled, Brown would monitor the dance floor and warn dancing couples to "show some daylight between you." [15]

Brown's extensive work in the black women's club movement widened her circle of black female friends. Among the prominent black women whom she called upon as a "personal friend" to help her raise $1,000 for a special fund for her school was bank president and clubwoman Maggie Lena Walker, who was the first black woman to hold the position of bank president. Walker sent Brown a check for $10, but promised to send more later. [16] In a follow-up letter, the savvy businesswoman asked Brown to recommend "a good, strong, hustling woman who isn't afraid to travel, talk, and work . . . and [she would] make the [terms] to suit her." [17]

Brown's network of black women included hair care magnate Madame C. J. Walker, with whom she had an active correspondence. Madame Walker wrote her in 1916, offering to visit and give a lecture to help Brown raise money during her trip to the South. In turn, Walker asked Brown to "work up" prospects who would join her company as sales agents. Following a fire on campus that destroyed several buildings, Madame Walker wrote a compassionate letter and enclosed a check for $25, while explaining that her obligations to her expansion projects prevented her from sending more.[18] Margaret Murray Washington, widow of Booker T. Washington, and Mary B. Talbert, president of the National Association of Colored Women, were also part of Brown's black women's network. Margaret Murray Washington was an ally in several women's organizations. She understood the responsibilities of maintaining a school, because of what she experienced at Tuskegee Institute following her husband's death in 1915. The women traded gossipy "secrets" in their letters as well as "school talk." Washington wrote Brown in November of 1918 expressing her hope that an old building on the Tuskegee campus could be restored "for future generations of young colored women," but she also commented on the ostentatious house of an unnamed black woman, writing "some people are all for show."[19] Another friend, the NACW's Mary Talbert, wrote Brown after a pleasurable visit to PMI, praising the school as "the full realization of [Brown's] dream."[20]

Brown turned to lifelong black women friends for advice and support, although her authoritarian temperament no doubt was too much for some. Ola Glover was not one of the faint-hearted. The Hampton graduate and PMI nurse was a match for Brown's strong personality. She helped Brown through several illnesses and was her close friend and confidante. Brown was devastated when Glover unexpectedly died. Another close associate and trusted friend was Wilhelmina Crosson, a talented Boston native and protégé of Brown who became her successor when she retired in 1952. The younger woman, a specialist in remedial education, revered Brown and attempted to follow her wishes in maintaining the school after Brown's death in 1961.[21]

As PMI gained prominence, Brown became known as a stickler for "the social graces," and advertised her school among the growing black middle and upper classes. To distinguish PMI as a private, college preparatory boarding school, Brown developed what she called "the Palmer triangle of achievement," which emphasized religion, culture, and educational excellence. Christian principles were important teaching tools for Brown and instilled into everyday campus life. By culture, Brown meant "ease, grace, and poise" that would make blacks social equals to all others. In her view, the combination of culture and religion produced "a refined person [who] is the masterpiece of God."[22] Educational excellence meant that her students were on par with students of any other race. However, in the interview with PMI graduates profiled in chapter 5, some students thought that culture received more emphasis than educational excellence. While Brown advocated education for all black children, her dedication to creating a gentry class of racial representatives distinguished her views from the more egalitarian concepts that school founders Laney, Bethune, and Burroughs espoused.

Black people generally applauded Brown's accomplishments in education and recognized her with honorary degrees from their colleges. She was a popular guest speaker at black middle class organizations and church functions. Her students and some teachers were mostly in awe of her. Leslie Lacey, a student at PMI in the 1950s, described Brown as "very distinguished. From head to shoes she was dressed in perfect taste; even the carnation on her well-tailored white suit was still slightly dripping with dew. She was short in stature, but from behind the podium she looked large and impressive."[23] Others, including scholar and activist W. E. B. Du Bois, questioned her racial tactics. Brown's declarations about becoming acceptable through an emphasis on manners led Du Bois to speak out and call her a naïve representative of the "white South."[24] To Brown, however, being acceptable to the "better class" of whites did not mean blind imitation of them. By her standards of proper social decorum, Brown considered white culture to be in decline. Furthermore, Brown's exacting manner and dominant personality probably undermined her ambition for national leadership among blacks. This fact may have contributed to the tensions in her friendship with the more conciliatory Bethune, who was considered by some as black America's first lady.

The criticism of Brown in parts of the black community may have been due to her exacting standards, but with her impeccable dress and flawless speech, she projected an aura that was admired. Despite her questionable tactics for race advancement, she remained an unquestioned authority on manners and morals for the up-and-coming black middle class. In addition to her book, *Mammy,* mentioned earlier, in which she painted a nostalgic picture of plantation life and "Mammy" as a trustworthy figure who created a lasting bond between the races, Brown also wrote a second book. *The Correct Thing to Do, to Say, to Wear (1941),* a widely circulated treatise on etiquette and required reading at PMI, was based in part on her frequent chapel talks to her students. The book expounded upon her view that black slaves provided the foundation of southern culture because they were entrusted with teaching the social graces to their white owners.[25] Among the social dictates that Brown championed was that a young lady must be "considerate, not overbearing or dictatorial, she must give the young man plenty of room to be gracious and chivalrous."[26] The doyenne of the social graces was a sought-after speaker and frequently quoted in the black press, especially after Howard University awarded her an honorary degree in 1944. In her well-attended public lectures, she warned black women not to follow the "vices" of white women.[27] Since her mission was to show black women as virtuous and equal, she exhorted them to disavow drinking, smoking, and being "modern" if they wished to fulfill their destiny to lead the race "into a fuller and freer atmosphere."[28]

Like Laney and Bethune, Brown used her prominence as a founding school principal to promote a wider agenda for the race as a whole, especially black women. One of her particular projects, as shown in her speeches and writings, was to launch a "Crusade for Character." She challenged black women to "first seek to stabilize the moral and cultural values of Negro womanhood so that society will be a fit place for your children."[29] Acceptability, she believed, was necessary simply to communicate with whites, not to imitate them. But she also defended the honor of thousands of upstanding black women against the malicious insults they received from white men. She said, "[T]hese women would bow to the lust of no man. They live their lives beyond reproach; their hands and their hearts are clean and they are equal in intelligence and character to women of any race."[30]

In her role as an intermediary between the races, Brown's network of women included the members of the Council on Interracial Cooperation, an organization that she founded to enlist prominent black and white Southerners in an effort to foster racial understanding. Yet studied civility and manners did not keep Brown from becoming increasingly outraged by the tactics used to suppress blacks. While on a train trip to an interracial women's meeting, she was denied a sleeping car because white people on the train objected to having a black woman in their midst. Brown was forcefully removed to the "Jim Crow" section.[31] When she arrived at the meeting, she blasted the hypocrisy of white clubwomen who talk about interracial cooperation but who remain silent as black women are continually victimized by white men. At such public forums she stressed the similarities between black and white women and told her audiences that the black woman "wants everything—education, power, influence—in fact everything that the white woman wants, except her white husband!"[32]

Having not experienced overt racism growing up in Massachusetts, she met her share of it as a black woman speaking out and fundraising in the public sphere, not only in the South, but in the North as well. Brown wrote about what a northern white woman told her when she objected to the woman's children calling her by her first name: "No matter what you or any other Negro may accomplish . . . you can never hope to be the equals of my children, and they shall not address you as 'miss.'"[33] Another incident occurred in New York City's Roosevelt Hotel when the elevator operator refused to take her to the eleventh floor, where her meeting was taking place. He directed the always well-dressed and proper Brown to the rear service elevator. She missed the meeting while trying to get to the eleventh floor by way of the rear elevator and the back stairs. Brown dealt with such indignities by appearing to rise above them. Her memorable response to such incidents was to declare: "I sit in a Jim Crow car, but my mind keeps company with the kings and queens I have known."[34]

A major fire, dwindling enrollment, and the effects of the black consciousness movement precipitated the closing of PMI in 1971. It was by then one of the longest surviving black, privately run, pre-collegiate (it was also a junior college) institutions. Although PMI came to be associated with black elitism and was featured in a 1947 issue of *Ebony* magazine as a "Finishing School," it was clearly more than that. Brown's emphasis on cultural and social equality with whites, in retrospect, can be viewed as an effort to subvert the entrenched narrative of black inferiority so prevalent in early twentieth-century America. Through her network of supporters, she mounted a public platform to promote interracialism, interdependence, and to promote a positive image of black women, while simultaneously attacking racism and sexism. In effectively using her women's networks along with other important funding sources, Brown achieved her primary goal, and that was to produce educated black youth whose contributions to society as teachers, lawyers, doctors, and business people, showed what *they* were capable of achieving.

## MARY MCLEOD BETHUNE'S NETWORK

Female supporters and networks were as central to Mary McLeod Bethune's development and success as a school founder as they were for her good friend Charlotte Hawkins Brown. That support began in her home community of Mayesville, South Carolina, where she was born in the final days of Reconstruction in 1875. Her mother, Patsy McLeod, a former slave, and Emma J. Wilson, her first teacher, were early influences. Bethune recalled that her mother, whom she said was a descendant of African royalty, had "a great philosophy of life. She could not be discouraged."[35] In Bethune's adult life, a sense of indomitability and optimism like her mother's became her own trademark. Emma Wilson, a graduate of Scotia Seminary for Colored Girls in North Carolina, helped young Mary obtain a scholarship to her alma mater offered by a white Quaker woman, Mary Crissman. Wilson was the first black woman that Bethune could remember who was addressed as "Miss" among all elements of the race-divided southern hamlet of Mayesville.[36] A student at Scotia from 1887 thru 1894, Bethune came of age there in its strict but nurturing female-centered community. Founded in 1867 by Presbyterian Church administrator Luke Dorland, the school employed a staff composed mostly of black and white women who taught a mainly domestic arts curriculum. The black teachers, some of them Scotia alumni, made a particularly strong impression on Mary. "My contact with the fine young Negro teachers—Hattie Bomar, Rebecca Cantey, and others gave me confidence in the ability of Negro women to be cultured, and the incentive that made me feel that if they could do it, I could, too."[37] Bethune's next strong female mentor was Lucy Craft Laney of Haines Normal and Industrial Institute, who also inspired Charlotte Hawkins Brown, Nannie Burroughs, and so many other women educators of the period. Bethune said Laney fired her with the ambition for service. As a teaching apprentice at Haines in 1898, Bethune said, "I studied her, watched her every move and gave myself full to the cause she represented."[38] When she founded the Daytona Normal and Industrial School for Colored Girls in 1904, she instituted many of Laney's practices and ideas, including outreach to the surrounding black community, teaching skills to create "better homes," and operating a farm and a hospital, while teaching a mix of industrial and academic courses to the girls. In an open fundraising letter published in the *New York Times*, Bethune wrote "that the greatest hope for the development of my race lies in the training of our women thoroughly and practically."[39] At the age of twenty-nine she opened the school and began to attract a resourceful and talented cadre of women teaching colleagues, supporters, and benefactors with whom she forged lifelong friendships.

A particularly interesting group of early supporters was the "fine club of white women" [who] formed the philanthropic Palmetto Club of Daytona. This women's club produced the nucleus of the school's board of supervisors, which was charged with conducting fundraisers and school improvement events. In a 1907 school bulletin, the board of supervisors was listed as "a special committee of the philanthropic department of the Palmetto Club."[40] Bethune installed the all-female board of supervisors, which was primarily a service and fundraising group. However, with the exception of herself, the board of trustees, charged with major fundraising and business affairs, remained all male. The trustees at first consisted of local businessmen, the city's mayor, a minister, James Gamble, and Bethune's then-husband, Albertus Bethune.[41] Dora E. Maley, a member of the Palmetto Club recalled that she met Bethune when the young woman first arrived in Daytona. She was so impressed with Bethune's vision for her school that she "collected a few odd pieces of furniture including a wide double bed in which the five little girls that made up her first class of students, slept crosswise."[42] Comparable to Alice Palmer's support for Charlotte Hawkins Brown, Dora Maley's friendship had a multiplier effect. Many of the wealthy clubwomen she introduced Bethune to also became supporters of the school.

As her school continued to take shape and grow, Bethune added two additional women to the faculty—Willie C. Byrd and Mattie M. West—in the second year. "I need strong women to help me realize this vision," she declared.[43] She sought to hire experienced women teachers such as star recruit Frances Reynolds Keyser, an honor graduate of Hunter College who left her secure job as supervisor of the White Rose Mission for delinquent girls in New York City to join Bethune at the fledgling school in 1909. Keyser took charge of the entire curriculum, freeing Bethune for administrative and fundraising duties.

Under Keyser's stewardship, the school earned state accreditation and a grade "B" academic reputation. In 1920, Bethune also hired Portia Smiley, a graduate of Hampton Institute and Pratt Institute in New York, to supervise the domestic science [arts] program. Smiley, who also was a practical nurse, was described as "an artist" in domestic arts and crafts. Frances Kyles, another experienced teacher, also joined the faculty that year. As the school continued to grow, Bethune hired more women teachers and assistants so she could diminish her teaching role in favor of fundraising, which increasingly involved more travel. Elizabeth R. Ody became the school's first business manager in 1907 and retained the title of personal secretary to Bethune. She was the predecessor to the long-serving Bertha Loving Mitchell, who in the 1930s and 1940s filled various management roles at the school that was eventually renamed and expanded to become Bethune-Cookman College.[44]

Bethune's appeal in the black community was enhanced by the enthusiasm of her female network, but it was never exclusive to one gender. Yet in her cultivation of helpful friends, aside from her major benefactors, she leaned heavily upon a broad constituency of women. For example, in a 1907 copy of the school's newsletter, *Industrial Advocate*, a list of visitors and contributors shows mostly women. If visits reflect interest in the school, women seemed most interested. The donations as listed in the newsletter included cash, furniture, dinnerware, and clothes. Some of the big names that Bethune attracted to her school in the early days were Chicago social reformer Jane Addams and Sarah Lawrence, who organized a "Sarah Lawrence Dollar Drive" for the school. Lawrence became an active supporter of Bethune after she and her philanthropist husband, William Van Duzer Lawrence who later founded Sarah Lawrence College in his late wife's honor, bought a vacation home in Daytona Beach. Sarah Lawrence agreed to contribute one dollar for every dollar that the school could raise from any person in the United States. "The dollar drive has helped us when we needed help most," wrote Bethune in the *Advocate*. Lawrence's daughter, Louise L. Meigs, remained a benefactor and deeply interested Bethune correspondent through the school's transformation into collegiate status in the early 1920s.[45]

Although black women were also staunch supporters, segments of both the black and white communities attacked the school, but for different reasons. Some blacks accused Bethune of "making servants of our children," and some whites charged that she was causing black children to "aim too high."[46] Being attacked from both sides, Bethune expressed appreciation for the steadfast help she received from many local black women:

> Many kind women stood by me faithfully through those early trying days, sharing their food and their clothes with me and helping me to bake cakes, potato pies, and to fry fish and chicken, by which we earned money to pay the first installment on the place which is now known as the Bethune-Cookman College. Dear good-hearted souls! Many a night they have helped wash and iron a shirtwaist and press a

skirt to wear the next day. Many a time they have helped me to cut and paste board soles to put in my worn shoes to keep my feet off the ground.[47]

Bethune received similar support among black women throughout the nation. A 1924 headline in the *Pittsburgh Courier*, a nationally circulated black newspaper, read: "Local Women Urge Cause of Mrs. Bethune." The article reported that the women, led by Mrs. Daisy Lampkins, formed a Daytona Club to work on behalf of the school.[48] The article reported that Bethune exhorted them: "We need your help! Women in Pittsburgh can do it. I believe in you. I know you will put the job over." The women applauded their approval, the article stated.[49] This same spirit permeated other Bethune gatherings and clubs called "Bethune Circles," similar in intent to the Laney Leagues formed to support Lucy Laney's Haines Institute, as discussed in chapter 3. They were founded in the 1930s by black women as a more formal outgrowth of communal efforts to help the school. The circles held regular meetings and drafted a constitution and by-laws. Their stated purpose was to "apply the model of Mary McLeod Bethune to the uplift of humanity and the fostering of her school,[50] and, of course, to hold fundraising events. The first Bethune Circle was organized by Ada Lee of Jacksonville. Bethune wrote Lee in 1932 expressing her appreciation:

> I want you to know how grateful we are for your efforts in behalf of Bethune-Cookman College. No other Negro woman in Florida has been more diligent in her interest. You have given of yourself in order that our work may go forward. I am grateful for your friendship and the interest you have manifested in my personal welfare. I don't have time to give . . . appreciative affection to my friends but I am sure they know that I have sincere regard for them.[51]

Showing her appeal across class lines, and the importance of reaching all black women, Bethune developed a strong relationship with Marjorie Joiner and the National Beauticians' Organization she led. She spoke at their conventions; they held meetings on the campus, and made substantial financial contributions to the college. This network of enterprising, business-minded women extended into eastern cities and into the Midwest. In the South, the Southern Federation of Colored Women's Clubs was another base of support for Bethune. Calling for "united action," she organized a meeting of regional club officers in Daytona and, unsurprisingly, was elected president of the new organization in 1920. Charlotte Hawkins Brown, also in attendance, was elected chair of the executive board. At the close of the meeting, the delegates gave "unstinting praise" to Bethune and her school and presented the grateful president with a check for $70.[52]

Another example of her broad-based support among women was illustrated in a letter from Eva R. Jackson of Detroit. It is written on her company's letterhead, "Eva's Housewife Bluing Soap Powder."[53] The company's motto is also inscribed: "Our soap dissolves instantly in hot or cold water. Saves times and hands." Enclosed in the letter is a $1 donation. Ms. Jackson concluded by advising Bethune to "take your proper rest and save your strength."[54]

Never losing touch with her base of ordinary black women, Bethune cultivated relationships with several influential and powerful women as well. None was more influential and helpful than First Lady Eleanor Roosevelt. Mrs. Roosevelt reportedly encouraged her husband, Franklin Delano Roosevelt, in his outreach to the black community. Bethune became a frequent visitor to the White House and was President Roosevelt's special adviser on minority affairs while also serving a sub-cabinet position as director of the Division of Negro Affairs of the National Youth Administration in the 1930s. A humorous story in the rich oral tradition surrounding Bethune emerged from one of her frequent visits to the White House during a time when the black people who entered were usually there as servants. One day a White House guard became too familiar with the dignified, pearl-wearing Mrs. Bethune and greeted her by calling out, "Hey, Auntie!" Bethune stopped in her tracks, turned slowly around to face the white man at the gate, and looked at him quizzically as though trying to remember him, then she calmly asked: "Now tell me, which one of my sisters' children are you?" Bethune sauntered into the White House, leaving the guard speechless.

Eleanor Roosevelt returned the favor of visiting by famously staying overnight at her friend's home on the Bethune-Cookman campus in the early 1950s—openly defying the city's segregationist policies (see chapter 4). A 1942 letter to Mrs. Roosevelt shows how Bethune negotiated such celebrity access and favorability among white women to her advantage. The subject of the letter was Bethune's brief hospital stay, during which she received lots of attention from friends, including author and Nobel laureate Pearl Buck, who sent roses. After thanking Mrs. Roosevelt "and our beloved president" for all you have done for "us all," she told the first lady not to worry about her hospital stay: "Now, don't you send roses [like Pearl Buck], but do come yourself on December 15 [to the Board of Trustees meeting]. I need you."[55]

"I need you," was a recurring refrain in Bethune's vocabulary of appeals. She used it often with women supporters, creating a sense of sisterhood while making the recipient of the plea feel that it would be a personal blow to Bethune if she did not respond. Bethune counted other high profile women—black and white—in her network of friends and benefactors. Among her other high profile backers were Madame C. J. Walker, the wealthy hair care manufacturer, and Maggie Lena Walker, the banker, both of whom were known for their support of black institutions and other black women.

## NANNIE BURROUGHS AND OTHERS

An important layer of the extensive Bethune network was her personal friendships with other black clubwomen, educators, and school founders. Two of her most sustained friendships were with like-minded contemporaries Nannie Helen Burroughs, who presided over the National Training School for Negro Girls in Washington, D.C. (renamed the National Trade and Professional School for Negro Women and Girls), and, of course, Charlotte Hawkins Brown. The three women—Brown, Bethune, and Burroughs—were nicknamed the "three B's of education."[56] Their schools and the many challenges they faced while trying to maintain them created a strong bond among them, but they were also connected through women's club work and the mandate of race uplift—the notion that the more fortunate and educated of the race had a duty to uplift the others. In personality, Nannie Burroughs was as blunt and direct as Mary Bethune was conciliatory and diplomatic. Burroughs often was at odds with the patriarchal leadership of the Baptist Convention under which the Women's Auxiliary that she led and that had founded her school was managed. She railed against some of their decisions and against black leaders she considered weak or cowardly, calling them "parasitic leeches and Uncle Toms who must be gotten rid of—the sooner the better."[57] However, like Bethune, the scripture-quoting Burroughs had a missionary zeal for serving the most vulnerable and downtrodden of the race, a category in which she placed black women. They had different temperaments, but Bethune and Burroughs shared a belief in practical education and an orientation toward helping less privileged blacks, and both geared their curriculums toward preparing women for the work world. In the early 1920s, Bethune and Burroughs also shared the officers' podium as president and vice president, respectively, of the National Association of Wage Earners. It was a short-lived labor organization dedicated to organizing the "migrant class of workers for better working conditions." Their goal was to raise the qualifications and pay in order to be treated like professionals.[58] In a 1934 letter to Bethune, Burroughs wrote, "God bless you; you are doing a big job, but my reaction to the whole thing is that you are working too hard."[59] Bethune wrote Burroughs in 1940 after learning that she was ill and said, "I am writing speedily to let you know how sorry I am to know this and how sincerely I hope that you will be yourself again soon. Understand that you are in His keeping."[60] During their years of correspondence, they often put small checks or pledges in the envelope to support each other. Their main topic, however, was their shared goals for their schools and the mutual respect and Christian love they expressed toward each other.

## COMPLEX FRIENDSHIPS

Brown's relationship with Bethune is better documented. Their long friendship—its high and low points—is disclosed through their correspondence, which began in the 1920s during their membership in the Southeastern Federation of the National Association of Colored Women's Clubs and through their joint tenure as president and vice president of National Association of Colored Women. It lasted until Bethune's death in 1955. As their letters show, Brown and Bethune had a complex friendship characterized by mutual love and respect, and empathy for each other's challenges in maintaining their schools—as well as fits of jealousy and competiveness. Alice Hurley, who was at PMI in the early 1950s, says the relationship was "extremely competitive." Brown would often mention Bethune in her chapel talks, noting that she was contributing in the same way as the more publicized Bethune.[61]

In a 1941 letter, Bethune acknowledged a check from Brown supporting one of her early fundraisers. It was one of the steady stream of small checks, usually $5 or $10, between them. Throughout their friendship they traded visits to each other's homes and gave speeches at each other's school. The tone of their written interchanges suggests that Bethune considered Brown to be the ultimate arbiter of culture, a role in which Brown exulted. Bethune was, no doubt, pleased to receive Brown's letter giving a positive review of her visit to Bethune-Cookman, as the keynote speaker for graduation. Brown, thanking Bethune for her hospitality, wrote, "The recent commencement service" was a "beautiful and highly cultural affair."[62] The two women shared donor lists and prayers, sent gifts to each other, and often chided one another about working too hard, a critique that both women ignored. There were also instances of frank advice, as in Brown's 1946 letter endorsing the intent of Bethune's million-dollar fundraising campaign, but warning Bethune of the difficulty of raising so much money: "Listen, Darling, go slow—you are no longer young. To raise a million dollars is a Herculean task, but if Bethune-Cookman is to live after you, you must do it!"[63] Bethune wrote Brown thanking her for her honest assessment, and ends the letter by telling Brown to "take care of your sore gum. Be lazy a little while and you will be all right."[64] When Bethune wrote Brown relaying her thoughts about taking over the management of the Hungerford School in Eatonville, Florida, in order to keep it under black control,[65] Brown wrote back saying, in essence, "Are you crazy?" But she said it very diplomatically, with these prescient words:

> I would like to do everything that you ask me to do, but I definitely feel that the day of the private high school is practically gone, and I believe you will be adding to the burden of the school if you attach this institution to it. I may be wrong, but it seems to me you have "found" enough

things, and I don't think your present state of health ought to warrant you trying to do anything else. If you insist, however, I will do anything that you want done.[66]

Bethune wrote back a week later, saying, "I think you are absolutely right!"[67]

Their letters impart their sense of themselves as doing important, historic work that they felt would be their legacy. Bethune wrote to Brown in 1951, "God has been marvelously good to us. When I think of you, Nannie Burroughs, Jane Hunter,[68] and myself—four women within a similar range of years, who have tried to inspire and help younger women—I feel a sense of deep gratitude for the opportunities that have been ours."[69] The most striking aspect of the letters is the compassion and empathy they expressed for each other. Bethune wrote to Brown, "I wish that Palmer was twice as large as it is. I know you are terribly crowded. It is grand to make a work so efficient and so demanding that you have to turn them away by the hundreds. . . . I want to see you very much and talk over school matters with you." In another letter, she included this: "I pray for you daily as I pray for myself. Your task has been hard and serious just as mine has."[70] However, this spirit of camaraderie was sometimes strained by either jealousy or misunderstanding, or both. In her letter, Bethune mentioned a newspaper interview in which Brown allegedly made sniping remarks about her by first praising Brown's long years of service and toil, and the selection of the "fine New England [women] who will succeed you." Then in classic Bethune style, she aims for the high ground with practiced humility and verve with this response:

> I wondered deep in my heart, what provoked any necessity for such remarks from a fine, well-rounded, balanced person such as you are. You have had full opportunity to reach heights toward which you aspired. What I have been able to accomplish, Charlotte, has been accomplished with great humility and very real desire for service. Your emphasis on my relationship to Franklin D. Roosevelt and the ironical statement about my being "first lady of the land," . . . seemed unnecessary to me. Surely, you know that I had not fantastical ideal of power in this association. I regret that you feel that the Southern women did not receive you because of your Northern training, while they accepted me and boosted me to the top; that you represent the classes, while I represent the masses. Thank God I do represent the masses. . . . My record speaks for itself, dear friend. There has never been a time and—never will—when I will say to the world that Charlotte Hawkins Brown, Jane Hunter or Nannie Burroughs or any woman struggling to make the world better, is making less of the contribution to which she is credited. What we have done and are doing is too greatly needed for there to be any insinuations on our service.[71]

Brown's prompt reply was a tartly worded telegram denying the charge, but it seems to reveal a long-held envy of Bethune's prominence:

> Am not guilty of no [sic] such statement. Your good common sense should have taught you better. I don't have your money but certainly have enough to have paid my carfare to ask you personally rather than send [an] unkind letter. I owe you nothing but I know I helped push you to the front [when] the people wanted me. You deserve it and I glory in it. I do not need politics to make me great. . . . Sorry that you count friendship of such little worth.[72]

This rift between the friends was apparently a brief one. Two months later, Brown concluded a letter to Bethune with these words: "Remember, I love you although I may not always agree with you. You are a fine example of the success of your thinking."[73] Bethune, the featured speaker at PMI's fiftieth anniversary program in 1952, promptly returned the honorarium, telling Brown to "please use this sum for yourself or whatever you desire. God bless you and the school."[74] Another example of the support that Bethune gave Brown and PMI came when she served as assistant director of the National Youth Administration in the Roosevelt administration. The registrar's report at PMI noted the extra help that Bethune sent to PMI via grants. In addition to the "regular quota," the report notes that "through the influence of Dr. Mary McLeod Bethune, an additional five scholarships were given to the institution."[75]

The depth of their bond also showed when Brown stood by Bethune when she was labeled a "communist sympathizer" in 1952 and disinvited from a planned speech at an Englewood, New Jersey high school. The "red scare" led by Senator Joseph McCarthy caused many to disavow friendships with those snared by that charge. After Bethune was vindicated and delivered the speech in Englewood, she shared her feelings about this episode with her "pal": "When I arose to speak they applauded me for three minutes; when I finished, they arose and applauded for five minutes. That was a hard accusation . . . but one thing, my dear, that we can all be assured of, the open record of our lives will either stand the test or fail. God bless you, Charlotte. . . ."[76]

Three months before she died on June 18, 1955, all traces of animosity had vanished, and a summing up was taking place. In what is probably her last letter to Charlotte Hawkins Brown, Bethune begins, "My old pal, I miss you so much and our comradeship in the days that have passed. Our paths have crossed so frequently, but both of us are slowing down now very rapidly and we find ourselves [knowing] that our years are behind us rather than in front of us. God has been wonderfully good to both of us. He has honored our efforts. So my dear, take your strides now slowly, but [be happy in knowing] the joy of having given your best.[77]

Inspired by Lucy Laney, Mary Bethune, Charlotte Brown, and Nannie Burroughs developed friendships and networks that supported their purposeful work as school founders. Their communication skills and the ability to impart their vision to others made them warriors for the cause of education and for better race relations, especially among women. Their correspondence reveals personal relationships not evident in their public lives. Yet, showing what historian Darlene Clark Hine termed "dissemblance,"[78] the content of their letters mainly focused on the work that they felt bound them together in a distinct and exclusive sisterhood. The inner lives of the never-married Burroughs and the failed marriages of Bethune and Brown—two for Brown, and one for Bethune—are notably missing in their letters. Among the first educated women of their race, they were mindful and protective of their legacy and wanted to ensure the survival of their institutions. Challenging the image of black women's unworthiness, inclined them to keep their emotional lives away from public scrutiny and their public demeanor confident, but measured. Yet, we do come to know these women by the company they kept and by what they fought so hard to build and maintain. Their women's networks show how resourceful they were in gaining the support of different races and classes by projecting vision and moral certitude. In this way, their public lives became inspirational to "the masses" and "the classes."

Brown felt victimized by racism yet focused most of her activism on changing black people's behavior. She clung to the idea that blacks could earn social acceptance, although her own experience disproved it. Bethune expanded her parameters of involvement to government service, while Brown focused on her school, and becoming an authoritative voice of social graces and a self-described ambassador between the races. Brown's successful school, her eloquence, and deep convictions gained her celebrity status and respect among the black middle class and many whites. She used her network of friends and supporters so effectively that her school was able to survive without major grants for her fifty-year tenure and grow her school into a collegiate institution. Brown, although a tenacious fundraiser, was not able to secure her school's future. The most lasting result of her activism was Palmer Memorial Institute and its high-achieving students, who in an era of low expectations for blacks came to symbolize for Brown not only class-conscious race uplift but also vindication of her sex.

Bethune's diplomatic skills and ability to cross class and race lines easily won her many allies and friends. The loyalty of her female network enabled and empowered Bethune and created a bond of mutuality, trust, and purpose. Moreover, her outreach to women energized them—"I need you!" she told both celebrity women and ordinary black women. This was, indeed, true. She needed all the help she could muster. Despite her persuasiveness, organized philanthropy placed its bets on male leadership in education while turning down many requests from women. Burroughs' initial hope that black community support would make appeals to white benefactors unnecessary was not sustained, but black

Figure 7.2.    Mary McLeod Bethune, Eleanor Roosevelt, and other notable women active in interracial cooperation, circa 1950s. Photo courtesy of Florida Memory, State Archives of Florida.

women, especially the Women's Auxiliary of the Baptist Convention, remained her most dependable source of financial and moral support.

The networks they developed confirm the conclusion of historians that friendships among women institution builders of this period enhanced their private lives, specifically historian Nancy Cott's suggestion that these friendships were a prerequisite to the feminist movement.[79] These particular founders soared, not above their very strong personalities, but above the low expectations placed on black women of that era. Sandwiched between the culmination of the struggle for women's suffrage and the beginning of the Civil Rights Movement, friendship and support among women were vital to the survival of their schools. The founders embraced Laney's view that the education of children was their duty. Concurrently, their success was a sign of women's broader leadership in the public arena.

Their women's networks challenged notions of female docility and acceptance of the status quo. To white women supporters, Brown and Bethune offered the promise of racial cooperation and of doing work that muted (but did not overcome) historical patterns of racial distrust and bigotry. To black women supporters it provided a light that reflected their own possibilities as well as what might be possible in their children's lives. "I believe in God, and in Mary McLeod Bethune," Bethune often said. To all—close friends, supporters, and the founders themselves—each school was a gauge of values that moved the classes and masses towards a common and lofty purpose.

## NOTES

1. Charlotte Hawkins Brown to Daisy Bright, Charlotte Hawkins Brown Papers, reel #2-B, Schlesinger Library, Harvard University.

2. Estelle Freedman, "Separatism as Strategy: Female Institution Building and American Feminism, 1870–1930," *Feminist Studies* 5, no. 3 (Fall 1979): 512–29.

3. Charles W. Wadelington and Richard F. Knapp, *Charlotte Hawkins Brown: What One Young African-American Woman Could Do* (Chapel Hill: University of North Carolina Press, 1999), 157.

4. McCluskey, "We Specialize in the Wholly Impossible," *Signs*, vol. 22, no 2 (Winter, 1997): 403–26. For a fuller account of the relationship between Brown and the Palmer family, see Constance Marteena, "Twig Bender of Sedalia" and other unpublished autobiographical documents in the Charlotte Hawkins Brown Papers, reel 1; 1–177; Schlesinger Library, Radcliffe Institute for Advanced Study, Cambridge, Mass. (hereafter: Charlotte Hawkins Brown Papers).

5. Wadelington and Knapp, *Charlotte Hawkins Brown*, 105–106.

6. Charlotte Hawkins Brown, "The Life Story of Charlotte Hawkins Brown," unpublished manuscript, Charlotte Hawkins Brown Papers, Schlesinger Library

7. McCluskey, "We Specialize in the Impossible," 403–26.

8. Leslie Lacey, *The Rise and Fall of the Proper Negro* (New York: MacMillan, 1970), 49.

9. Wadelington and Knapp, *Charlotte Hawkins Brown*, 132.

10. Constance Marteena, *The Lengthening Shadow of a Woman: A Biography of Charlotte Hawkins Brown* (New York: Exposition Press, 1977); unpublished version in the Charlotte Hawkins Brown Papers, reel 1, 21.

11. Frances Guthrie to C. H. Brown, 1906, the Charlotte Hawkins Brown Papers.

12. C. H. Brown to Mrs. Stone, 7 April 1921, the Charlotte Hawkins Brown Papers.

13. Brown, "What the Negro Woman Asks."

14. Alice and Anthony Hurley, interviewed by Audrey T. McCluskey, 14 August 2011.

15. Hurley interview, 14 August 2011.

16. Maggie Lena Walker to C. H. Brown, 17 December 1916, the Charlotte Hawkins Brown Papers.

17. Maggie Lena Walker to C. H. Brown, 5 January 1917, the Charlotte Hawkins Brown Papers.

18. Madame C. J. Walker to C. H. Brown, 1916; Walker to Brown, 9 January 1918, the Charlotte Hawkins Brown Papers.

19. Margaret Murray Washington to Charlotte Hawkins Brown (18 November 1918).

20. Mary Talbert to C. H. Brown, 12 April 1917, Charlotte Hawkins Brown Papers.

21. Wadelington and Knapp, *Charlotte Hawkins Brown*, 98.

22. "Twig Bender of Sedalia," the Charlotte Hawkins Brown Papers, reel 1; 1–177.

23. Lacey, *Rise and Fall*, 48.

24. Tera Hunter, "The Correct Thing: Charlotte Hawkins Brown and the Palmer Institute," *Southern Exposure* (September/October 1983): 37–43.

25. Charlotte Hawkins Brown, "The Negro and the Social Graces," box 94, folder 51, Joel Spingarn Papers, Moorland-Spingarn Research Center, Howard University.

26. Charlotte Hawkins Brown, "Negro Women Not Freed by Emancipation," *Buffalo Progressive Herald*, 15 March 1939; Charlotte Hawkins Brown papers, reel 1, 1–2.

27. "Crusade for Character," *Norfolk Journal and Guide*, 19 December 1942, C. H. Brown vertical file, M-SRC.

28. "Crusade for Character."

29. Charlotte Hawkins Brown, "Where We Are in Race Relations," Charlotte Hawkins Brown Papers.

30. "Where We Are in Race Relations."

31. "Made to Dress as a Maid," *Norfolk Journal-Guide*, 14 September 1935, C. H. Brown vertical file, M-SRC.

32. McCluskey, "We Specialize," 417.

33. Charlotte Hawkins Brown, "Where We Are in Race Relations," Charlotte Hawkins Brown Papers.

34. Charlotte Hawkins Brown Museum, North Carolina Historic Sites, North Carolina Department of Cultural Resources, http://www.nchistoricsites.org/Charlotte Hawkins Brown Papers/history.htm (10 August 2009).

35. Mary McLeod Bethune, interviewed by Dr. Charles S. Johnson (1939), microfilm, Mary McLeod Bethune Papers, Bethune-Cookman College Collection, University Publications of America.

36. Mary McLeod Bethune interviewed by Dr. Charles S Johnson.

37. Mary McLeod Bethune interviewed by Dr. Charles S. Johnson.

38. Mary McLeod Bethune interviewed by Dr. Charles S. Johnson.

39. Mary McLeod Bethune to editor, *New York Times*, 16 April 1920, BCCC.

40. *The Daytona Industrial Advocate* l, no. 1, 5 (March 1907), General Education Board Archives, Rockefeller Foundation, Sleepy Hollow, N.Y. Two copies of this newsletter were included in Bethune's application for funding from this powerful funding organization.

41. Albertus Bethune attended Avery Institute in Charleston. He married Mary McLeod in 1898 and left the family in 1907, but the couple never divorced.

42. Dora E. Maley, letter on the occasion of the 50th anniversary of Bethune-Cookman College, 15 March 1955, Mary McLeod Bethune vertical file, Halifax Historical Society, Daytona Beach, Fla.

43. Rackham Holt, *Mary McLeod Bethune*, 104.

44. McCluskey, "Education of Black Girls," 165.

45. The *Daytona Industrial Advocate* 1, no. 5.

46. Frances Keyser, unfinished biography of Mary McLeod Bethune, BCCC, reel 1.

47. Keyser, unfinished biography.

48. "Local Women Urge Cause of Mrs. Bethune," *Pittsburgh Courier*, 12 December 1924, Mary McLeod Bethune Papers, Amistad Research Center, Dillard University, New Orleans, Louisiana.

49. "Local Women Urge Cause of Bethune."

50. By-laws of the Bethune Circle, BCCC, reel 3.

51. Mary McLeod Bethune, letter to Mrs. Ada Lee, in McCluskey and Smith, *Mary McLeod Bethune: Building a Better World*, 107.

52. Minutes, meeting of Southern (Southeastern) Federation of Colored Women's Clubs—formed at Daytona (16 January 1920), BCCC.

53. Eva R. Jackson to Bethune, BCCC, reel one.

54. Jackson to Bethune, BCCC.

55. Bethune to Eleanor Roosevelt (8 December 1942), BCCC.

56. Wadelington and Knapp, *Charlotte Hawkins Brown*, 135.

57. Nannie Helen Burroughs, "Unload the Leeches and Parasitic 'Toms' and Take the Promised Land," Nannie Helen Burroughs Papers, Library of Congress, box 46.

58. Higginbotham, *Righteous Discontent*, 219.

59. Nannie Helen Burroughs to Bethune, 24 January 1934, NHB Papers, Library of Congress.

60. Bethune to Burroughs, 29 February 1940, Library of Congress, box 34.

61. Brown to Bethune, August 20 (no year), BCCC part 2, reel 2.

62. Hurley interview, 14 August 2010.

63. Brown to Bethune, 20 August 1946, Bethune Papers, Foundation Collection, part 2.

64. Brown to Bethune, August 20 (no year).

65. Bethune to Brown (September 4, 1945), BCCC, part 2, reel 2.

66. Bethune to Brown, 4 September 1946, BCCC.

67. Brown to Bethune, 14 April 1950, BCCC, part 2, reel 2.

68. Bethune to Brown, 22 April 1951, BCCC.

69. Jane Edna Hunter (1882–1971) trained as a nurse at Hampton Institute before moving to Cleveland and becoming one of the leading settlement house workers and institution-builders in the country.

70. Bethune to Brown, 28 August 1951, BCCC, reel 2.

71. Bethune to Brown, 28 May 1951, BCCC.

72. Brown to Bethune, 6 September 1951, BCCC.

73. Brown to Bethune, 6 November 1951, BCCC.

74. "Report of the registrar," *Palmer Memorial Institute*, 1941, Charlotte Hawkins Brown Papers

75. Bethune to Brown, 24 June 1952, BCCC.

76. Bethune to Brown, 18 June 1955, BCCC.

77. Darlene Clark Hine, "Rape and the Inner Lives of Black Women in the Middle West," *Signs* 14, no. 4 (Summer 1989): 912–20.

78. Wadelington and Knapp, *Charlotte Hawkins Brown*, 135.

79. Nancy Cott, *The Bonds of Womanhood: Women's Sphere in New England, 1790–1835* (New Haven, Conn.: Yale University Press, 1977), chap. 1.

# EIGHT

## Passing into History

### *Commemorations, Memorials, and the Legacies of Black Women School Founders*

> *She was a woman who stood for the best and noblest things in life, and gave herself unstintingly to the work of lifting her poor, struggling, and oppressed race out of the ignorance and degradation in which 250 years of slavery had left it.*
>
> —from a eulogy for Lucy C. Laney

In his eulogy for Lucy Craft Laney, Rev. Francis J. Grimke, the prominent black Presbyterian minister, provided an example of "ceremonial rhetoric" that has historically functioned to enhance the shared public regard for the deceased.[1] At Laney's funeral on Thursday, October 26, 1933, in Augusta, Georgia, Grimke's presentation of her as the incarnation of idealized womanhood correlated with the one that the educator had prescribed for black women. Realizing the challenges ahead for blacks in the new century, Laney placed black women in the vanguard of a movement to teach "the black babies" and to lighten the racial "burden" of prejudice, immorality, and lack of education.[2] Laney's life of self-sacrifice and duty was a model for aspiring black women of her era. She revised the nineteenth-century ideal for white women that stressed being "true," pure, and submissive to male authority by focusing on the communitarian goal of uplift of family and race.

Among black women teachers and school founders, until well into the twentieth century, many viewed teaching as service to the race and a sacred calling, with Lucy Laney as their standard bearer. The outpouring of spoken and written regard that followed her death exalted her in eulogies, newspaper editorials, and other expressions that functioned as a first draft of history and reflected the community's high regard for her life of inspired service, as she passed into history. Her legacy became institutionalized through ongoing testimonies, commemorations, and memorials that presented Laney to the general public and helped to preserve her legacy.

This concluding chapter, beginning with Laney, discusses the legacies of the four school founders as forged in the voices of their contemporaries and preserved via various public displays of commemoration and memorialization of the women and their work. These events and testimonies serve as interventions into contested and racially restricted public space and memory.

Some scholars distinguish between the "golden virtues, virtuous women, and sterling events" of ceremonial rhetoric, such as eulogies, and what is considered the more historically trustworthy collective and cumulative record necessary for critical memory.[3] Yet public memorials, while seldom presented as critical scholarship, engage community consciousness as acts of preservation. The recent dedication of the Martin Luther King, Jr., Memorial on the National Mall in Washington, D.C., is an example. The gendered dimension of such events is invoked by the unveiling of the Rosa Parks statue in 2013 in the Statuary Hall of the U.S. Capitol—the first woman to be so honored—and the planned Harriet Tubman Underground Railroad Monument to be built on Maryland's Eastern Shore, as recently announced by the Obama administration.[4] The latter two are new historical insertions of heroic black women into public space and memory. Memorials of black women in public space can serve as symbols of integrity and accomplishment and challenge pervasive negative representations of black women that have long saturated the popular imagination.[5] Conversely, when used for hagiography and stripped of context, they can serve to prescribe and confine black women within an idealized, one-dimensional public space. Yet, the presence of such representations in public space can incite discussion and continued reexamination of their lives and work.

Although memorializing as a community discourse is a well-established practice in African American communities, in the aftermath of the Civil Rights movement there was increased interest in reaching broader audiences. The momentum generated by the push to memorialize the martyred Dr. Martin Luther King, Jr., began after his assassination in 1969 and culminated in a national holiday in his honor and the national monument; it also brought about a wider acceptance of the effort to fill the racial void left by a century of Jim Crow segregation and policies that confined blacks to a narrow and restricted public space. Such public memorials increase black visibility as subjects and may counter existing ideas and stereotypes that many Americans hold about African Americans.[6] The memorialization of black women school founders, which began with community recognition of their work, benefitted from this effort. When

Lucy Laney passed into history on October 24, 1933, from the effects of nephritis and hypertension, the school she founded in 1883 and presided over for over forty years survived her and defined her legacy as a highly revered national figure. At the time of her death, the country was in the throes of the Great Depression, and for blacks in her home state of Georgia, times were especially hard. More lynching of blacks occurred in Georgia than almost any other state, prompting an outcry from national black leaders like W. E. B. Du Bois.[7] As a result, the migration of blacks from Georgia and other southern states to the North in search of a better life was in full swing. Part of the stature that Laney achieved in life and death was due to her determination to stay put and run her school despite these conditions.

The news of her death was carried in the national press in articles of varying lengths, most of which mentioned her years of service to Haines Institute, along with a biographical sketch that noted her slave heritage. News accounts, especially in the black press, leaned toward hagiography, repeating the basic story of her racial pride and exceptional accomplishment in maintaining a school that became a model of black progress. The *Pittsburgh Courier*, a national black weekly, covered her death and funeral with several articles, including one that began, "It has been given to few women of any race or generation to so largely enhance the welfare fortune and of as many people as was true of Miss Lucy Laney." The article noted her "moral integrity, creative imagination [and] spiritual enthusiasm."[8] In a companion article in the same edition, the newspaper called Laney "America's most interesting and useful character." She was, the article continued, "a fearless champion of the rights of her people." She had a penchant for considering the needs of others before her own. Laney was, the article concluded, "unselfish and broad-hearted."[9] The *Chicago Defender*, the most influential national black newspaper of the day, founded by fellow Georgia native Robert S. Abbott, called Laney "a pioneer in the development of the race . . . [and a] fight[er] for educational advancement for the youth of the South." The newspaper, a long-time supporter, had previously run ads for her fund drives.[10] A headline article in the *Philadelphia Tribune* announced, "Lucy Laney, Founder of Haines Institute Was One of the Greatest Teachers."[11] Her funeral rites, held in the school chapel in McGregor Hall, were a spectacle befitting royalty. Scholar Karla Holloway notes the "culturally distinct" funeral practices of African Americans that stress "putting away" the dead in style.[12] Although Laney had a known preference for simplicity, her funeral rites were on a grand scale. Her casket, a gift from an alumnus, was described as an engraved "metal gray, lined with velvet, banked by flowers from all over the country."[13] Following the African American cultural practice of not rushing a funeral, the service featured over two dozen speakers and several musical numbers performed by an alumni chorus of fifty voices. Descriptions of the funeral noted the attendance and partici-

pation of the diverse, interracial constituencies she cultivated: the Presbyterian Board of Missions; the Baptist Ministers Alliance; white citizens of
Augusta; Haines Alumni; the Young Women's Christian Association of
Indianapolis; the Lincoln University president; as well as representatives
of Atlanta University, South Carolina State, the Lamar Nursing School,
and Palmer Memorial Institute. The ceremony, "more of a coronation
than a funeral," made her life ripe for lyrical and allegorical appropria-
tion, such as the following by Haines alumnus Dr. S. S. Johnson:

> Clods of the campus rest quietly on her remains,
> Disturb not her peaceful rest;
> We loved her well but Jesus loved her best.
> Her life was as pure as the falling flakes of snow,
> As unapproachable as the distant star;
> Cold in the dust the perished heart may lie,
> But the love that warmed it once can never die.[14]

Reports differed on the number of people who "paused to pay tribute
to respect at the bier of that God-sent woman," with the *Afro-American*
reporting 10,000 mourners, while the hometown white-owned *Augusta
Chronicle* listed the number at 1,000. The contradictory numbers are probably due to the rarity of such a large funeral, with an influx of mourners
and dignitaries from other states. Charlotte Hawkins Brown, who was
one of the speakers, called Laney "the outstanding model of Negro womanhood in the world . . . and the woman who was the inspiration of my
childhood dreams, the fulfillment of my ideals for a useful life."[15] Mary
McLeod Bethune, who had already credited Laney with being her inspiration, issued a statement declaring that Laney was "our heroine in the
field of Christian education. . . . She blazed the way to higher things."[16]
She was "a spiritual symbol of vision, sacrifice and devotion," said her
friend Nannie Helen Burroughs. Among the most memorable and stir-
ring tributes was from Howard University President Mordecai Johnson,
who had presided over the bestowal of an honorary master of arts degree
on Laney in 1930. This is a digest of his remarks at her funeral:

> Farseeing spirit and idea; mother of the children of the people; pure
> hearted teacher; founder and vigorous sustainer of the educational
> community; evoker of faith and ambition; inspirer of conscientious and
> unremitting discipline; all things renouncing, all work obediently do-
> ing, eloquently begging on behalf of your Holy cause; simple, indefati-
> gable, indomitable, woman—creative.[17]

Reaction among whites in Augusta can be gauged by the *Augusta
Chronicle*'s October 25, 1933, editorial titled simply "Lucy C. Laney." It
praised her for a "a life of sacrifice and service," and called her "great."
"She believed that all God's children had wings. . . . [T]hat is why she
gave her life for her own, the colored race. She was a pioneer for prohibi-
tion; for women's rights; and the rights of all mankind. It was not for self-

glory that she labored but for her people." It went on to say that she was a woman of "sacrifice, service, and character," echoing sentiments of the black community in its "News About Colored People" column that was published expressly for black consumption. The newspaper also referred to her as "Miss Laney," an uncommon honorific for a black woman by a white newspaper. Thus, both black and white communities, although split on many matters of substance, contributed to the near-deification of Lucy Laney following her death. In a concluding editorial, the *Chronicle* printed these words: "The whole population, white and colored, felt a kindly interest in Lucy C. Laney and respected her for her unselfish work and there are any on the streets of Augusta who, at the mention of her name, will rise up and call her blessed for what she has done."[18] Perhaps the greatest tribute to Lucy Laney immediately after her death was from former students whose lives she had touched. Ten such students who were then enrolled at Lincoln University signed a letter of appreciation, stating, "Miss Laney was both mother and inspiring teacher. Her life was a daily sacrifice for the salvation of others. As we go on and upwards in our struggles in life, we shall forever be inspired by the lofty goals of Miss Laney."[19]

Eulogies, as a first draft of history and memory, have contributed to the more recent and ongoing living memorials to Laney, of which the Lucy Craft Laney Consolidated High School that sits on the original site of Haines Institute is an example. Her gravesite, located near the entrance of the high school, holds one of two eternal flames erected in the state of Georgia; the other one is at the gravesite of Martin Luther King, Jr., in Atlanta. The inscription on the gravestone reads: "Lucy Craft Laney, 'Intrepid leader, faithful teacher, loyal friend.'" According to the Haines Jubilee program of 1936, such a gravesite was envisioned as a destination for future pilgrims, who would be inspired and strengthened by her example of "courage and wisdom."[20]

Across the street from the public high school, Laney's original home at 1116 Philips Street now houses the Lucy Craft Laney Museum of Black History and Conference Center. The mission of the museum is to honor Laney's legacy through the arts and history. The building was purchased in 1987 from the city for $10,000 by Delta House, Inc., a nonprofit organization sponsored by the Delta Sigma Theta Sorority. After extensive renovation, it opened in 1991, anchoring the revitalization of the historic downtown district where most black Augustans once lived. According to its director, Christine Betts, the operations budget comes mostly from the city of Augusta. The museum owns few Laney artifacts and documents, owing to a devastating fire that took the life of Laney's surviving niece and onetime principal of Haines, Margaret Louise Laney. It invokes Laney mainly through its programming and commitment to serving the people of the city, particularly its youth, which was Laney's mission. Youth art exhibits are held that feature the work of Laney High School

Students, plus several permanent collections, including the Lamar nurses' exhibit that recalls the nursing school founded by Laney in 1892 that was the first in the city.[21] The museum also houses art and photographic exhibits documenting the rich history of black Augustans as well as other black historical figures. It sponsors conferences and after-school programs that include job preparation and computer skills. With a full-time executive director, a librarian, and a part-time staff of professionals and volunteers, the museum engages the community by connecting history, memory, and present-day issues. Among the museum's inner-city neighbors are descendants and representatives of those who bore witness to Laney's educational and social mission. Mrs. Lucille Laney Ellis Floyd, in her eighties when she was interviewed in 2003, attended Haines in the early 1930s. Floyd, whose mother named her after the revered teacher, remembered that "Miss Laney taught all the classes," and would find an idle student and ask him or her what was her next class and then to open that book, be it Greek, Latin, math, or the Bible. Laney would then, without notes, teach that chapter to the student.

Floyd also remembered an incident in which Laney was arrested at the school in front of the children. It happened, according to Floyd, when a white Western Union messenger entered the school without taking off his hat. After repeating her instructions to him to please remove his hat, Laney "knocked it off of his head." The police came and arrested her, but she spent no time in jail, and as Floyd remembers, the case was dropped.[22] Mrs. Magnolia Donahue, another member of the community and Haines graduate, entered Haines Institute the year after Laney died in 1934. She remembered that the Haines environment reflected Laney's uncompromising standards. "It was like a university," she said. Under A. C. Griggs, who assumed the presidency after Laney's death, every student was required to take black history, combined with the classics, and vocational courses in sewing and cooking, she recalled.[23]

In Laney memorials, living memory and recorded past events combine to engage with the present and encourage the critical discussion of both past and present realities. The Lucy Craft Laney High School built on the site of the original Haines Institute and the eternal flame that marks her grave on the campus, are constant reminders of her deeds and ideals. Christine Betts, of the Lucy C. Laney Museum, illustrates this. She defines her mission as director as one that focuses "not on the person, but the legacy." Lucy Laney's legacy, she feels, can be used to teach, to inspire, and to strengthen the present community.[24] This notion of the past engaging with the present is also behind the naming of and mission of the Lucy Craft Laney School at Cleveland Park Community School in Minneapolis, founded in 2000. The well-constructed, brightly lit school, just one of several institutions and commemorations that honor her work, recalls Laney's visit to the Presbyterian General Assembly meeting in Minneapolis seeking financial support for her new school. The mission at

Lucy Craft Laney School at Cleveland Park—to "nurture young minds" and to minister to "the whole child," as well as to engage the community—is helping to keep Laney's legacy alive well beyond her native Georgia.[25]

Mary McLeod Bethune, the best known protégé of Lucy Laney, passed into history in her Daytona home on May 18, 1955, after a massive heart attack. Her reverence for her mentor is shown in words and deeds. As venerated figures, both women found a place in collective racial memory. But unlike Laney, who kept a low profile and never sought public attention as a transformer, Bethune had swag and established a high profile nationally, especially in the nation's capital. Like Laney, Bethune in her role as an educator evoked narratives of service and spiritual motherhood, but the generation of change that occurred between the two women's deaths meant that the Victorian view of women as primarily nurturing mothers or spiritual mothers was fading. Laney, a spinster who found marriage incompatible with her life's work, was memorialized as a spiritual mother to all the "children of the people." Bethune, who separated from Albertus Bethune after a few years of marriage that produced a son, probably came to agree with Laney. The memorials to Bethune reflect the changing status of women in the public sphere. She is pictured with children in the Lincoln Park memorial discussed below, but she is also remembered as a political leader, with links to a U.S. president and first lady, and as an activist for women, jobs, and civil rights. Although Jim Crow segregation was still a fact of southern life during both women's lifetimes, Laney could only imagine a "separate but equal" scenario of racial justice, while Bethune imagined complete racial equality.

Months before her death, Bethune celebrated the *Brown v. the Board of Education* Supreme Court decision that overturned the doctrine of "separate but equal" in public education. In her final column in the Chicago *Defender* she urged blacks to "keep up the pressure" for full citizenship rights.[26] She also wrote "My Last Will and Testament," a digest of her moral philosophy and aspirations for black America that was published in *Ebony* Magazine, in which she advised the upcoming generation to "be ever vigilant" in the cause of justice.[27] Her sense of history and her place in it are shown in efforts to preserve her work. These included setting up the Bethune Foundation at Bethune-Cookman College in 1954, a year before she died. Located at her Daytona homestead, she envisioned the foundation as "a sacred place," that will bring people together from all walks of life to work together on solving the world's problems. It would also be a place where materials on her life would be gathered for those who would want to write about her in the years to come.[28] The U.S. Postal Service issued a commemorative Mary McLeod Bethune postage stamp in 1985, which was one of the first to honor African Americans leaders.

Bethune's passing was headline news throughout the nation. "One of the titans fell," declared the Norfolk *Journal and Guide*. "So great were her dynamism and force that it was almost impossible to resist her," the *Washington Post* added. The *New York Times* credited Bethune with fostering interracial goodwill. The *Pittsburgh Courier* touted her "indomitable soul." As when Laney died, both black-owned and white-owned newspapers sang her praises. The black press, a longtime fan of Bethune, was especially effusive. "One of the truly great women leaders in world history. . . . Big and little, rich and poor, all creeds and colors, professional and unskilled, came to pay tribute to the woman who founded the college with $1.50 and a prayer. Her home will undoubtedly become a national shrine."[29] However, unlike Laney, Bethune had surpassed the label of "educator" and was remembered as a "great American and world citizen."[30] The giant statue of her that graces the campus of Bethune-Cookman University, where she is buried, reminds everyone who passes by of the fact that it was Bethune who grew the tiny Florida girls' school into the accredited four-year coeducational liberal-arts college and provided the foundation for its continued development and present status as a university.

Although her emphasis on race uplift and respectability was born out of an earlier period, defined by segregation and restrictions on women, Bethune's advocacy stressed both the civil rights and uplift of the oppressed and the ascendancy of African American women. Her role in the advancement of women is memorialized in several settings, including a women's residence center at Howard University. The most visible memorial that acknowledges her leadership in the advancement of black women is the Bethune Council House, her former Washington, D.C., residence. It is the headquarters of the National Council of Negro Women, the organization that she founded in 1935. It is now a national historic site run by the United States Park Service that houses the organizational files of the NCNW and is part of the National Archives for Black Women's History. It serves as a meeting place for women's conferences, seminars, and other events and supports a gift and book shop.[31] The Council House is the best realization of what Bethune envisioned for the continuation of her work. The archive is accessible to researchers doing black women's history, especially women's organizations. Washington, D.C., is also the city from which Bethune's name became known to households across America and is where a bronze statue by sculptor Robert Berks was erected in 1974. The Mary McLeod Bethune Emancipation Memorial, as it is called, was commissioned by the NCNW after a long fundraising campaign and winning federal approval for the site.[32] Bethune is portrayed with one hand on the cane given to her by President Franklin Delano Roosevelt and the other outstretched holding a "scroll of learning" that is being offered to a girl and boy who are reaching for it. "Let her work praise her" is inscribed on the front of the statue. Lines from "My Last Will and Testament" are also inscribed around the base of the structure.

In the decades following her death, memorials and commemorations to Bethune proliferated, with streets, monuments, buildings, schools, and scholarships honoring her, including a women's residence center at Howard University and a senior citizen housing development in New York City. Particularly notable were the commemorations in her home state of Florida on the tenth anniversary of her death. Governor Haydon Burns proclaimed her birth month, July, "Dr. Mary McLeod Bethune Month," and in Dade County (Miami), local churches launched a weeklong commemoration with special sermons and activities.[33] Her birthplace of Mayesville, South Carolina, has opened the Dr. Mary McLeod Bethune Memorial Park, located on land purchased by the Lee County chapter of the NCNW, which includes the site where Bethune was born. The long range mission of the park is to develop a "state of the art" attraction that will include a reconstruction of the one-room McLeod family cabin, a botanical garden with classes in horticulture, walking trails, and a community learning center.[34] It is the result of years of planning and fundraising by South Carolinians to commemorate their native daughter.

Bethune's funeral also held true to the African-American tradition of putting away the dead in style. It was held on the Bethune-Cookman College campus and attended by several thousand people who packed the auditorium and the grounds to say goodbye and shower her with accolades. Bethune was described in the eulogy as having five lives: "her family, her college, her National Council of Negro Women, Bethune-Volusia Beach [development project], and the Bethune Foundation." Howard Thurman, the popular theologian and Bethune-Cookman graduate, noted that her handicaps—being a woman in a male-dominated society, and a Negro in a white-dominated society—did not deter her. He continued, "She was a thinker. She had the uncanny ability, by clear reflective ability, to move to the center of an issue while the rest of us nibbled at the edges.[35] Former first lady Eleanor Roosevelt, her friend of many years, memorialized Bethune with these words: "a really great American woman. . . . I will cherish the spirit she lived by and try to promote the causes she believed in, in loving memory to a very wonderful woman."[36]

Bethune's friend of more than half a century and fellow school founder Charlotte Hawkins Brown of Palmer Memorial Institute, passed into history on January 11, 1961, in Sedalia, North Carolina. She left behind nearly sixty years of single-minded devotion to her school. PMI was her priority and, like Bethune, she traced her inspiration for uplifting the race through education to trailblazer Lucy Laney, and determined to follow in her footsteps.[37]

Brown, eight years Bethune's junior, was a stickler for "doing and saying the right thing," while the more politically ambidextrous Bethune although regal in her bearing displayed a common touch. When Brown passed into history from complications of diabetes, she was profiled in both local and national newspapers. News accounts described her as the woman who transformed a tiny school in the backwoods of North Carolina into a nationally respected college preparatory, known for educating the sons and daughters of the black elite. Some news accounts mentioned that the childless Brown was survived by nieces whom she helped to raise, including Maria Cole, wife of singer Nat King Cole. Singer Carol Brice was also mentioned among her surviving relatives. Other obituaries noted her insistence on teaching the social graces and the "meaning of culture" to girls and boys.[38] The *New York Times*'s obituary mentioned that the founding of her school had been precipitated by the then-teenager's striking ability "to read aloud from her Latin book" as she was wheeling a neighbor's baby in her hometown of Cambridge. The babysitter caught the eye of Wellesley College president Alice Palmer, who became her mentor and helped her secure admission to Salem State University.[39] However, Brown's students remember her on a much more personal level—as recounted in chapter 5. They uniformly admired her and the high standards she imposed that they still recall and live by today. They admired the way she stood up to white people in segregated North Carolina. She even corrected a white male visitor who had the habit of calling blacks "negras" (see chapter 6).

Although her success at PMI made her an admired national figure, she became a household name in black communities for her popular lectures on the social graces, which she delivered at schools and churches across the nation. However, Brown's fame in her later years was eclipsed by the blossoming of the Civil Rights and Black Power movements, as more politically oriented students disavowed what many considered her conformist and outdated white middle class value system. Interestingly, the black college student sit-in to integrate the Woolworth lunch counter that ignited the student protest against segregation throughout the South took place in 1960 in Greensboro, a few miles from the Sedalia campus a year before Brown died. In the changing social and political climate and under new leadership at PMI, students rebelled against the school's strict discipline. Several fires caused damage and destruction to campus buildings, including the girls' dormitory.[40] After several attempts to keep the school open, a combination of factors led to PMI closing ten years after Brown's death.

As had been the case when Laney and Bethune died, Brown's funeral was held on campus and she was buried there on a site she had selected ten years earlier.[41] The overflow crowd in the Alice Freeman Palmer building heard the main eulogy delivered by former Howard University president Mordecai Johnson. He extolled her virtues as an educator and a "race woman" who raised the standard for black education in the state. Those closest to Brown remembered another side of her that was often overlooked—her humor and pithy way of making her point. Wilhelmina

Crosson, Brown's close associate who succeeded her as president of PMI, compiled some of Brown's aphorisms that are emblematic of her legacy and style, including these:

> Never let a fool kiss you, and never let a kiss fool you.
> A Boston physician once said that in fifty years kissing would be a thing of the past; in fifty years your children won't care.
> The laziest cook in the world is the one who puts popcorn in her pancakes so they will turn over by themselves.
> Clothes often *fake* the man.
> Two black boys saw an engine passing by. One boy said, "If I were white, I could learn to run that engine." The second boy said, "give me half a chance to learn, and I will run it—black as I am."[42]

The fact that Brown's death coincided with the onset of black militancy probably delayed a fuller appreciation of her because of her emphasis on the social graces rather than political action for racial advancement.[43] Yet, time and a deepening sense of history have combined to refocus attention on preserving the legacy of Charlotte Hawkins Brown as a visionary institution builder whose accomplishments deserve wider appreciation. That is the mission of the Charlotte Hawkins Brown Historical Foundation, which was incorporated in 1983 to help the state of North Carolina plan and develop a state memorial in her honor on the site of PMI. A $400,000 grant from the state was used to acquire forty-one of the original 350 campus acres and to begin the process of building and restoring, deteriorating structures. The Charlotte Hawkins Brown Museum at Historic Palmer Memorial Institute opened to the public in 1987, with a small exhibit and visual programs. By 1994, three of the fourteen buildings had been restored. Tracey Burns-Vann, the first director of the museum, believes that this restoration project has helped to revitalize the predominately black community of Sedalia and fulfills a broader mission that Brown would be proud of—promoting educating the populace and interpreting African American history.[44] She feels that Brown would be proud of what is being preserved in her name, including her private residence, Canary Cottage, which contains some of her original furnishings.[45] Today, the museum is the only state-designated African American historic site in North Carolina. The initial state support in 2002 was $249,000,[46] and the site attracted 16,000 visitors. With an upgrade in infrastructure and public programming, the attendance in 2012 was 17,098, according to present site director Frachele Scott, although budget cuts due to the poor economy have meant minimal funding increases from the state.[47] The work of preserving Brown's legacy, since the school closed in 1971, is aided by an active PMI alumni association that hosts a biennial meeting attended by over 100 former Palmerites. It is similar to the Haines Institute alumni association in its dedication to preserving the legacy of the founder and of the school itself. The website, newsletter, and the all-class reunions support that effort.

Nannie Helen Burroughs was the last of this quartet of school founders to pass into history: on May 26, 1961, just four months after the death of her friend Charlotte Hawkins Brown. Along with Mary McLeod Bethune, they were dubbed "the three B's of education."[48] Burroughs's death also marked the passing of an era, with the main stalwarts of the early black women's movement, including the school founders, clubwoman Mary Church Terrell, and author-educator and feminist, Anna Julia Cooper, all deceased.

Burroughs gave her total devotion to her school and church work. She became a symbol of women's empowerment through that work, launching her advocacy and social mission from within those structures. The news accounts of her death, although a national story, garnered front-page headlines in her hometown, Washington, D.C. In the Washington *Afro-American* the headline featured a photograph of mourners weeping at Burroughs' coffin. "The Nation Pays Tribute to Miss Burroughs,"[49] it read. The news story also reported that ninety-five ministers were in attendance, with nine of them paying an oral tribute and the others sitting among the audience of 800. The three-hour funeral, held at the venerable Nineteenth Street Baptist Church where Burroughs had held membership since 1892, was long even by Baptist standards, where length of service is often equated with stature of the deceased. The extended coverage and details of the funeral in the black press reinforced that correlation. She "lay in a bronze sealed casket with eggshell interior, [and] with a near white veil over her form, in a dress of blue lace over powder blue sateen, a corsage of pink gladioli in her hands, and her Delta Sigma Theta pin on her bosom,"[50] the *Afro-American* reported. Among those remembering her deeds and character were the following: "She was clear-thinking, had a sense of humor, and [was] a fine Christian[51] spirit," said Mrs. Jessie Ford of the Baptist World Alliance of the woman who initiated Women's Day as a fundraiser in the black Baptist church. "She was a world leader among women," said Dr. C. C. Adams of the Foreign Mission Board, "but her influence was felt . . . everywhere." Dr. Mordecai Johnson of Howard University, who had eulogized both Lucy Laney and Mary Bethune, mentioned Burroughs's down-to-earth personality, "[T]here was no important people or places to her,"[52] he said in his remarks. Washington's mainstream white-owned newspapers covered her death with more detachment, including the *Washington Post*'s B section article that noted understatedly, "she trained Baptist missionaries for service in Africa."[53]

As a reminder of the changing times and to place this closing era in context, an unrelated editorial in the *Afro-American* on the same day called upon President Kennedy to send federal troops to Alabama to protect the Freedom Riders, who were being harassed and threatened by white segregationists as they rode buses through the South in protest of Jim Crow laws. Burroughs, rebellious and defiant against unjust laws, would have found solidarity with the emerging black resistance. Part of her legacy was her militant stance against racism and her simultaneous appeal to black self-sufficiency. Burroughs's prominence in black Baptist communities nationwide, and her star status among blacks in the Washington, D.C., area ensured her legacy. Given her prominence in the nation's capital, it is not surprising that most of the memorials and commemoration of Burroughs are in and around Washington, D.C. In 1964, the board of trustees of the National Trade and Professional School voted to rename the school in Burroughs's honor.

The leadership transition to Rebekah J. Callaway (1961–1968) and Aurelia R. Downey (1968–1988), the second and third presidents, enhanced and transformed the school and preserved Burroughs's legacy.[54] The school operated as a coeducational private Christian school for pre-K through sixth grade and advertised itself as offering a strong academic program, cultural enrichment and sound Christian teachings.[55] In 1981, the land was assessed at $3,000,000 and has increased since then. "Our school has been black-owned since 1909," Mattie Robinson, a trustee, proudly asserts. An annual parade is held in the city to commemorate Burroughs and her work and to publicize the school. Fundraising efforts focus on the black community, in whose interest the school continues to operate. As a continuing memorial to its founder, a bust of Burroughs occupies a prominent place on the campus and in advertisement for the school. After celebrating the 100 year anniversary in 2012, the small Christian school found it hard to stay financially afloat. The school, still bearing the name, Nannie Helen Burroughs offered a proposal to reorganize as a public charter school. However, at present, it is closed.

Both together and separately, the commemorations and memorials for these women school founders and race leaders serve as historical and cultural markers of an evolving black feminine ideal. Although representatives of a bygone era of mores and customs, their legacies provide a standard for meaningful and continued engagement with themes of struggle and triumph. Concurrently, the claim of black memorializing is one that jettisons the marginality of invisibility suffered by oppressed groups. Instead, such recognition reflects the need to preserve history while claiming ownership of public space. This preservation through both the immediacy of eulogy spoken by those who knew or remember them, and the permanence of the events, structures, and installations that honor them, recites their virtues as well as the ideals that the community thrust upon them. They inspire allegory and nostalgia, but also can incite critical discourse and rediscovery. While public memorials and commemoratives for these women may include aspects of idealized gender roles for women as self-sacrificing spiritual mothers, the innovative, self-starting women who emerge defy easy categorization.

They were institution-builders, activists, and public figures who constituted a forgotten sisterhood who individually and collectively made a difference in the lives of African Americans. They were women who defied obstacles of race and gender and forged ahead to realize their visions of a more just and educated nation. Having passed into history, the continued recovery and revisiting of their lives and work ensure that they will no longer be forgotten.

**Figure 8.1.   Portrait of Lucy C. Laney in Georgia state Capitol, installed, 1992. Photo courtesy of the Georgia State Archives.**

**Figure 8.2.    Statue of Mary McLeod Bethune, in Lincoln Park, Washington, DC, installed, 1972. Photo courtesy of the Florida State Archives.**

## NOTES

1. Michael L. Kent, "The Rhetoric of Funereal Oratory and Eulogy: Reconciling Rhetorics of Past and Present" (PhD diss., University of Oklahoma, 2007), 1–12.

2. Lucy Craft Laney, "Burden,"

3. Houston Baker, "Critical Memory and the Black Public Space," in *The Black Public Sphere: A Public Culture Book,* ed. Black Public Sphere Collective (Chicago: University of Chicago, 1995), 7.

4. The Dr. Martin Luther King, Jr., Memorial, http://www.nps.gov/mlk; John M. Broder, "Obama to Name New National Monuments," http://thecaucus.blogs.nytimes.com/2013/03/22/obama-to-name-new-national-monuments/ (22 March 2013).

5. This is a reference to several volumes of scholarship over the last twenty-five years that show how black women have been stereotyped by controlling images, such as "mammies; Jezebels, matriarchs," welfare queens, and other negative representations that remain a part of the popular imagination. Examples include Patricia Hill-Collins, *Black Feminist Thought: Knowledge, Consciousness, and the Politics of Empowerment* (New York: Routledge, 1990); bell hooks, *Ain't I a Woman* (Boston: South End Press, 1990); Deborah Gray White, *Too Heavy a Load: Black Women in Defense of Themselves, 1894–1994* (New York: W. W. Norton, 1999).

6. Michael C. Dawson, "A Black Counterpublic?: Economic Earthquakes, Racial Agenda(s), and Black Politics," in *The Black Public Sphere,* 195–227.

7. John Dittmer, *Black Georgia in the Progressive Era, 1900–1920* (Chicago: University of Illinois Press, 1977), 3.

8. "Lucy Laney," *Pittsburgh Courier,* 4 November 1933.

9. "Lucy Laney," *Pittsburgh Courier,* 4 November 1933.

10. "Open Drive to Aid Laney School," *Chicago Defender,* 21 July 1928.

11. "Lucy Laney, Founder of Haines Institute Was One of the Greatest Teachers," *Philadelphia Tribune*, 28 October 1933.

12. Karla Holloway, *Passed On: African American Mourning Stories: A Memorial* (Durham, N.C.: Duke University Press, 2003), 152.

13. Haines Institute "Golden Jubilee Program" (1936), Lucy C. Laney vertical file, Richmond County Historical Society, Augusta, GA.

14. Haines Jubilee Program, 1936.

15. "Lucy Laney," *Augusta Chronicle*, 5 November 1933, 15.

16. "Lucy Laney," *Augusta Chronicle*, 5 November 1933, 15.

17. Lucy C. Laney Funeral Program, Lucy C. Laney file, Lincoln University Archives.

18. "Lucy C. Laney," *Augusta Chronicle*, 25 October 1933; 29 October 1933.

19. Student-signed letter, 25 October 1933, Lincoln University Archives.

20. Haines Jubilee Program, 1936.

21. Christine Betts, interview with the author, at Lucy Laney Museum, Augusta, Ga., 25 April 2003.

22. Lucille Laney Ellis Floyd, interview with the author, Augusta, Ga., 25 April 2003.

23. Magnolia Donahue, interview with the author, Augusta, Ga., 25 April 2003.

24. Christine Betts, interview with author.

25. The Lucy Craft Laney at Cleveland Park Community School serves a pre-K through eighth-grade population of more than 600 students that is 87 percent African American, with the remaining 13 percent comprising Asian, Latino, and white students, http://lucylaney.mpls.k12.mn.us/home (2 April 2013).

26. Mary McLeod Bethune, "U.S. Will Make 'the Grade' in Integrating All Its Schools," *Chicago Defender* [column] 4 June 1955, 10.

27. Mary McLeod Bethune, "My Last Will and Testament," *Ebony* magazine, August, 1955, reprinted in McCluskey and Smith, *Building a Better World*, 58–61.

28. Bethune, "My Foundation," in McCluskey and Smith, *Building a Better World*, 270.

29. "Bethune" *Washington Afro-American*, 28 May 1955; also see Audrey Thomas McCluskey, "Representing the Race: Mary McLeod Bethune and the Black Press in the Jim Crow Era," *Western Journal of Black Studies* 23, no. 4 (1999): 236–45.

30. *Norfolk (Va.) Journal and Guide*, 28 May 1955, 10; *Washington Post*, 21 May 1955, 16; *New York Times*, 19 May 1955, 29; *Pittsburgh Courier*, 28 May 1955; *Washington Afro-American*, 21 May, 1955.

31. The Mary McLeod Bethune Council House, http://www.nps.gov/mamc/index.htm.

32. The Mary McLeod Bethune Monument was dedicated in 1974. It is located in Lincoln Park near Capitol Hill and was sponsored by the organization that Bethune founded, the National Council for Negro Women.

33. Bethune vertical file, Dade County (Miami) Public Library.

34. Mary McLeod Bethune Memorial Park brochure, National Council of Negro Women, Mayesville, S.C., n.d.

35. "Mary McLeod Bethune," *Daytona Beach Morning Journal*, 24 May 1955.

36. "Mary McLeod Bethune Remembered," Eleanor Roosevelt, *Washington Daily News*, 21 May 1955.

37. "Some Incidents in the Life and Career of Charlotte Hawkins Brown," Papers of Charlotte Hawkins Brown, 1900–1961, Scheslinger Library, Radcliffe College, microfilm, reel 1.

38. "Charlotte Hawkins Brown," *Pittsburgh Courier*, 21 January 1961.

39. "Charlotte Hawkins Brown," *New York Times*, 12 January 1961, 29(L).

40. Charles W. Wadelington and Richard F. Knapp, *Charlotte Hawkins Brown and Palmer Memorial Institute* (Chapel Hill: University of North Carolina, 1999), 206.

41. Wadelington and Knapp, 196.

42. Constance Hill Marteena, *The Lengthening Shadow of a Woman: A Biography of Charlotte Hawkins Brown* (Hicksville, N.Y.: Exposition Press, 1977), 89.

43. "Some Incidents in the Life and Career of Charlotte Hawkins Brown," Charlotte Hawkins Brown Papers, microfilm, reel 1.

44. Tracy Burns-Vann (site manager of the Charlotte Hawkins Brown Museum), in telephone interview with author, 21 May 2003.

45. Tracy Burns-Vann, telephone interview, 21 May 2003.

46. Frachele Scott (site manager of the Charlotte Hawkins Brown Museum), in telephone interview with author, 17 April 2013.

47. Frachele Scott, telephone interview, 17 April 2013.

48. "The Three B's of Education," http://www.nchistoricsites.org/chb/three-bs.htm (5 April 2013).

49. "The Nation Pays Tribute to Miss Burroughs," *Washington Afro-American*, 27 May 1961, 1.

50. "The Nation Pays Tribute."

51. "The Nation Pays Tribute."

52. "The Nation Pays Tribute."

53. "Nannie Helen Burroughs," *Washington Post,* 21 May 1961 6(B).

54. Downey, *Tale of Three Women.*

55. Nannie Helen Burroughs School, http://www.greatschools.org/washington-dc/washington/200-Nannie-Helen-Burroughs-School/ (5 April 2013).

# Milestones and Legacies

SELECTIVE CHRONOLOGY OF FOUR BLACK WOMEN SCHOOL
FOUNDERS

Lucy Craft Laney

1854: Born in Macon, Ga., to formerly enslaved parents, David and Louisa Laney.

1860s: Attended Lewis (later Ballard) High School in Macon.

1869: Admitted to Atlanta University.

1873: Member of first graduating class, Atlanta University (normal course for future teachers).

1873–1883: Taught in Macon, Augusta, Milledgeville, and Savannah.

1883: Founded and served as principal, school for black children at Christ Presbyterian Church, Augusta.

1886: Chartered Haines Normal and Industrial Institute, named for benefactor Francine F. Haines, president of Women's Dept. of Presbyterian Assembly.

1888: First graduating class of Haines Institute.

1889: Marshall Hall, girls dormitory dedicated. First permanent building, named for donor, Mrs. Marshall of Minneapolis.

1890: Established the first kindergarten in the Southeast.

1892: Established training program for black nurses in Augusta.

1895: Named honorary chairperson, National Association of Colored Women; Mary McLeod Bethune appointed apprentice teacher at Haines (1895–1896); Mary Jackson (McCrorey) named associate principal at Haines.

1899: Hampton Institute speech, "The Burden of the Colored Woman"; received honorary degree from Lincoln University, PA.

1900–1930: Member of the southern black women's network, which included Mary McLeod Bethune, Charlotte Hawkins Brown, and Nannie Helen Burroughs.

1905: Established first athletic teams for black secondary schools.

1906: Philanthropy of Mrs. McGregor of Detroit, for construction of McGregor Hall.

1908: Visit of President-elect William Howard Taft.

1912: Founder, Augusta chapter of National Federation of Colored Women's Clubs.

1916: Established Negro History as required course at Haines; attended Amenia Conference on black leadership (Nannie Helen Burroughs also attended).

1918-1919: Cofounded Augusta chapter of National Association of Colored People.

1920s: Active in black women's club activities, working against lynching and for voting rights.

1933: Passed into history on October 23 in Augusta. Thousands attended her funeral; Charlotte Hawkins Brown gave tribute. Buried on Haines Institute campus.

1949: Haines Alumni Association leased property to Richmond County Board of Education; Haines Institute merged with A. R. Johnson High School to be become Lucy Craft Laney High School (public).

1951: New building constructed on original site.

1953: Construction of Lucy Craft Laney High School completed on grounds of Haines.

1967: Lucy Craft Laney Hall dedicated at Lincoln University, PA.

1974: Lucy C. Laney portrait commissioned by Gov. Jimmy Carter to hang in Georgia state capitol.

1987: Lucy C. Laney home purchased by Delta House, Inc. (Delta Sigma Theta Sorority), becomes Lucy Craft Laney Museum of Black History.

1992: Inaugural inductee, Georgia Women of Achievement.

1997–1998: Haines Institute Alumni Association installed eternal flame at Laney gravesite.

2000: Lucy Craft Laney Community School at Cleveland Park (Minneapolis) among other memorials across the nation named in her honor.

Mary McLeod Bethune

1875: Born in Mayesville, SC, to formerly enslaved parents Samuel and Patsy McLeod.

1885: Attended Presbyterian Mission School, Emma Wilson first teacher.

1894: Graduated from Scotia Seminary for Negro Girls (Concord, NC) teacher training course.

1895–1896: First teaching job, at Haines Institute under Lucy C. Laney.

1898: Married Albertus Bethune in Sumter, SC.

1899: Gave birth to only child, Albertus, Jr., in Savannah, GA.

1901: Taught at Palatka (FL) Mission School.

1904: Opened the Daytona Educational and Industrial Training School for Negro Girls.

1912: Established McLeod Hospital and Nurses Training School in Daytona.

1917–1928: Rose to leadership and presidency of state (FL.) and national black women's clubs (National Association of Colored Women) and educational organizations (National Association of Colored Teachers).

1918: Dedication of White Hall classroom and office building on Dayton School campus.

1923: Merged Daytona Institute with Cookman Institute of Jacksonville, sponsored by Methodist Episcopal to become Bethune-Cookman Collegiate Institute.

1931: Bethune-Cookman College received "B" rating from Southern Association of Colleges and Secondary Schools.

1935: Founder and president of the National Council of Negro Women; recipient of Spingarn Medal for meritorious service to the black race.

1936–1944: Held appointments in Franklin D. Roosevelt's administration with National Youth Administration, Negro Affairs.

1942: Resigned presidency of Bethune-Cookman College; resumed presidency in 1946–1947.

1944: Presided over the dedication of National Council of Negro Women headquarters, Washington, DC.

1949: Received honorary Doctor of Humanities degree from Rollins College, Winter Park, FL.

1953: Dedication of the Mary McLeod Bethune Foundation at Bethune-Cookman College.

1955: Passed into history on May 18 after heart attack at home on Bethune-Cookman College campus.

1904–present: Daytona School for Girls evolved into Bethune-Cookman College; now Bethune-Cookman University.

1944–present: Bethune Council House present site of Mary McLeod Bethune Memorial Museum and National Archives for Black Women's History, national historic site through National Park Service.

1974: Bethune Memorial Statue erected on public land in Lincoln Park, Washington, D.C.

1982: Mary McLeod Bethune Community Child Care Center, Daytona, FL.

2000: Dr. Mary McLeod Bethune Park, Mayesville, SC, located near Bethune's birthplace and featuring replica of the McLeod family cabin.

2003: Mary McLeod Bethune Day Academy, public charter school, Washington, D.C., became one of many educational facilities in towns and cities across the nation named in her honor.

Charlotte Hawkins Brown

1883: Born Lottie Hawkins in Henderson, NC.

1888: Brown family moved to Cambridge, MA.

1900: Met benefactor Alice Freeman Palmer (president of Wellesley College); attended Massachusetts State College at Salem.

1901: Inspired by Lucy Laney's example, accepted teaching position at American Missionary Association's Bethany School in Sedalia, NC, which closed after one year.

1902: Opened Alice Freeman Palmer Memorial Institute (PMI) in Sedalia.

1905: Memorial Hall was dedicated.

1907: PMI received formal charter.

1909: Founded and served as president of North Carolina Federation of Colored Women's Club.

1911: Married Edward S. Brown; separated after one year.

1916: Total number of PMI graduates reached fifty-five; campus had four main buildings, Memorial Hall, Grinnell Cottage, Grew Hall, Mechanical Hall.

1919: Published first book, *Mammy: An Appeal to the Heart of the South*.

1922: Academic year average attendance at PMI rose to 250 students.

1927: Stone Hall and Kimball Hall dedicated.

1923: Briefly married to John W. Moses.

1930: PMI advertised as a "finishing school."

1932: PMI opened junior college division.

1933: Sedalia Singers of PMI performed at the White House.

1939: PMI junior college closed.

1935: Founding member of the National Council of Negro Women, with founding president Mary McLeod Bethune serving as vice president.

1940: Published *The Correct Thing to Do, to Say, to Wear*.

1944: Delivered lecture at Tuskegee Institute, "Character and the Social Graces"; Howard University bestowed honorary doctorate.

1952: Retired as president of PMI.

1961: Passed into history on January 11 in Greensboro, NC.

1956: First Charlotte Hawkins Brown Day observed in Sedalia, NC.

1971: Palmer Memorial Institute closed.

1987: Charlotte Hawkins Brown Museum planned after the state of North Carolina purchased PMI campus; became state's first historic site commemorating African American heritage.

1988: Dedication of Charlotte Hawkins Brown Highway on U.S. 70.

2010: Charlotte Hawkins Brown banquet room at O. Henry Hotel, Greensboro, NC.

Nannie Helen Burroughs

1879: Born in Orange, VA, to John and Jennie Burroughs, farm owners.

1896: Graduated with honors from M Street high school, Washington, D.C.; joined the newly established National Association of Colored Women.

1897: Worked as associate editor of the *Christian Banner* in Philadelphia.

1900: Delivered influential speech, "How the Sisters are Hindered from Helping," at National Baptist Convention meeting, Richmond, VA; elected secretary for the Foreign Mission Board of the National Baptist Convention, Louisville, KY.

1906: Presented idea for Women's Day at the National Baptist Convention, Memphis, TN.

1909: Founded and served as principal, National Training School for Negro Girls, Washington, D.C.; Mary McLeod Bethune was opening day guest speaker for missionary training program.

1918: Published "Open Letter to [Rev.] Billy Sunday."

1921: Founded as president the National Association of Wage Earners, with Mary McLeod Bethune as vice president.

1927: Delivered keynote speech at meeting of National Association for Study of Negro Life and History (Mary McLeod Bethune was vice president of NASNLH).

1928: Published, "12 Things the Negro Must Do for Himself" and "12 Things White People Must Stop Doing to the Negro."

1931: Chairwoman, National Advisory Board on Negro Housing, appointed by President Herbert Hoover.

1933: Delivered speech, "How White and Colored Women Can Cooperate in Building a Christian Civilization," Richmond, VA.

1954: Invited Rev. Martin Luther King, Jr., to speak at the Women's Day Program of the Baptist Women's Auxiliary. His topic: "The Vision of the World Made New."

1961: Passed into history on May 20, in Washington, DC.


1964–present: National Trades and Professional School renamed the Nannie Helen Burroughs School. The private, Christian elementary school that offered "strong academic programs in a safe, Christian environment," on the original site closed in 2012. The new proposed Nannie Helen Burroughs public charter school expects to serve K–5th grade, http://www.dcpcsb.org/data/images/nhb%20pages%20from%20part%201-1.pdf (15 June 2014).

1975: Mayor Walter Washington declared Nannie Helen Burroughs Day in Washington, D.C.; legislation passed to rename part of Minnesota Avenue Nannie Helen Burroughs Avenue.

2000s: The Nannie Helen Burroughs Project—Values and Vision, a website "devoted to increasing the exposure to this American hero," at http://www.nburroughsinfo.org/files/52552739.pdf (14 June 2014).

# Bibliography

## BOOKS

Allen, Carol. *Black Women Intellectuals: Strategies of Nation, Family, and Neighborhood in the Novels of Pauline Hopkins, Jessie Fauset, and Marita Bonner*. New York: Garland Publishing, 1998.

Anderson, James D. *The Education of Blacks in the South, 1860–1935*. Chapel Hill, N.C.: University of North Carolina Press, 1988.

Bacote, Clarence. *The Story of Atlanta University: A Century of Progress, 1865–1965* Princeton, N.J.: Princeton University Press, 1969.

Black Public Sphere Collective, editors. *The Black Public Sphere: A Public Culture Book*. Edited by Black Public Sphere Collective. Chicago: University of Chicago Press, 1995.

Bowie, Walter Russell. *Women of Light*. New York: Harper and Rowe, 1963.

Bradstock, Andrew, and Anne Hogan, eds. *Women of Faith in Victorian Culture: Reassessing the Angel in the House*. New York: St. Martin's Press, 1998.

Brawley, Benjamin. *Negro Builders and Heroes*. Chapel Hill, N.C.: University of North Carolina Press, 1974.

Campanella, Richard. *Benville's Dilemma: A Historical Geography of New Orleans*. Lafayette, La.: Center for Louisiana Studies, 2008.

Carson, Clayborne, ed. *The Papers of Martin Luther King, Jr., Vol. 4: Symbol of the Movement, January 1957–December 1958*. Berkeley, Calif.: University of California Press, 2000.

Cashin, Edward J. "Paternalism in Augusta: The Impact of the Plantation Ethic upon an Urban Society," in *Paternalism in a Southern City: Race, Religion, and Gender in Augusta, Georgia*, edited by Edward J. Cashin and Glenn T. Eskew. Athens, Ga.: University of Georgia Press, 2001.

Cashin, Edward. *The Quest: A History of Public Education in Richmond County, Georgia*, Augusta, Ga.: Richmond Board of Education, 1985.

Cook, J. Lawrence. *An Autobiography of the Early Years, 1899–1922*, edited and annotated by Jean Lawrence Cook, M.D. (1972), http:/doctorjazz.co.uk/page16.html (30 August 2005).

Cooper, Anna Julie. *A Voice from the South* [1892]. New York: Oxford University Press, 1988.

Cott, Nancy. *The Bonds of Womanhood: 'Woman's Sphere' in New England, 1790–1835*. New Haven, Conn.: Yale University Press, 1977.

Daniel, Sadie Iola, and Hallie Quinn. *Women Builders*, rev. ed. Washington, D.C.: G.K. Hall, 1997.

Davis, Elizabeth Lindsay. *Lifting as They Climb*. New York: G. K. Hall, 1996.

Deutrich, Mabel E., and Virginia C. Purdy, eds. *Clio Was a Woman: Studies in the History of American Women*. Washington, D.C.: Howard University Press, 1980.

Dittmer, John. *Black Georgia in the Progressive Era, 1900–1920*. Chicago: University of Illinois Press, 1977.

Downey, Aurelia R. *A Tale of Three Women: God's Call and Their Response*, Baltimore: Brentwood Publishers, 1993.

Du Bois, W. E. B. *Black Reconstruction*. Reprint of Harcourt Brace edition. Millwood, N.Y.: Kraus Thomson, 1935.

Du Bois, W. E. B., ed. *Second Atlanta University Conference.* New York: Octagon Books, 1968.

Du Bois, W. E. B. *The Souls of Black Folk.* Chicago: A. C. McClurg, 1903.

Fairclough, Adam. *A Class of their Own: Black Teachers in the Segregated South.* Cambridge, Mass.: Harvard University Press, 2007.

Fields, Mamie Garvin, with Karen Fields. *Lemon Swamp and Other Places: A Carolina Memoir.* New York: Free Press, 1983.

Fitzgerald, T. E. *Volusia County, Past and Present.* Daytona Beach, Fla., 1937.

Flemming, Sheila Y. "Bethune-Cookman College," in *Black Women in America: An Historical Encyclopedia,* vol. 1, edited by Darlene Clark Hine. Brooklyn: Carlson Publishing, 1993.

Gaines, Kevin. *Uplifting the Race: Black Leadership, Politics, and Culture in the Twentieth Century.* Durham: University of North Carolina Press, 1996.

Giddings, Paula. *When and Where I Enter: The Impact of Black Women on Race and Sex in America.* New York: William Morrow, 1984.

Hanson, Joyce Ann. *Mary McLeod Bethune and Black Women's Political Activism.* Columbia, Mo.: University of Missouri Press, 2003.

Harper, Frances E. W. *Iola Leroy; or, Shadows Uplifted.* Philadelphia: Garrigues Brothers, 1893.

Harrison, Earl L. *The Dream and the Dreamer: An Abbreviated Story of the Life of Dr. Nannie Helen Burroughs and the National Trade School.* Washington, D.C.: unknown binding, 1956.

Hartshorn, William, ed. *An Era of Progress and Promise, 1863–1910.* Boston: Priscilla Publishing Co., 1910.

Haynes, Elizabeth Ross. *The Black Boy of Atlanta.* Boston: House of Edinboro, 1952.

Higginbotham, Evelyn Brooks. *Righteous Discontent: The Women's Movement in the Black Baptist Church, 1880–1920.* Cambridge, Mass.: Harvard University Press, 1993.

Hill-Collins, Patricia. *Black Feminist Thought: Knowledge, Consciousness, and the Politics of Empowerment.* New York: Routledge, 1990.

Hofstadter, Richard. *Social Darwinism in American Thought.* Philadelphia: University of Pennsylvania Press, 1955.

Holloway, Karla. *Passed On: African American Mourning Stories: A Memorial.* Durham, N.C.: Duke University Press, 2003.

hooks, bell. *Ain't I a Woman.* Boston: South End Press, 1990.

Johnson, Charles S. 1930s Oral History Project on Black Leaders, BCCC.

Johnson, Karen A. *Uplifting the Women and the Race: The Lives, Educational Philosophies, and Social Activism of Anna Julia Cooper and Nannie Helen Burroughs.* New York: Garland Publishing, 2000.

Jones, Tommy Jesse. *Study of Private and High Schools for Blacks.* Washington, D.C.: U.S. Printing Office, 1901.

Lacy, Leslie. *The Rise and Fall of the Proper Negro.* New York: MacMillan, 1970.

Laney, Lucy C. "General Conditions of Mortality," in *Atlanta University Papers Series,* edited by W. E. B. Du Bois. Atlanta: Atlanta University, 1896.

Laney, Lucy C. "Address Before the Women's Meeting," in *Second Annual Atlanta University Conference Proceedings, 1897.* New York: Arno Press, 1968.

Lerner, Gerda, ed. *Black Women in White America: A Documentary History.* New York: Vintage Books, 1973.

Logan, Rayford W. *The Negro in American Life and Thought: The Nadir, 1877–1901.* New York: Dial, 1954.

Lyford, Carrie Alberta. *A Study of Home-Economics Education in Teacher-Training Institution for Negroes.* Washington, D.C.: Federal Board of Vocational Education, 1923. Reprint 1969.

Majors, M. A. *Noted Negro Women: Triumphs and Activities.* Chicago: Donohue and Henneberry, 1891. Reprint by Books for Libraries Press, 1971.

Marteena, Constance Hill. *The Lengthening Shadow of a Woman: A Biography of Charlotte Hawkins Brown.* Hicksville, N.Y.: Exposition Press, 1977.

McCluskey, Audrey Thomas. "Most Sacrificing Service," in *Women of the American South: A Multicultural Reader*, edited by Christie Anne Farnham. New York: New York University Press, 1997.

McCluskey, Audrey Thomas, "Manly Husbands and Womanly Wives: The Educational Leadership of Lucy Craft Laney," in *Post Bellum, Pre-Harlem Renaissance: African American Literature and Culture, 1877–1919*, edited by Carolyn Gebhard and Barbara McCaskill. New York: NYU Press, 2006.

McPherson, James M. *The Struggle for Equality: Abolitionists and the Negro in the Civil War and Reconstruction*. Princeton, N.J.: Princeton University Press, 1964.

Meltzer, Milton. *Mary McLeod Bethune: Voice of Black Hope*. New York: Viking, 1987.

Murray, Andrew Murray. *Presbyterians and the Negro: A History*. Philadelphia: Presbyterian Historical Society, 1966.

Neverdon-Morton, Cynthia. *Afro-American Women of the South and the Advancement of the Race, 1895–1925*. Knoxville: University of Tennessee Press, 1989.

Ovington, Mary White. *Portraits in Color*. New York: Viking Press, 1927.

Patton, June O. "Augusta's Black Community and the Struggle for Ware High School," in *New Perspectives on Black Educational History*, edited by Vincent P. Franklin and James D. Anderson. Chapel Hill: University of North Carolina Press, 1978.

Peare, Catherine Owens. *Mary McLeod Bethune*. New York: Vanguard, 1951.

Perkins, Linda M. "Education," in *Black Women in America: An Historical Encyclopedia*, edited by Darlene Clark Hine et al. New York: Carlson Publishing, 1993.

Pickens, William. *Nannie Burroughs and the School of the Three B's*. New York: 1921.

Preston, Lloyd, and Stephens C. Terrell, *Blacks in Augusta: A Chronology, 1741–1977*. Augusta, Ga.: Preston Publications, 1977.

Richardson, Clement, ed. *The National Cyclopedia of the Colored Race*, vol. 1. Montgomery, Ala.: National Publishing Co., 1919.

Rouse, Jacqueline Ann. *Lugenia Burns Hope: Black Southern Reformer*. Athens: University of Georgia Press, 1989.

Salem, Dorothy. *To Better Our World: Black Women in Organized Reform, 1880–1920*. Brooklyn: Carlson Publishing, 1990.

Scott, J. Irving E. *The Education of Black People in Florida*. Philadelphia: Dorrance, 1974.

Shaw, Stephanie J. "Black Club Women and the Creation of the National Association of Colored Women," in *"We Specialize in the Wholly Impossible": A Reader in Black Women's History*, edited by Darlene Clark Hine, Wilma King, and Linda Reed. Brooklyn, N.Y.: Carlson Publishing, 1995.

Smith, Elaine M. "Mary McLeod Bethune and the National Youth Administration," in *Clio Was a Woman: Studies in the History of American Women*, edited by Mabel E. Deutrich and Virginia C. Purdy. Washington, D.C.: Howard University Press, 1980.

Tygiel, Jules. *Baseball's Great Experiment: Jackie Robinson and his Legacy*. New York: Oxford University Press, 1983.

Wadelington, Charles W., and Richard F. Knapp. *Charlotte Hawkins Brown and Palmer Memorial Institute*. Chapel Hill: University of North Carolina, 1999.

Washington, Booker T. *The Story of the Negro: The Rise of the Race from Slavery*, vol. 2. New York: Doubleday, 1909. Reprinted by Negro Universities Press, 1969.

White, Deborah Gray. *Too Heavy a Load: Black Women in Defense of Themselves, 1894–1994*. New York: W. W. Norton,1999.

Williams, Fannie Barrier. "The Club Movement among Negro Women," in Progress of a Race [1902], edited by J. W. Gibson and W. H. Crogman. Miami: Mnemosyne Publishing Co., 1969.

Woodson, Carter G., ed. *The Works of Francis J. Grimke*, vol. 4. Washington, D.C.: Associated Publishers, 1942.

Woodward, C. Vann. *The Strange Case of Jim Crow*. New York: Oxford University Press, 1957.

## ARTICLES AND THESES

African-American Religion: Documentary History Project. "African-Americans and Billy Sunday in Atlanta," http://www3.amherst.edu/~aardoc/Atlanta_1.html (15 May 2011).

Bethune, Mary McLeod. "U.S. Will Make 'the Grade' in Integrating All Its Schools." *Chicago Defender* (4 June 1955): 10.

Blount, Jean. Interview with Margaret Louise Laney. "Miss Lucy Laney and Early 20th Century Education." *Oral Memoirs of Augusta's Citizens*, vol. 3. Augusta Regional Library (6 February 1975): 1–26.

Burroughs, Nannie H. "How Does It Feel to Be A Negro?" *Black Dispatch* (16 July 1938).

Burroughs, Nannie H. "Legitimate Ambitions of the Negro." *Missionary Review of the World* 45 (1922): 454–56.

Burroughs, Nannie H. "The Negro Woman and Suffrage." *The West Virginia Woman's Voice.* (15 June 1923). Nannie Helen Burroughs Papers, box 46, Library of Congress.

Burroughs, Nannie H. "The Negro Home." *Outlook* 144 (September 1926): 84.

Carby, Hazel V. "On the Threshold of Woman's Era: Lynching, Empire, and Sexuality in Black Feminist Theory." *Critical Inquiry* 12 (Autumn 1985): 262–77.

Cottingham, Britt Edward. "The Burden of the Educated Colored Woman: Lucy Craft Laney and the Haines Institute, 1886–1933." Master's thesis, Georgia State University, 1995.

*The Crisis.* "Haines Institute: The Spirit of Lucy Laney Marches On." Vol. 47, no. 8 (August 1940): 342.

Douglass, Robert J. "Climbing Upward—She Lifted Others," *Abbott's Monthly* (June 1931): 32–34.

Du Bois, W. E .B. "Editorial." *Crisis* 13, no. 6 (April 1917): 269.

Eskew, Glenn T. "Black Elitism and the Failure of Paternalism in Post-bellum Georgia: The Case of Bishop Lucius Henry Holsey," *Journal of Southern History* 58, no. 4 (Nov. 1992): 637–66.

Fleming, Harold G. "Victorian Reformer." *Southern Changes* 11, no. 5 (1989): 18–19.

State of Florida, Biennial Report of the Superintendent of Public Instruction (Tallahassee, 1912): 22.

Freedman, Estelle. "Separatism as Strategy: Female Institution Building and American Feminism, 1870–1930," *Feminist Studies* 5, no. 3 (Fall 1979): 512–29.

Griggs, A. C. "Notes: Lucy Craft Laney," *Journal of Negro History*, vol. 1, no. 19 (June 1934): 97–102.

Harley, Sharon. "Nannie Helen Burroughs: The Black Goddess of Liberty." *Journal of Negro History* 18 (Winter–Autumn 1996): 62–71.

Higginbotham, Evelyn Brooks. "African-American Women's History and the Metalanguage of Race." *Signs* 17, no. 2 (Winter 1992): 251–74.

Hine, Darlene Clark. "Rape and the Inner Lives of Black Women in the Middle West." *Signs* 14, no. 4 (Summer 1989): 912–20.

Hunter, Tera. "The Correct Thing: Charlotte Hawkins Brown and the Palmer Institute." *Southern Exposure* (September/October 1983): 37–43.

Kendall, Anne. "Lucy Craft Laney." Lucy C. Laney File, Atlanta University Center Library (1972): 1–10

Kent, Michael L. "The Rhetoric of Funeral Oratory and Eulogy: Reconciling Rhetorics of Past and Present." PhD diss., University of Oklahoma. 2007.

Kousser, Morgan J. "Separate But *Not* Equal: The Supreme Court's First Decision on Discrimination in Schools." *Social Science Working Paper*, no. 204 (March 1978): 1–46.

Laney, Lucy Craft. "The Burden of the Educated Colored Woman." *Southern Workman* (1989) 28, no. 9: 41–44.

Linsin, Christopher E., "Something More Than a Creed: Mary McLeod Bethune's Aim of Integrated Autonomy as Director of Negro Affairs." *Florida Historical Quarterly* 76, no. (Summer 1997): 20–41.

Ludlow, Helen W. "The Bethune School." *The Southern Workman* 41 (March 1912): 144.

Maley, Dora E. Letter to unknown, 17 March 1955, on the occasion of the 50th anniversary of Bethune-Cookman College. Mary McLeod Bethune file, Halifax Historical Society, Daytona Beach, Fla.

Marshall, Mary Magdalene. "Tell Them We're Rising: Black Intellectuals and Lucy Craft Laney in Post Civil War Augusta, Georgia." PhD diss., Drew University, 1998.

McCluskey, Audrey Thomas. "Mary McLeod Bethune and the Education of Black Girls in the South, 1904–1923." PhD diss., Indiana University, 1991.

McCluskey, Audrey Thomas. "Representing the Race: Mary McLeod Bethune and the Press." *Western Journal of Black Studies* 23, no. 4 (Winter 1999): 236–45. New Orleans.

McCluskey, Audrey Thomas. "'We Specialize in the Wholly Impossible': Black Women School Founders and Their Mission." *Signs: Journal of Women in Culture and Society* 22, no. 2 (Winter 1997): 403–26.

McCrorey, Mary Jackson. "Lucy Laney." *The Crisis* 41, 6 (June 1934): 161.

McPherson, James M. "White Liberals and Black Power in Negro Education, 1865–1915." *American Historical Review* 75, no. 5 (June 1970): 1374.

Meier, August. "The Vogue of Industrial Education." *The Midwest Journal* no. 7 (Spring 1955): 241–66.

Perkins, Carol O. "The Pragmatic Idealism of Mary McLeod Bethune." *Sage* (Fall 1988): 30–35.

Perkins, Linda M. "The Impact of the 'Cult of True Womanhood' on the Education of Black Women." *Journal of Social Issues* 39, no. 3 (1983): 17–28.

Rashidi, Runoko, and Karen Johnson. "A Brief Note on the Lives of Anna Julia Cooper and Nannie Helen Burroughs: Profiles of African Women Educators." *Global African Community History Notes,* http://aalbc.com/reviews/anna.htm (12 March 2009).

Roane, Florence L. "A Cultural History of Professional Teacher Training at Bethune-Cookman College." PhD diss., Boston University, 1985.

Roosevelt, Eleanor. "Mary McLeod Bethune Remembered." *Washington Daily News* (21 May 1955).

Ross, B. Joyce. "Mary McLeod Bethune and the Administration of the National Youth Administration: A Case Study of Power Relationships in the Black Cabinet of Franklin Delano Roosevelt." *Journal of Negro History* 40 (January 1975): 1–28.

Sargent, Edward D. "Nannie Helen Burroughs School: Keeping a High Profile." *Washington Post* (23 July 1981).

Smith, Daniel Scott. "Family Limitation, Sexual Control, and Domestic Feminism in Victorian America." *Feminist Studies* 1, no. 3/4 (Winter–Spring 1973): 40–57.

Smith, Marjorie E. W. "Putting First Things First," Board of Missions of the Presbyterian Church. Reprint in *Haines Journal* (April 1934): 8–9.

Smith, Sandra N., and Earle H. West. "Charlotte Hawkins Brown." *Journal of Negro History* 51, no. 3 (Summer 1983): 191–206.

Stillman, Clara. "A Tourist in Florida." *The Crisis* (February 22, 1924): 173.

Towns, George A. "The Source of the Traditions of Atlanta University." *Phylon* 3, no. 2 (1942): 118–19.

Walker, Audrey. *Nannie Helen Burroughs: A Register of Her Papers in the Library of Congress.* 1982: 1–6.

Williams-Way, Gloria T. "Lucy Craft Laney: 'The Mother of the Children of the People.'" PhD diss., University of South Carolina, 1998.

Yee, Shirley J. "Finding a Place: Mary Ann Shadd Cary and the Dilemmas of Black Migration to Canada, 1850–1870." *Frontiers: A Journal of Women Studies* 18, no. 3 (1997): 1–16.

# Special Collections

## ABBREVIATIONS:

ARC: Amistad Research Center, Tulane University
BCCC: Bethune-Cookman College Collection (Mary McLeod Bethune Papers)
CHB: Charlotte Hawkins Brown Papers, Schlesinger Library, Harvard
LLC: Lucy Craft Laney Papers
LOC: Library of Congress
M-SRC: Moorland-Spingarn Research Center, Howard University
NHB: Nannie Helen Burroughs Papers


## ARCHIVES AND SPECIAL COLLECTIONS:

Charlotte Hawkins Brown Papers, Schlesinger Library, Harvard University, Cambridge, Mass.
Edward Twichell Ware Records, Woodruff Library, Atlanta University Center
General Education Board Archives, Rockefeller Foundation, Sleepy Hollow, N.Y.
Lucy C. Laney vertical file, Library of Congress Manuscript Division
Lucy C. Laney file, Reese Library, Augusta (Ga.) College
Mary McLeod Bethune Collection, Dade County (Fla.) Public Library
Mary McLeod Bethune Papers, Amistad Research Center, Tulane University, New Orleans
Mary McLeod Bethune Papers, Bethune-Cookman College Collection, Bethesda, Md.
Moorland-Spingarn Research Center, Howard University, Washington, D.C.
Nannie Helen Burroughs Papers, Library of Congress, Manuscript Division
Presbyterian Historical Society, Philadelphia
Richmond County (Ga.) Historical Society


## INTERVIEWS BY THE AUTHOR:

Christine Betts, Augusta, Ga.
William "Bill" Brooks, Brandon, Fla.
Tracy Burns-Vann, Sedalia, N.C.
John T. Daniel, M.D., Durham, N.C.
Ida Daniel Dark, Ph.D., Durham, N.C.
Magnolia Donahue, Augusta, Ga.
Lucille Ellis Floyd, Augusta, Ga.
Olga Black Fluker, Little Rock, Ark.
Naomi M. Holmes, Virginia Beach, Va.
Alice and Antony Hurley, Columbia, S.C.
Robert Lipscombe, Denver, Colo.
Olvin McBarnette, Alexandria, Va.
H.M. "Mickey" Michaux, Durham, N.C.
Alma Grace Morland Motley, Charlotte, N.C.

Jeanne Lanier Rudd, Sedalia, N.C.
John Scarborough, Durham, N.C.
Frachele Scott, Sedalia, N.C.

# Index

# About the Author

**Audrey Thomas McCluskey** is emerita professor of African American and African Diaspora Studies, Indiana University-Bloomington. There she served alternately as director of graduate studies, director of the Black Film Center/Archive and the Neal-Marshal Black Culture Center. In 2000, she published, with co-editor, Elaine M. Smith, *Mary McLeod Bethune: Building a Better World* (Indiana University Press). Her publications on black women educators and activists have appeared in *Signs: A Journal of Women in Culture; Black Scholar; Feminist Teacher; Florida Historical Society,* as well as chapters in several anthologies and encyclopedias. Her publications in film studies include: *Imaging Blackness: Race and Racial Representation in Film Poster Art* (2007); *Frame by Frame III: A Filmography of the Black Diasporan Image* (2007); *Richard Pryor: The Life and Legacy of a "Crazy" Black Man* (2008); and *The Devil You Dance With: Film Culture in the New South Africa* (2007).